JUDAISM

Key Words in Jewish Studies

Series Editors
Deborah Dash Moore, University of Michigan
MacDonald Moore, Vassar College
Andrew Bush, Vassar College

JUDAISM

The Genealogy of a Modern Notion

Daniel Boyarin

RUTGERS UNIVERSITY PRESS

New Brunswick, Camden, and Newark, New Jersey, and London

Library of Congress Cataloging-in-Publication Data

Names: Boyarin, Daniel, author.

Title: Judaism : the genealogy of a modern notion / Daniel Boyarin.
Description: New Brunswick, New Jersey : Rutgers University Press, [2018] |
Series: Key words in Jewish studies | Includes bibliographical references and index.
Identifiers: LCCN 2018004644 | ISBN 9780813571621 (cloth) | ISBN 9780813571614 (pbk.)
Subjects: LCSH: Hebrew language—Etymology. | Judaism.
Classification: LCC PJ4801 .B69 2018 | DDC 296.01/4—dc23
LC record available at https://lccn.loc.gov/2018004644

A British Cataloging-in-Publication record for this book is available from the British
Library.

∞ The paper used in this publication meets the requirements of the American National
Standard for Information Sciences—Permanence of Paper for Printed Library Materials,
ANSI Z39.48-1992.

www.rutgersuniversitypress.org

Manufactured in the United States of America

For Chava שתחיה, on our fiftieth, קיין עין הרע
זיבציק ער און זיבציק זי

We must set out on the slow road of detailing, and we must renounce the idea that detail means trifle.
— Max Weinreich, *History of the Yiddish Language*

Contents

Foreword

The Rutgers book series Key Words in Jewish Studies seeks to introduce students and scholars alike to vigorous developments in the field by exploring its terms. These words and phrases reference important concepts, issues, practices, events, and circumstances. But terms also refer to standards, even to preconditions; they patrol the boundaries of the field of Jewish Studies. This series aims to transform outsiders into insiders and let insiders gain new perspectives on usages, some of which shift even as we apply them.

Key words mutate through repetition, suppression, amplification, and competitive sharing. Jewish Studies finds itself attending to such processes in the context of an academic milieu where terms are frequently repurposed. Diaspora offers an example of an ancient word, one with a specific Jewish resonance, which has traveled into new regions and usage. Such terms migrate from the religious milieu of Jewish learning to the secular environment of universities, from Jewish community discussion to arenas of academic discourse, from political debates to intellectual arguments and back again. As these key words travel, they acquire additional meanings even as they occasionally shed long-established connotations. On occasion, key words can become so politicized that they serve as accusations. The sociopolitical concept of assimilation, for example, when turned into a term—assimilationist—describing an advocate of the process among Jews, became an epithet hurled by political opponents struggling for the mantle of authority in Jewish communities.

When approached dispassionately, key words provide analytical leverage to expand debate in Jewish Studies. Some key words will be familiar from long use, and yet they may have gained new valences, attracting or repelling other terms in contemporary discussion. But there are prominent terms in Jewish culture whose key lies in a particular understanding of prior usage. Terms of the past may bolster claims to continuity in the present while newly minted language sometimes disguises deep connections reaching back into history. Attention must be paid as well to the transmigration of key words among Jewish languages—especially Hebrew, Yiddish and Ladino—and among languages used by Jews, knitting connections even while highlighting distinctions.

An exploration of the current state of Jewish Studies through its key words highlights some interconnections often only glimpsed and holds out the prospect of a reorganization of Jewish knowledge. Key words act as magnets and attract a nexus of ideas and arguments as well as related terms into their orbits. This series plunges into several of these intersecting constellations, providing a path from past to present.

The volumes in the series share a common organization. They open with a first section, Terms of Debate, which defines the key word as it developed over the course of Jewish history. Allied concepts and traditional terms appear here as well. The second section, State of the Question, analyzes contemporary debates in scholarship and popular venues, especially for those key words that have crossed over into popular culture. The final section, In a New Key, explicitly addresses contemporary culture and future possibilities for understanding the key word.

To decipher key words is to learn the varied languages of Jewish Studies at points of intersection between academic disciplines and wider spheres of culture. The series, then, does not seek to consolidate and narrow a particular critical lexicon. Its purpose is to question, not to canonize, and to invite readers to sample the debate and ferment of an exciting field of study.

Andrew Bush
Deborah Dash Moore
MacDonald Moore
Series Co-Editors

Preface

This is a book about a word, a key word, arguably one of the most key of key words for Jewish studies. We scholars talk about "Judaism" constantly, and nonscholars do too. There is Second-Temple Judaism, rabbinic Judaism, medieval Judaism, modern Judaism, even orthodox Judaism. It seems highly significant, however, that there is no word in premodern Jewish parlance that means "Judaism;" indeed, from a linguistic point of view, only modern Judaism could be said to exist at all. When the term *Ioudaismos* appears in non-Christian Jewish writing—to my knowledge only in 2 Maccabees—it doesn't mean "Judaism," the "religion," but the entire complex of loyalties and practices, including dress, speech, *and also* sacrifice, that mark off the people of Judea (what we call now "Jewishness"); after that, it is used as the name of the Jewish "religion"—itself a highly problematic term—only by writers who do not identify themselves with and by that name at all, until, it would seem, the nineteenth century.[1]

Paul, né Saul, is an excellent example.[2] Although, for sure, a *Ioudaios* and remaining one forever, he only uses *Ioudaismos* as something from which he has distanced himself, from which he is other as it is (now) other to him; it clearly no longer has for him quite the sense it had in Maccabees. This will be discussed in some detail in the following text. It might seem, then, that "Judaism" has not, until sometime in modernity, existed at all, that whatever moderns might be tempted to abstract out, to disembed from the culture of Jews and call their "religion," was not so disembedded or ascribed particular status by Jews until very recently, perhaps in some sites in the eighteenth century, in others, the twentieth. In this book, I will claim with some theoretical justification up front that it is highly problematic to ascribe to a culture a category or abstraction that it does not know or show in its language. On the other hand, and this is crucial too, for sure for a study of "Judaism" as a key word, it is equally apposite to remark that for Christian writers, Greek and Latin *Ioudaismos* and *Iudaismus* and their vernacular cognates were in fairly constant usage from at least the second century on. This further complicates matters and makes them interesting.

As made clear in the editors' foreword to each volume in the series, the books are expected to divide into three sections:

> The volumes of this series share a common organization. They open with a first section, Terms of Debate, which defines the key word as it developed over the course of Jewish history. Allied concepts and traditional terms appear here as well. The second section, State of the Question, analyzes contemporary debates in scholarship and popular venues, especially for those key words that have crossed over into popular culture. The final section, In a New Key, explicitly addresses contemporary culture and future possibilities for understanding the key word.

My book on one of the most basic and ubiquitous of all key words for the study of *Jews*, is both a scholarly study of a word (and concept) as well as a metareflection on the principles and meanings of such studies. In my actualization of the three sections, I have thematized this doubled nature. In a sense, moreover, my entire book fits best the rubric of the first section as defined by the series. With the sweet complicity of the editors, who have become accessories before the fact and after as well, I have interpreted the mandate to have three sections in my own way (indeed, that very mandate/stricture seems to spur creativity). My first section is, therefore—perhaps overly *raffiniert*—dubbed "The Debate of the Terms," in which I both introduce the major claim of the book, to wit that "Judaism" is not a *Jewish* term, and also lay the theoretical groundwork for my urging that research ought to be based on the categories recognized in the language(s) of the objects of our research and not on anachronistic terms applied a priori. The second, two chapters continuing the conceit (or at any rate, self-regard) of the first is "The State of the Lexicon: Questioning the Archive," in which I attempt to make good on the promise of the first section to show that "Judaism" is not a word/concept used in any *Jewish* language before modernity (at some place or time), and finally my "A New Dispensation: The Christian Invention of 'Judaism'" consists of a genealogy in two chapters of the notion that there is a "religion" called "Judaism"—or better put, an *Ekklesia* (*Synagoga*) called "Judaism"—arguing that it is a product of Christian semantic necessity and production, not that of *Jews*. This final chapter ends up in a somewhat preliminary account of the consequences of converting a people "Israel" to an *Ekklesia*, "Judaism," and a further meditation in the form of an epilogue, returning to where we began, on the effect of applying, or refusing to apply, anachronistic terms to the study of *Jews* or other human collectives. As the preceding paragraphs might indicate to certain assiduous readers of my work, this relatively slim volume represents the culmination, the final statement from me (בלי נדר) of nearly twenty years' thinking on the "Judaism question."

Parts of some of the chapters in the final section of the book, "The Christian Invention of 'Judaism,'" are significant revisions—indeed, in part a palinode—of papers that I published as early as 2000; Chapter 2 represents in large part the lectures that I delivered at Columbia University in 2015 as the Bampton Lectures in America (and the present publication should be considered, therefore, the publication of those lectures—the permission for which I am grateful to the current stewards of the Bampton legacy). Other parts of the middle section represent brand-new research for this book based on the methodology and theoretical reflections of the first part, which are themselves quite new for me, having been first delivered in 2015 at the University of Chicago as the Sigmund H. Danziger Jr., Distinguished Lecture in the Humanities and published in *Critical Inquiry*, to which journal I am grateful for the opportunity to use this text as the first section of the current book.

PART I

THE TERMS OF THE DEBATE

1 The Debate of the Terms

The Western construction of religion creates a world beyond which it cannot see.

—Daniel Dubuisson, *The Western Construction of Religion: Myths, Knowledge, and Ideology*[1]

Whoever uses terms like transcendence, capitalism, superstition, imperialism, heresy, slavery, and liberty without considering what they mean in a particular time and place (or whether they are even legitimate categories in certain times and places) is already a shoddy historian.

—Arnaldo Momigliano, "The Rules of the Game in the Study of Ancient History"[2]

Teaching English to Speak Hebrew; or, the Key Word Issue

Very far from a shoddy historian—indeed, a superb one—Seth Schwartz defends the necessity for such scholarly usages condemned by Momigliano: "Finally, our modern western language is necessarily inadequate to describe the realities of a radically different culture." I concur completely, and it will be noted that I refrain, more consistently lately than formerly, from bandying about terms such as "ethnicity" or "culture" as well. He goes on, however, to add, "But our job is precisely to translate and explain, which necessarily requires that we make use of inherently misleading modern language to describe our subjects. There is simply no choice."[3] Agreeing with Schwartz in principle that we must translate, I would suggest that it is our concept of "translation" itself that needs reforming.[4] Rather than trying to "translate" into *our* language, we must seek unceasingly to learn *their* language(s) and find the words, as many as it takes, in our language to describe what we have learned.[5] That is translation, as Talal Asad imagines it. Attacking anthropologist Ernest Gellner, who had claimed that those who wish to describe the "coherence" of "primitive cultures" do so out of "tolerance," Asad writes, "He appears unaware that for the translator the problem of determining the relevant kind of context in each case is solved by *skill* in the use of the languages concerned, not by an a priori 'attitude' of intolerance or tolerance. And skill is something that is *learned*—that is, something that is necessarily circular, but not viciously so. We are dealing not with an abstract matching of two sets of sentences, but with a social practice rooted in modes of life."[6] As Walter Benjamin, citing Rudolph Pannwitz, writes, "Our translations, even the best ones, proceed from a wrong premise. They want to turn Hindi, Greek, English into German instead of turning German into Hindi, Greek, English."[7] Lilith Acadia has put her finger on the issues at stake: "Viewing non-Western society through the lens of a Western concept is misleading and reveals an epistemological power asymmetry: the West sets the terms of the debate, becomes the norm, unreciprocatingly expects others to assimilate to the West, and belongs everywhere while others are 'uprooted' when not in their historically limited 'local place of origin.' The western concept of religion's power in history-making skews the narrative."[8]

Asad's essay, "The Concept of Cultural Translation in British Social Anthropology,"[9] provides one of the most significant recent interventions in this question. Early in his paper, Asad quotes approvingly a statement of Godfrey Lienhardt:

> Eventually, we try to represent their conceptions systematically in the logical constructs we have been brought up to use; and we hope, at the best, thus to reconcile what can be expressed in their languages, with what can be expressed in ours. We mediate between their habits of thought, which we have acquired with them, and those of our own society; in doing so, it is not finally some mysterious "primitive philosophy" that we are exploring, but the further potentialities of our own thought and language. The problem of describing to others how members of a remote tribe think then begins to appear largely as one of translation, of making the coherence primitive thought has in the languages it really lives in, as clear as possible in our own.[10]

Substituting "collective" for "tribe" and "other" for "primitive" as well as "sense" for "coherence," since we now strongly prefer to assume that "to get at any culture's thoughts you need to locate both its coherencies and its incoherencies,"[11] I would subscribe to this description of the task of the cultural translator.

The first thing to note is how different this is from the procedure enjoined by J. Z. Smith, who insists that we must translate into the terms of *our* analytic thought:

> Giving primacy to native terminology yields, at best, *lexical* definitions that historically and statistically, tell how a word is used. But lexical

definitions are almost always useless for scholarly work. To remain content with how "they" understand "magic" may yield a proper description but little explanatory power. How "they" use a word cannot substitute for the *stipulative* procedures by which the academy contests and controls second-order specialized usage.[12]

This view of cultural translation could not, I think, be more at odds with Lienhardt's position as explained and defended by Asad.[13] Asad himself builds on Lienhardt, making, moreover, the key point that in cultural translation, properly conceived, the target language must always be shifting to accommodate—to make sense of—the new *Lebensform* that it is translating.[14] The languages of dominated groups have always done this, and on a more neutral plane, languages in contact have always done this as well, shifting their semantics in response to contact with other forms of life and thus languages. The eventual development of the concept of "religion" in many forms of life—including the modern Jewish one—under the impact of colonialism is only a case in point. The task of the cultural translator is to make our powerful modern European language submissive to the language of the past, of the other, to let English speak Hebrew or ancient Greek or Hindi.[15] Putting it perhaps less metaphorically, anthropological theorist Eduardo Viveiros de Castro has written, "I would add that to translate is always to betray, as the Italian saying goes. However, a good translation—and here I am paraphrasing Walter Benjamin (or rather Rudolf Pannwitz via Benjamin)—is one that betrays the destination language, not the source language. A good translation is one that allows the alien concepts to deform and subvert the translator's conceptual toolbox so that the *intentio* of the original language can be expressed within the new one."[16]

Most of Asad's paper is an astute explication and defense of Lienhardt's thesis against some less than seasonable attack that it suffered. In defending Lienhardt against some quite absurd statements by his antagonist, the aforementioned Gellner, Asad hits what is for me the nail right on the head, remarking, "But if the skilled translator looks first for any principle of coherence in the discourse to be translated, and then tries to reproduce that coherence as nearly as he can in his own language, there cannot be a general rule as to what units the translator will employ—sentences, paragraphs, or even larger units of discourse."[17] Note that nothing in this account of cultural translation suggests in any way, shape, or form the necessity to find a word in "our" language that matches up with, for better or worse, a word in the language of the other collective.[18] Once again, and with what is to my ears a distinctly

Wittgensteinian ring, "We are dealing not with an abstract matching of two sets of sentences, but with a social practice rooted in modes of life."[19]

The point is *not* the mutual unintelligibility of languages or forms of life but the very hard work necessary to render them intelligible to each other and the necessity to do so, as much as possible, without imposing the terms of one on the other.[20] As one of Wittgenstein's most perspicacious interpreters puts it, "Grammar owes no homage to reality. It is, in this sense, autonomous. It does not reflect objective necessities. On the contrary, it *determines* what we conceive of as necessary. We *can* understand different colour geometries. We *can* understand different number systems."[21] We *can* understand different ways of imagining the world and dividing up practices into categories, and to do so is the task of the translator: to make our languages capable of speaking the language of others. The purpose is to develop a third way between the extremes of assuming unintelligibility—radical Sapir-Whorfianism—on the one hand and a kind of universal science-speak on the other. I do believe that we can learn to understand others with a great deal of difficulty and that the effort is worth it. Neither to leave the texts in ancient Greek nor to translate them into English but to make English speak Greek. Lest this proposal sound unworkable or even Borgesian, I want to point out a method (developed by Carlin Barton) for doing this—namely, the method, adumbrated herein, of presenting as much of the context as practical of a given usage, translating all of the context *except* for the key words being studied and doing that over and over for the key word in question. Adorno has perfectly described the procedure that we propose:

> The way the essay appropriates concepts can best be compared to the behavior of someone in a foreign country who is forced to speak its language instead of piecing it together out of its elements according to rules learned in school. Such a person will read without a dictionary. If he sees the same word thirty times in continually changing contexts, he will have ascertained its meaning better than if he had looked up all the meanings listed, which are usually too narrow in relation to the changes that occur with changing contexts and too vague in relation to the unmistakable nuances that the context gives rise to in every individual case. This kind of learning remains vulnerable to error, as does the essay as form; it has to pay for its affinity with open intellectual experience with a lack of security that the norm of established thought fears like death.[22]

Both as a research program and as a mode of conveying results, this holds the promise of developing a sense of the range of usage—not lexical meaning—that a word can show within a given state of the language.

The question, thus, remains of how far one can "reduce the unknown to the known," following J. Z. Smith's famous injunction,[23] before one loses the irreducible difference of "the unknown." Note that I am not claiming, not at all, that the "external" observer can never see things that are occluded from the member of the culture itself. Any given culture makes distinctions that are not articulated (that are tacit, that "go without saying") and makes categories and distinctions that do not operate "on the ground." (For instance, informants might tell an ethnographer that we do not marry first cousins but only second cousins, and then the ethnographer discovers many first-cousin marriages.) Such discrepancies are well known to ethnographers, but this hardly marks an opposition between subjective and objective or insiders' and outsiders' perspectives. One would have to demonstrate *in either case* on the basis of the same kind of evidence whether a distinction or category is operative within the culture.

If I want to learn something about Jewish practice—oral, textual, embodied in antiquity, late antiquity, or the Middle Ages—I contend that I cannot do so by reducing those unknowns to the known. Such a practice will inevitably (as I hope to show here) result in a description that assimilates them, in one way or another, to modern "Judaism."[24] Once more, as Adorno has written, "Thought's depth depends on how deeply it penetrates its object, not on the extent to which it reduces it to something else."[25] If, as argued by Walter Capps, religious studies is founded on the Enlightenment postulate that "the objects of investigation have essences, which are discrete and unchangeable," then this is precisely what I deny about "religion." I feel instinctively sure that utilizing terms like "religion" to delineate the concept worlds of people who had no such concepts, or words, is a practice of self-replication and not translation. Benson Saler reminds us that "the power of religion as an analytical category, we might well affirm, depends on its instrumental value in facilitating the formulation of interesting statements about human beings, the phenomenal subjects of anthropological research."[26] It is the claim of my work that "religion" obscures much more than it reveals for the formulation of interesting statements about ancient Greek or Judean human beings, which is to be taken as a synecdoche for all humans before or outside of the hegemony of modern Euro-American forms of life.[27] Avoiding as much as possible Smith's vaunted "stipulative procedures by which the academy contests and controls second-order specialized usage" and precisely (in the sense of *davka*) trying, as much as possible, to determine "how *they* use a word" is what we need to do. To return to Wittgenstein for a moment, "we must do away with all *explanation*, and description alone must take its place" (PI 109). Pace Smith, who seems to take this as an intellectually nugatory practice, translation understood thus requires no little industry and acumen, including theoretical sophistication, and of course, it never reaches final results by its very nature.[28] Indeed, I would suggest that the work of describing in more detail than previous accounts, accounting for more confounding data, painstakingly and inductively looking for patterns where in the beginning only chaos seems to lie, is itself redescription. Note that I am not claiming, not at all, that the "external" observer can never see things that are occluded from the member of the collective itself.[29] I wish to repeat and emphasize that any given collective makes distinctions that are not articulated (that are tacit, that "go without saying"), but the possibility of discovering such for a form of life so distant from ours that all that is left are words in texts and artifacts is not likely to yield these secrets.[30] Utilizing terms like "religion" and "Judaism" to delineate the concept worlds of people who had no such concepts, or words, is a practice of self-defeat—pure or not. We will never find the other as long as we persist in reducing the unknown to the known.[31]

This needs, however, to be articulated with a history of the present. As Ian Hacking has written, "But I as philosopher am decidedly Whiggish. The history that I want is the history of the present. That's Michel Foucault's phrase, implying that we recognize and distinguish historical objects in order to illumine predicaments."[32] The Foucauldian project, as conveyed by Hacking, of seeking to illumine our own predicaments through investigation of the past is one that I have made my own for decades. My present project is somewhat different but, I think, not inimical to the "history of the present"; in fact, it may simply be the other side of the coin.

I wish now to understand as best as I can the different ways that human beings—and, paradoxically, especially those we see as our ancestors—have chosen to pursue their existence as humans. This is not discrepant with Foucauldian practice, for he too looked for the radical otherness and the genealogies of modern formations. The project is not to be construed as even an attempt at an "objective" and true description of the other's form of life; indeed, the very form of the questions "Does *Ioudaismos* mean 'the religion Judaism'?" or even "What does *Ioudaismos* mean?" is generated from the present. It is quite possible, even probable, that "natives" would consider this quite an uninteresting set of questions and want to tell us something entirely different about their language, their form of life, their selves. In her wonderful pseudonymous book about the actual experience of fieldwork, Laura Bohannon relates repeatedly how the people she was studying considered it most important (repeatedly) that she learn to distinguish between different grasses in their ecosystem, while she wanted only to learn kinship terms.[33] I grant then—not only grant but assert con brio—that this project is generated in and from the present and may answer to present needs and concerns as well.

Nonetheless, the presentist vantage offered here is quite distinct from the sort of questions usually asked in religious studies—namely, What can we say about ancient religion? How do Judaism and Buddhism compare? From one point of view, the kind of comparatism (between "us" and "them," as it were) proposed herein enables the "other" language to function as a "language game," one that enables us to "envisage a world in which people's natural reactions are different in certain striking ways from ours . . . , or in which people's powers of surveying things was greater or lesser than with us. Reflection on the language-games that might be played in such circumstances by such people helps us to shake the grip of the thought that our concepts are the only possible ones, or that they are uniquely correct."[34] For me, at any rate now, history is that which we strive to write ourselves out of, looking for the differences, which doesn't necessarily imply ruptures. To be sure, the search for difference has to be predicated on sameness as well; there is no absolute otherness.[35] It is a practice, moreover, in which we find ourselves transformed in the effort to listen to the other, in which we become strangers to ourselves, promoting the known to the unknown.[36] Observing carefully a language (form of life) that doesn't have "religion" might problematize the seemingly settled notion, "religion," in our own language as well.[37] Manifestly, I do not mean to short circuit the hermeneutical circle or to take a positivist stand on historical truth or the interpretation of texts; indeed, the opening to "usage" without putting the particular unit of meaning into a lexical box opens hermeneutical possibilities rather than closing them down.

To the Matter at Hand

Annette Yoshiko Reed writes, "Today, 'Apocalypticism' and 'Mysticism' are no longer taken for granted as neutral or universal categories of historical and comparative analysis. As with many other rubrics once common in Religious Studies—such as 'Gnosticism,' 'esotericism,' 'paganism,' 'magic,' 'superstition,' and even/especially 'religion'—both categories were subject to reassessment, destabilization, and deconstruction, especially since the 1970s."[38] In our recently published book, *Imagine No Religion*,[39] Carlin Barton and I have argued philologically what many have suspected and even asserted—namely, that there is no term or even set of

terms in Ancient Greek (including Hellenistic Greek) or Latin that corresponds even roughly to our modern term "religion," thus joining the
crowd of reassessors, destabilizers, deconstructors of that term.

Let me clarify this last point somewhat, as it's key to the argument
that follows throughout this book. Without attempting to "define" religion, an impossible task as has been recognized by most scholars, let me
give some examples of its modern usage, drawn almost at random from
various sources:

- "Religion does not encourage people to 'stop thinking.' In fact, religion
  encourages people to think about how they can re-bind themselves or
  re-connect with a God who is infinitely more intelligent and loving."
- "On one definition, a religion is an apparently universal social phenomenon
  involving some or all of the following:
      a distinctive worldview
      doctrines, beliefs, or traditions
      practices, rituals, rules, shared experiences, and other behavioral
      expectations
      attention to the divine, holy, mysterious, sacred, supernatural, or
      ultimate concerns
      group identity
      social institutions
      promotional and legal claims to be a religion"
- "Religion is any cultural system of worship, including designated behaviors
  and practices, world views, texts, places, ethics, or organizations, that
  relates humanity to the supernatural or transcendental."
- "At a fundamental and basic level, religion consists of (1) a community of
  individuals (2) who share representations, ideas, and perhaps beliefs about a
  supernatural realm and the forces or beings inhabiting this realm, (3) who
  practice both individual and collective rituals addressing supernatural
  beings and forces inhabiting a sacred realm and (4) who are often organized
  into small or big *cult structures* (religious corporate units) with specific
  practitioners charged with organizing the community and their ritual
  practices (cf. Geertz 2013)."[40]

Although this is not the venue to go into detail, it is by now notorious
that none of these "definitions" fits all or even most of the human collectives of the world. In fact, it is well-established that there is no working
definition of "religion" that picks out one thing that is common to all
humans.[41] After briefly demonstrating the mutual incompatibility of
various attempts at modern scholarly definitions of "religion," Brent
Nongbri concludes in a declaration that feels quite right to me (especially
fitting the last of the aforementioned citations), "Because of the

pervasive use of the word 'religion' in the cultures of the modern western world (the 'we' here), we already intuitively know what 'religion' is
before we try to define it: Religion is anything that looks sort of like
modern Christianity. Such a definition might be seen as crass, simplistic,
ethnocentric, Christiano-centric, and even a bit flippant; it is all these
things, but it is also highly accurate in reflecting the uses of the term in
modern languages."[42] Given this usage—and it is beyond the scope of the
present book to justify it here further—it is not surprising that there isn't
such a word or category outside of "modern Christianity" (with all the
diversity of that aggregation) or that only with the advent of modern
Christianity was it necessary to produce such a category virtually everywhere that Europe touched. There is no word in any premodern Jewish
text or in any Jewish language that matches in meanings and offered
definitions to the usage and definitions of "religion" as just sampled
in English.

Reed further explains:

> Personally, I still remain skeptical as to the utility of these particular
> categories—in my case: primarily because of their lack of fit with the
> full range of the relevant data now known to us and because of their
> resultant simplification of what we increasingly know to be much more
> interesting, dynamic, and complex phenomena. In part, however, my
> skepticism reflects my own scholarly temperament: I tend to be wary
> of temptations to frame our inquiries into the past in terms defined
> foremost by disembodied "-isms" of modern invention, at the expense
> of taking seriously our premodern sources and their capacity to sur-
> prise us—not least by confronting us with potentially quite different
> ways of ordering knowledge, categorizing texts and ideas, and theoriz-
> ing experience. Here as elsewhere, I tend to try to use such categories
> as sparingly as possible, only when able to articulate precisely how they
> prove useful, and always anxious about the dangers of collapsing the
> diversity of the premodern sources thereby labeled into anachronisti-
> cally modern assumptions about which similarities and continuities are
> and are not meaningful or worthy of study.[43]

In this book, I intend to show that "Judaism" as a name that Jews use
is just such an "ism" of modern invention. I would confess to preferences
almost identical to those of Reed—that is, avoiding such anachronisms in
studying the past—and will make some arguments to that effect herein. I
will not claim, however, the necessity of the second argument. One
can accept the results of the first—that "Judaism" is a modern
term—without acceding to the second that using it to refer to the past is
problematic. In other words, one could conceivably grant that the

concept of "Judaism" is modern and still assert its utility for scholarly, historical research. I will try to show that this is not the case but grant that my argument on this point is not indefeasible.[44] The first point, however, that "Judaism" is a modern invention, is a matter for the philological record. The term "Judaism," the very subject of this book, does not appear in Reed's list—to be sure, not meant to be exhaustive, so this is no critique. It would seem, nonetheless, that this term has not yet been reassessed (sufficiently), destabilized, or deconstructed—yet.

I enter the lists.

The Pitfalls of Anachronism; or, "Judaism" as a Normative Concept

Let me begin with an account of the vicissitudes of the condition of "Judaism" to date. Since, as will be argued, the statement "Judaism exists" makes no ontological sense and only has meaning in a language in which the word "Judaism" (or cognate) exists, it would follow that any talk of "Judaism" in antiquity, or in the Middle Ages for that matter, is *eo ipso* an ideological intervention, an assertion precisely of the timelessness of the abstract entity of Judaism, a Form in the Platonic sense that can exist without anyone knowing that it does. As Adorno has written in a somewhat different context, "This kind of writing does not criticize abstract fundamental concepts, aconceptual data, or habituated clichés; instead, it presupposes them, implicitly but by the same token with all the more complicity."[45] In general, users of the language who utilize "Judaism" to refer to something that persists from Moses Our Rabbi to Moses Mendelssohn are indeed willy-nilly speaking normatively. They have an idea of that of which Judaism consists, believe that a certain essence can be traced in all forms of the alleged "religion" throughout this history and that, therefore, even if "Judaism" be a modern term, it picks out some unique thing in the world. This is a perfectly legitimate sort of normative statement, a theological claim if you will—and, as such, is successful within a given language game but hardly one that is justifiable within the language game of historiography.

The best example of such an approach outside of the pulpit would be George Foot Moore's works, especially as signified by his aptly titled "The Rise of Normative Judaism." Moore (October 15, 1851–May 16, 1931) was one of the most respected scholars of his time (with good reason) and taught generations of students at Harvard. It is easy to get a sense of Moore's approach from the very opening of this extended essay:

> The centuries which we designate politically by the names of the
> dominant powers of the age successively as the Persian, Greek, and

Roman periods of Jewish history constitute as a whole an epoch in the religious history of Judaism. In these centuries, past the middle of which the Christian era falls, Judaism brought to complete development its characteristic institutions, the school and the synagogue, in which it possessed, not only a unique instrument for the education and edification of all classes of the people in religion and morality, but the centre of its religious life, and to no small extent also of its intellectual and social life. Through the study of the Scriptures and the discussions of generations of scholars it defined its religious conceptions, its moral principles, its forms of worship, and its distinctive type of piety, as well as the rules of law and observance which became authoritative for all succeeding time. In the light of subsequent history the great achievement of these centuries was the creation of a normative type of Judaism and its establishment in undisputed supremacy throughout the wide Jewish world.[46]

It is clear already, and Moore goes on to state explicitly, that this stipulative "normative Judaism," which really for him means "Judaism" *tout court*, is the Judaism defined by the Mishna. Startlingly, for Moore, "Judaism" is so reified that it can actually have agency: "Judaism saw in [Ezra] the restorer of the law."[47] This "Judaism" manifests for Moore as "rabbinic texts," as becomes lucidly explicit in his further citations. Thus with respect to the introduction of the Mishna known as the Chapters of the Fathers, Moore writes, "With the authenticity of these utterances we are not here concerned; what is beyond question is that they are set down at the beginning of the Sentences of the Fathers as recognized fundamentals of Judaism, and if anyone should choose to rename the collection 'Maxims of the Pharisees,' the significance of the sayings would not be diminished."[48]

Moore's work is admirable, and his scholarship is excellent in its studious effort to redeem "Judaism" from the prejudiced anti-Judaism of many of his peers and predecessors among Protestant Bible scholars, and in part that effort conditions his very exclusive identification of the ideologies and practices of the Rabbis (= the Pharisees) with the very essence of "Judaism." His view of things on this score is entirely consonant with that of Orthodox Jewish tradition. Since it has been established by historians by now that it was not the case that even after Yavne the Pharisees and then the Rabbis were the de facto leaders of Palestinian Jewry, let alone world Jewry, acceptance of this narrative must be counted a normative judgment of normativity, one that a historical scholarship cannot countenance. What is more to the point is that, as I would suggest, any assertion of there having been a "Judaism" as an essential object involves such normative judgments.

In another crucial paper, Moore shows that he understands well the issue itself, even if, of course, not as applicable to his own work, writing that "Christian investigation and discussion of the terms Memra and Shekinah have thus in all stages been inspired and directed by a theological motive, and the results come around in a circle to the theological prepossessions from which they set out."[49] Thus in this very paper, for instance, Moore excludes a particular interpretation implying a divine intermediary owing alone to the alleged total absence of a comparable idea in any "exoteric teaching of Judaism."[50] By this he must indeed mean, as I have already shown, the putative "Judaism" of the Mishna and its sequels, for had he had recourse to the texts known as Pseudepigrapha, he would have found ample evidence for the ideas of divine intermediaries.[51] As Reed sums up Moore's intervention, she finds him "refracting Second Temple Judaism through yet another later lens and claiming Rabbinic sources as the crux of a timelessly normative Judaism from which 'pseudepigrapha' (and earliest Christianity) are categorically excluded." It would hardly be inapposite to refer to Moore's linear history of the rise of "normative Judaism" and its eventual triumph over all, false, rivals as exactly what Walter Benjamin has famously elegized: "The nature of this sadness stands out more clearly if one asks with whom the adherents of historicism actually empathize. The answer is inevitable: with the victor." Put more crudely, Churchill described this as writing the history of the winners. My contention here is that hypostases such as "Judaism" when they are not attested within the language of a given culture nearly inevitably—try as we might to avoid this result—lead to consequences structurally like those of Moore.

The "Judaisms" Problem

Recognizing well the overweening normativity of the category "Judaism" when applied to antiquity, some major scholars of the twentieth century sought to disturb that normativity by introducing the term and concept of "Judaisms"—pluralized. In such fashion, they meant to disrupt both traditional and scholarly (such as Moore's) assignment of the term "Judaism" to the norms, leadership, and practices of the Rabbis. The initial moves in this direction came from Erwin Goodenough via his recognition that the "Judaism" of Philo and other Hellenistic Jews was significantly different from that of the Palestinians.[52] Pride of place in this movement certainly goes, however, to Jacob Neusner, who provided the first attempt at an actual definition of a "Judaism," one that would purportedly be neither essentialistic nor normative.[53] Here is, perhaps, Neusner's most succinct attempt at a definition:

[A Judaism] is composed of three elements: a world view, a way of life, and a social group that, in the here and now, embodies the whole. The world view explains the life of the group, ordinarily referring to God's creation, the revelation of the Torah, the goal and end of the group's life in the end of time. The way of life defines what is special about the life of the group. The social group, in a single place and time, then forms the living witness and testimony to the system as a whole and finds in the system ample explanation for its very being. That is a *Judaism*.[54]

Oddly enough, it seems that the alleged "Judaism" of the Mishna and the Talmuds, inherited by medieval Jewry and passed on to modernity, would not qualify as a "Judaism" on Neusner's account, since, according to him, in the same site, "the first requirement is to find a group of Jews who see themselves as 'Israel.' . . . That same group must tell us that it uniquely constitutes 'Israel,' not *an* Israel."[55] The Rabbis, of course, contend that they have the true and correct interpretation of Torah but explicitly deny that others—who may be sinners in their eyes—are not "Israel." This is particularly salient because, as Michael Satlow, Neusner's successor in the teaching of ancient Jewish culture in religious studies at Brown, makes clear, for all Neusner's talk of "Judaisms," it is essentially the history of the rabbinic tradition that he is setting out.[56] In any case, it is clear that Neusner's monothetic definition will not serve to include all the entities that he himself (and certainly we) might be tempted to incorporate as Judaisms were we engaging in that very practice.

Satlow has attempted to improve on Neusner's view by tempering it with the proposal of J. Z. Smith that we move toward a polythetic definition—virtually identical to Wittgenstein's "family resemblances"— that is a "map[ping] of characteristics that may or may not be shared by the members of a group. Two specific members of a group might share several of these characteristics, some overlapping set, or even none at all."[57] To put it in Smith's own language, "We need to map the variety of Judaisms, each of which appears as a shifting cluster of characteristics which vary over time."[58] Taking Smith's call as a program, Satlow proposes to carry it out.

Satlow begins by positing three maps: "A polythetic description of Judaism, I suggest, comprises of three maps that for heuristic purposes I would label, Israel, discursive tradition, and practice."[59] Attempting to finally get rid of the lingering (or actually clear and present) essentialisms of Neusner's approach, Satlow argues that "'Israel,' then, first and foremost indicates a mode of determining the scope of the data: for the academic student of religion, any Jewish community or individual that self-identifies as 'Jewish,' or part of Israel, 'counts' to the same degree as any other."[60] The other two maps are defined by Satlow as, "How do they [the given 'Israels'] accept or reject their received texts and their discourses, and how do they use (or not) this tradition to authorize and inform their beliefs and values?" and then, "What are their religious practices, and how do they justify and explain them?"[61] I shan't go into the details of Satlow's working out of his proposal, as I wish to query its very foundations even while recognizing how much of an advance it is over Neusner's essentialism or the grosser normative essentialisms of early scholarship such as Moore's. The most salient difficulties that I find with Satlow's proposal are that, beginning with any community that self-identifies with "Israel," it then proceeds to posit and investigate precisely the same set, beliefs and "religious" practices that mark nearly any other praxis of the study of "religions." It has given, in fact, a monothetic definition of a "Judaism" to wit that it must identify itself as an Israel. In fine, we end up with "Israels"—monothetically, if expansively defined—and their "religions."[62] On my view, a genuinely polythetic analysis starting from the data and not from any preconceived definition would lead, in a grossly cropped example, to something like the following results:

	Rabbis	Matthew	Sadducees	Marcion
Resurrection	+	+	−	−
God of Israel as Creator	+	+	+	+ (The Evil Creator)
Jesus as Savior	−	+	−	+
Call Themselves "Israel"	+	+	+	−

This is a synecdochal sample of a polythetic or family resemblance classification. Each of these entities shares at least one characteristic with at least one other, but none of them share all characteristics. Even the one characteristic that seems to be shared by all, Israel's God as creator, is so sharply different in Marcion for whom Israel's God is not the true God but some evil underling as to constitute a difference rather than a shared feature. There are ways in which the Rabbis and the Gospel of Matthew are closer to each other than the Rabbis and the Sadducees (as pointed out by Justin Martyr, lo these two millennia ago). Unless we decide to identify one characteristic as marking off something that we nominate Judaism and something that we nominate Christianity, an anachronistic and/or normative move, there is little reason to see the Gospel and Marcion as belonging to one group and the Rabbis and the Sadducees to another. Note please that there is no feature that joins the Rabbis and Marcion. Nevertheless, the Gospel shares distinctive features with the Rabbis that differentiate the Gospel from Marcion. The Gospel *does* share with Marcion the feature of Jesus as savior. Therefore, all these entities belong in the same family (polythetic aggregate), a family that I would hesitate to call Judaisms (Marcion indeed!), still less, Judaism! Now of course this analysis would need to be much more extensive with many other known groups included and many other parameters as well, but this is sufficient, I think, to indicate what a polythetic (family resemblance) classification would look like and why it wouldn't produce "Judaisms" without some dogmatic border being advanced.

While Satlow makes some progress over earlier monothetic versions of defining "Judaism," either inchoate or explicit, he nevertheless leaves us with the question of why we should seek to define something that no one knows of at the time about which the research is being done. If "Israels" are the object of study, then why not just say that? We end up with a polythetic definition of a word that didn't exist. What is gained by adding another layer of abstraction between us and the data by referring to them as "Judaisms"? It is considerations like these, inter alia,[63] that first led me to consider the possibility that it is not helpful to think in terms of "Judaisms."

"No Judaism" and Its Discontents

Steve Mason famously argued against the meaningful usage of the term "Judaism" in antiquity. I have strongly assented to his position, which I am developing further here partly in response to scholars who have rejected it. Seth Schwartz makes two arguments against the claim that there is no "Judaism" as the name of a "religion" in antiquity. The first is based on Shaye Cohen's argument from so-called conversion.[64] The argument runs as follows: if there was a "religious" ceremony by which others became Jews, then Judaism was necessarily a religion. To be sure, this argument begs the question by assuming the existence or relevance of a "religious" ceremony as opposed to some other kind of ceremony. Furthermore, Schwartz, in defending Cohen against Mason, somewhat misunderstands Mason's point, in my opinion. The point is not that peoplehood [*ethnos, genos,* or even *polis*] did not incorporate a strong cultic component in antiquity but precisely that worship and peoplehood are so inextricably tied to each other in antiquity that moving from one people to another (or even from the province of one *polis* to another) necessarily involved adopting new gods and new practices associated with them.[65] As Elizabeth Castelli has well phrased it, "From the vantage point of a post-Enlightenment society that understands the separation of the political and the religious as an ideal to be protected, the Roman imperial situation requires careful attention to the myriad ways in which 'Roman religion' might, it could be defensibly argued, not quite exist. That is, insofar as practices that could conventionally be called 'religious' intersected so thoroughly with political institutions, social structures, familial commitments, and recognition of the self-in-society, there is very little in ancient Roman society that would not as a consequence qualify as 'religious.'"[66] If "religion" does not pick out anything in the form of life that is distinguished from anything else there, identifying some doings as "religion" only means imposing our ideological divisions ("post-Enlightenment") on another form of life. For the most part, this inextricable tie holds with respect to Judaeans in antiquity as well, with only one nonconclusive exception. On the one hand, the case of the so-called conversion (forced) of the Idumeans and similar cases fits this notion of an inextricable linkage well; they were annexed to the Judaeans and thus required to behave accordingly. On the other hand, Cohen and Schwartz are undoubtedly correct to point to the conversion of Antiochus in 2 Maccabees 9:17 who "becomes a Jew" (Ἰουδαῖον ἔσεσθαι)[67] as a case in which he "becomes a Jew" without stopping to be a Seleucid, providing us with one interesting but far outlying case, as we know no other case in antiquity of one who becomes a *Ioudaios* and retains a non-*Ioudaios* "ethnic" identity. The second case adduced by them, however, goes exactly in the opposite direction, for Achior in Judith (14:10) does not become a Jew but "becomes added to the House of Israel"—"When Achior saw all that the God of Israel had done, he believed firmly in God. So he was circumcised, and was added to the house of Israel, remaining so to this day"[68]—which, if anything, strongly supports Mason's point. Achior didn't convert to a religion, but having learned to trust its god, he joined a collective. Following Cohen's reasoning adopted by Schwartz, after all, one could conclude that the book of Ruth is evidence for conversion to "Judaism" as well. Moreover, as has been recently shown, the rejection of any notion of the possibility of assimilation to the Jewish People was much more widespread than Schwartz recognized at the time of his writing.[69] Acknowledging, then, the significance of the single case in Maccabees as perhaps a harbinger of something yet to come, it remains the case that Mason was correct in seeing Judaean identity as parallel, grosso modo, with such identities as Ephesian, Athenian, and Roman.

Schwartz, however, makes yet another point against Mason (and thus implicitly against me as well). Arguing that "the Jews' religion was unusually tightly integrated and its administration was concentrated in the hands of an unusually unified clerisy," he wishes to derive from this point the conclusion that the Jews did, in fact, have a religion that we might as well name "Judaism." Formally, at least, this is a classic example of *petitio principi*, otherwise known as "begging the question," assuming the conclusion in the premises themselves. Beginning his sentence with the subject "The Jews' religion" disqualifies it a priori as an argument for the existence of such an entity. What of the substance of the argument, however? Schwartz finds it very telling that the Jews around the world converge in certain practices and diverge in others. The question still remains whether the name for the practices in which they converge ought to be Judaism, a religion, or not. The actual evidence for Schwartz's claim that "even before the rise of Christianity some people did think in terms of Judaism, in a sense much like the modern one"[70] is to all intents and purposes nonexistent or, at any rate, so rare as to be inconsequential. Moreover, his sequel, "and others thought that allegiance to the Jewish God and acceptance of his laws made you not simply pious but Jewish," actually serves better the argument of this book than his.

In the next section of this chapter, I will present the argument for avoiding the use of anachronistic terminology, such as "Judaism" in the scholarly description of ancient or otherwise other cultures.

Thrēskeia; or, Making an Example of "Religion"

> It is perhaps the case that for some [scholars] the category religion is analogous to the religion that William James discerns among many religionists: it "exists," that is, "as a dull habit."[71]
> —Benson Saler, "Religio and the Definition of Religion"

New Testament scholar Edwin Judge has enjoined, "When one encounters the word 'religion' in a translation of an ancient text. First, cross out the word whenever it occurs. Next, find a copy of the text in question in its original language and see what word (if any) is being translated by 'religion.' Third, come up with a different translation: It almost doesn't matter what. Anything besides 'religion.'"[72] In the philological tradition, the Greek word most often cited as meaning "religion" is *thrēskeia*, and that is how the word has been routinely translated. In a multiyear research project just published as a book cowritten with my colleague in Roman studies, Professor Carlin A. Barton, we have established a philological basis for denying the meaning of "religion" to any classical lexical item.[73] To prepare my part of that study, I read every extant passage from ancient Greek between Herodotus and the Greek Christians of the second century AD in which the word *thrēskeia* appears.[74] Barton pursued, in her turn, *religio*.[75] Barton and I have, moreover, tried to show how using a kind of semantic mapping, a description of the metonymic relations of usages, answers better to the way meanings actually work in languages and reveals more of their respective semantic categories than does the usual lexical division of a word into subheadings as dictionaries do. We thus propose, at least for all important words, family-resemblance style mappings of usage to replace dictionaries.

Some scholars are much friendlier to lexica than I am (we are). Leading—justly so[76]—historian of the Second-Temple period, Daniel R. Schwartz dissents on the question of "religion" in ancient Greek and thinks to prove its existence from dictionaries and extant traditions of scholars:[77] "Although it is true that translators of ancient texts sometimes use 'religion' even when the Greek does not require it, it is also the case that dictionaries, and scholars of ancient Greek, regularly render the Greek term *thrēskeia* as 'religion.'"[78]

Schwartz's reliance on the dictionaries reminds one of nothing so much as Wittgenstein's remark that "we do not analyze a phenomenon (for example, thinking) but a concept (for example, that of thinking), and hence the application of a word. So it may look as if what we were doing were nominalism. Nominalists make the mistake of interpreting all words as *names*, and so of not really describing their use, but only, so to speak, giving a paper bank draft on such a description [PI 384]." In translating a word without fully describing its use, we are only, to use Wittgenstein's wonderful metaphor, giving a check, promising something, something that we must finally deliver. Now to be sure, Schwartz, fine scholar that he is, takes pains to demonstrate the correctness of this translation in several passages of Josephus. Shortly, however, I will contend that his argument on this point fails with respect to Josephus as well. The check is still not cashed. Only as full a laying out and mapping of the usages of the key words as possible will cover such a check.

Here I propose to afford from my own research for the book (and in the book[79]) two examples out of many, coming back briefly to Josephus before concluding with more methodological reflections. The first example is drawn from the Roman-Greek writer Plutarch and the second from the Greek-writing Jew Philo. In both of these, I will show that the translation of "religion" is actually precluded (notwithstanding the lexicons and some scholarly translators).

Thrēskeia *as* Superstitio

Plutarch (c. 46–120 AD) writes of ideal wifely behavior: "A wife ought not to make friends of her own, but to enjoy her husband's friends in common with him. The gods are the first and most important friends. Therefore it is seemly for a wife to fear [*sebesthai*] and to know only the gods that her husband honors [*nomizei*], and to shut the outer door against all *periergoi thrēskeiai* and *xenai deisidaimoniai*" (Plutarch *Coniugalia praecepta* 140d).

This is a particularly rich passage, as it explicitly draws a contrast between proper *sebas* (*sebomai* = to show awe, fear, revere with respect to gods, persons, and objects) and improper *thrēskeia* and *deisidaimonia*, both of which are associated explicitly with negative adjectives; *thrēskeia* with *periergos* (taking needless trouble, useless) and *deisidaimonia* with *xenos* (alien, strange, unusual), an opposition we find in other texts as well. This is a common enough pattern to show that Greek culture had a certain similarity to the Roman culture in the form of a balancing system in which the midpoint between extremes is seen as the ideal,[80] one in which too much fear of the god was as negative a moment as too little. Karen King has referred to this as the Goldilocks Principle. We frequently find the word *eusebeia*, literally "good fear"—that is, that which is appropriate and within measure, not over-the-top or otherwise useless, in contrast to *deisidaimonia* and *thrēskeia* and as the perfect midpoint between those excesses and *asebeia*, impiety. *Thrēskeia* frequently functions in Greek much like *superstitio* in Latin: fearing the gods too much in Cicero's terms. *Deisidaimonia* and *thrēskeia* in this exemplary text represent the disdained extreme, too much of the proper *sebas* of "good fear"—that is, appropriate piety / reverence.

Thrēskeia *as Mere Outward Observance*

In some Hellenistic Jewish writers, moreover, we also find *thrēskeia* used in opposition to *eusebeia*. My example here is drawn from Philo (25 BC to 50 AD). There is frequently in this writer, as in Plutarch, a kind of negative tinge to the use of the term *thrēskeia*, or better put, he uses it in contexts that have a negative charge.[81] Thus within Philo's writings, we find instances in which *thrēskeia* is more marked with the overtones of the useless sort of observances that we have just seen in Plutarch. In the following context, it is clearly and explicitly marked by Philo as nearly the opposite of *eusebeia*. Philo speaks of one "who has more money than he knows what to do with" and founds a temple and sacrifices unceasingly, providing expensive votive offerings with all manner of rich furnishings. Nonetheless, "let him not be inscribed with the *eusebeis*, for he has wandered from the way of *eusebeia*; thinking it [*eusebeia*] *thrēskeia* as opposed to *hosiotēs* [*anti hosiotētos*], and giving gifts to the unbribable one who will never take them and flattering the unflatterable, the one who welcomes [all] that which belongs to the genuine class of *therapeia*—the genuine class being the soul bearing simply and entirely truth—while he rejects counterfeit ones. [*Quod deterius potiori insidiari soleat* 21]."[82] This unrighteous person has been led to his hypocrisy by mistakenly thinking that proper reverence (*eusebeia*) is *thrēskeia*, glossed here explicitly as sacrifices, offerings, and the like as opposed to appropriate *hosiotēs*, glossed explicitly as a movement of the soul bearing truth. We have several sharp semantic contrasts here. *Thrēskeia* is defined as neither *eusebeia* nor *therapeia* ("proper" divine service) and especially not *hosiotēs* but rather as that which is only external and hence "counterfeit," as he is not bringing truth from his soul as his sacrifice.[83] *Thrēskeia* here is the error of thinking that one can bribe God with material gifts.[84] The text could not be clearer or more explicit than it is in its valuation of *thrēskeia* as the inferior or even negative term and as the contrary of *eusebeia*. These instances are exemplary of numerous Greek literary usages of the word from the Hellenistic era. Were we attempting a map of the semantic field in which this word appears, we would tag it as (1) excessive, nonsensical, or even harmful cultic practice, in opposition to good cultic practice, and (2) as mere outer cultic practice, in opposition to inner piety. *Thrēskeia* is not used as "religion" in its modern European sense (*mutatis mutandis*) and thus it is very difficult, if even possible at all, to ascribe the *concept*, "religion," to those ancient folks. Some further thinking about language in a theoretical vein will help clarify my point of view.

Language as "Form of Life"

Ludwig Wittgenstein famously remarked: "For a *large* class of cases—though not for all—in which we employ the word 'meaning' it can be defined thus: the meaning of a word is its use in the language" (PI 43). This basic statement is what underlies the significance of Wittgenstein's contribution: a change from a conception of meaning as representation to a view that looks to use as the crux of the matter. A commentator on Wittgenstein has helpfully phrased it as follows: "Traditional theories of meaning in the history of philosophy were intent on pointing to something exterior to the proposition which endows it with sense. This 'something' could generally be located either in an objective space, or inside the mind as mental representation. Rather, when investigating meaning, the researcher must 'look and see' the variety of uses to which the word is put."[85] Without going into excessive detail here, it will be seen that if the project of assessing meaning is the observation of the usage of a word, then, without a word, it is nearly impossible to ascribe a meaning, a concept.[86]

If the meaning of the word is its use, then the interpretation of the word for both the speaker/writer and the hearer/reader is affected by all the myriad ways that the word has been used before, setting up an endless oscillation of meaning effects.[87] Again, taking this very seriously as a plausible description of actual natural language, I suggest that Wittgenstein implies that we don't walk around with a lexicon in our heads, a list of words and definitions, but with a *Zettelkasten* (box of note slips) of thousands and thousands of half-remembered prior uses of words and phrases that we pull out of our memories in appropriate (or seemingly appropriate) contexts. As one important Wittgenstein scholar has put it, "The point is that words are ultimately connected to the world by training, not by translation."[88] Stanley Cavell has articulated essentially the same point: "Instead, then, of saying either that we *tell* beginners what words mean or that we *teach* them what objects are, I say: We initiate them, into the relevant forms of life held in language and gathered around the objects and persons of our world."[89]

Another of Wittgenstein's philosophical investigations sharpens our philological investigation:

If "X exists" is meant simply to say: "X" has a meaning,—then it is not a proposition which treats of X, but a proposition about our use of language, that is, about the use of the word "X."

In other words, if the statement "Red exists" is true, then this means that "Red" has a meaning in a given language, and the statement "red does not exist" means the opposite:

But what we really *want* is simply to take "Red exists" as the statement: the word "red" has a meaning. Or perhaps better: "Red does not exist" as "'Red' has no meaning." (Wittgenstein 28–29)

Closet Platonists that we are, we are tempted to take "red exists" as an ontological statement, one that would necessitate something like, or at least analogous to, an Idea or Form. What Wittgenstein is claiming, in a non-Platonic thinking, in contrast, the sentence "red exists" ought really to be understood as a statement about a given language—namely, that within that language, the word "red" has meaning. If, for example, the sentence "religion exists" only means that the term "religion" has meaning, the term "religion" cannot have meaning in a language that doesn't have a word for it. Since the sentence is only a statement about language (and not about the metaphysical being of "redness"), then where there is no word for "red," redness is not meaningful. Where there is no word for "religion," religion is not meaningful as a concept, ergo "religion" does not exist in that linguistic-cultural system and similarly for "Judaism."[90] This helps us begin to answer what difference it makes when a language has no word that is used as we use "religion," or more specifically for the current case, "Judaism." I fully subscribe to this Wittgensteinian position, here only barely sketched in, of course.

When we divide the usage of a word into distinct and discrete meanings and submeanings as the practice of traditional lexicons, we are not actually describing the usage of the other language and its accompanying conceptual system but imposing the abstractions and categories of our language and conceptual system on them.[91] Thus, frequently enough, when we say that a given word has two meanings in some foreign language, all we are saying is that English has no word that matches the semantic range of that foreign tongue.[92] Only the usage of the other language will teach us what its living speakers consider to be within single categories and divided into separate ones. Asserting the existence of ancient religion or ancient Judaism is an imposition of our language on theirs, one valid for the pulpit perhaps, but not for describing a form of life.[93]

Wittgenstein has brilliantly formulated what was for me, before reading him, a hunch:

> It is easy to consisting only of orders and reports in battle.—Or a language consisting only of questions and expressions for answering Yes and No—and countless other things.—And to imagine a language means to imagine a form of life [PI §19].[94]

Although the meaning of "forms of life" in Wittgenstein is much contested,[95] I have found most helpful the account given by P. M. S. Hacker.[96] Crucial to understanding Wittgenstein here is the recognition that, already, "Wilhelm von Humboldt in his On Language (1836) linked the idea of forms of life with customs and habits of a language-using community."[97] As Hacker emphasizes—correctly, in my view—this is *not* a philosophical term of art but common German usage. And Hacker explicitly remarks that Wittgenstein is using the term in this "humdrum" fashion. "Form of life" is, therefore, something quite close to our notion of culture while bypassing many of the theoretical problems that have arisen with that term.[98] (In fact, in my work henceforth, I intend to use "form of life" precisely where I once would have written "culture.")[99] The novelty of Wittgenstein's §19 is not in the concept of "form of life," but only this: that to investigate a language means to investigate a form of life:

> To conclude: the expression "form of life" plays a very small role in Wittgenstein's later philosophy. No aura or mystique should be allowed to attach itself to his notion of a form of life. In itself it is of no great moment. What *is* of great moment is the larger body of thought of which the concept of a form of life is merely a surface ornament. That larger body of thought is the ethnological conception of language as a form of activity embedded in the ways of living of a language-using community. That activity is normative, i. e. rule-governed—but not in the manner of a calculus; rather in the manner of a game.[100]

In order to make sense of Hacker, I would insist that his statement that "form of life" is not of great moment comes simply to claim that Wittgenstein himself is neither coining nor referring to a new philosophical concept with that usage (of no great *moment*) but deploying it to make an argument that is of great moment at that moment.[101] It would follow, therefore, that what the language lacks, the form of life cannot comprise.[102]

As Hacker sums up, as lucidly as could be hoped for, "In short, human beings in different epochs, in different cultures, have different forms of life. Different educations, interests and concerns, languages, different human relations and relations to nature and the world constitute distinct forms of life. For different cultures form different conceptual structures, adopt distinctive forms and norms of representation, limited only by the vague boundaries of the concept of a form of representation or a language."[103] In investigating a language, we are investigating a form of life. A form of life that has no word that means "religion" cannot have religion in it nor can there be a "Judaism" without a word that refers to it.

What's at stake in claiming that there was no "religion" in the ancient Jewish concept world? Professor Richard Neer has shown the way to one part of an answer in his response to a draft of this chapter:

> It has to do with the relation between your . . . account of θρησκεία, which might be seen as tending to a behaviorism of ritual, and the place of early Judaism relative both to later Judaism and to medieval and later Christianity. I have in mind the charge, which one finds in St Paul and so on, and which Auerbach describes in "Figura," that the (early) Jews were carnal literalists who lacked true salvific religion. Paul's suggestion that "the letter killeth," his call for circumcision of the heart, the typological or figural reading of Jewish history, and so on—all maintain

that ancient Judaism was merely going through the motions, so to speak.

Yes, indeed, that is the point. One of the dangers of invoking the term "religion" where it is not wonted, so to speak, is precisely evaluating a form of life by its nearness or distance to Christianity, especially of the Pauline variety in which personal salvation is the very center of value. Among Jews, Indians, Romans, and myriad—nearly all—others, it is exactly the value of the "doings" that count: group adhesion, cohesion, effervescence (to use Durkheimian language), participation in a sacralized narrative, intimacy with the "ancestors" by doing their doings, and not individual emotion, belief, or the "salvation" of the individual.[104]

Josephus: *Thrēskeia* as *Eusebeia*

Philo's near-contemporary, Flavius Josephus the Judean historian, exhibits different usage of *thrēskeia*. In contrast to other Hellenistic writers, Josephus frequently uses *thrēskeia*, not in contrast to *eusebeia* but as a close congener or near synonym. There is no room here to expand on the historical background of such usage; suffice it to say here that it seems to be well attested in epigraphic sources from the northeast of the Greek-speaking area—namely, Thrace and Bythinia—and virtually only there.[105] It is this variance in use from other writers that has tempted scholars to see in Josephus the meaning "religion" for this word. Daniel Schwartz has provided several examples of what he takes to be knockout cases for the meaning "religion" in Josephus. I will analyze what I take to be his strongest example in order to show why it is not probative—indeed, almost the opposite—of that which he seeks to prove.

To be sure, most of Schwartz's examples are actually irrelevant, as they admittedly (by him) serve to prove only nuances of meaning like "piety" (= *eusebeia*) or something stronger like "devotion" but not "religion."[106] This sense for *thrēskeia* is very well attested in Josephus as documented in *Imagine No Religion* and does not match in any sense any of the varied usages of "religion." So here is what I take to be Schwartz's best relevant example. He argues that at *Antiquities* 12.269, when Mattathias and his sons declare that they will never abandon their ancient *thrēskeia*, "Josephus is rendering in indirect speech, Mattathias' declaration, according to Josephus' *Vorlage*, 1 Macc. 2:20, that he and his sons and brothers will continue 'to walk in the covenant [*diathēke*] of our fathers' and that sounds as if it refers to the whole ancestral tradition, and not just to worship."[107] Schwartz goes on, moreover, to cite a passage in the immediate sequel in which Josephus again renders "covenant" by *thrēskeia* and concludes, "Thus, in these passages *thrēskeia* seems to have a meaning more general than 'cult' for Josephus, referring to whatever the Jews' covenant with God entails—which is much more than 'worship.' In English, 'religion' is the general category of which 'worship' is an element."[108] The question is not whether "worship" is an element of "religion" in English but of what it was an element in Josephus's Greek, in Josephus's Judean form of life. Schwartz's own example and his argument here prove the opposite of what he wishes to prove, since the very *Vorlage* to which he refers, 1 Maccabees, has "covenant" (διαθήκη), which is, of course, a term not even close to being a semantic congener for modern "religion." This hardly supports a rendering of Josephus's *thrēskeia* as "religion." In short, as I have amply demonstrated elsewhere, *thrēskeia* is, for Josephus, frequently an equivalent for Torah or the Covenant, as it is—demonstrably and explicitly—here. Schwartz is thus checkmated by his own pawns, and the bottom line is that Josephus—and everyone else in his day and age—had no word for "religion." "Religion" is not part of the form of life of these folks. *Eusebeia* and *thrēskeia* in the fullness of time become the two Greek words most commonly used in later Greek to roughly approximate English "religion,"[109] but this fact hardly justifies anachronistically reading this meaning back before it is attested.[110]

Some scholars will object to the aforementioned conclusion, and some already have, to the effect that whether or not Josephus and his brothers had a *concept* of religion, they did have practices (verbal and embodied) that match *our* concept of religion, so why should we not call those "Josephus's religion" and just get on with it? In its most sophisticated version, this takes the form of asserting, with J. Z. Smith, that "religion is a product of the scholar's study," and, therefore, we may define it however we want for the purposes of comparative research. (Because my disagreements here are sharp, I would like to express here my deep appreciation of Smith's work, for all my dispute about some significant points of his approach. I could say that I have learned much from Smith's own "double project of appreciation and criticism of Eliade."[111])

The fundamental problem is that by dividing that which a given collective did not apparently divide and by joining together that which they did not, we run the serious risk of misinterpreting the doings of that collective. Let me give for this context one very quick but telling example. Josephus tells us that when the Judeans came to Jerusalem to observe the festival in the Temple, they discussed plans for the rebellion against Rome. Since in our modern cultural formation we have constructed separate realms called "religion" and "politics," the way has been open, all too open, for historians either to praise the wiliness of the Jews,

camouflaging their "political" motives with "religious" ones, or, alterna-
tively, to condemn their hypocrisy for this. There is, however, no reason
in the world to imagine that for the Judeans, offering a sacrifice and plan-
ning a revolt belonged to separate, axiologically distinct realms or
spheres.[112] Various strands of recent anthropological research have,
indeed, shown that the practices surrounding the war band and rebellion
are virtually identical to those that mark off what we call "religions."
Given the precise nexus between the practices that sacralize leaders,
groups, and commitments (even, not infrequently, unto death) in the war
band and the practices that sacralize leaders, groups, and commitments
(even, not infrequently, unto death) in cultic formations (indeed, the
impossibility—frequently—of telling these apart at all), it becomes even
more clear why the imposition of our categories of "religion" and "politics" on ancient cultures results in ghastly distortions.[113]

Steve Mason has written to this point:

> Josephus has often been criticized for presenting his teacher Bannus
> as well as the Pharisees, Sadducees, and Essenes as philosophical
> schools, because of our modern assumption that they were obviously
> religious groups. But there was no such terminology available to
> Josephus that would be intelligible to his audiences. He could say that
> these groups or individuals were concerned with piety, simple living,
> contempt for suffering and death, and expectation of a certain afterlife,
> and that is what he does. But these were what philosophical schools
> did, and that is why he calls them philosophies. There was no genus
> called religion, of which any of these could be a species. (Mason, ms.)

This revealing point made by Mason exposes perfectly what is at stake
in this investigation. As Mason shows, the application of anachronistic
categories and abstractions leads to a fundamental misapprehension of
Josephus's very text and results in him being accused of a flaw in understanding his own culture, as it were. Such accusations by historians of
category error on the part of Josephus—anatomized by Mason—remind
one of nothing so much as the repeated historians' critiques directed at
the Romans for not distinguishing clearly enough between the sacred
and the profane or between religion and politics, as if these were "real"
entities, Platonic forms, and not the constructs of particular cultures and
always different in configuration. Even as sophisticated a scholar as Tessa
Rajak partially falls into this trap, as shown by the following example:
"There is nothing more difficult, in writing about the Palestine of this
period, than to form an adequate conception of the relation between
religion and other spheres of life," she writes. Perhaps, I would suggest,
the difficulty lies in the fact that there is no such distinction made by the

people in the culture—least of all, Josephus. As Rajak herself notes elsewhere, "What is even more interesting is that prayer could be converted on the instant into a political meeting: 'We were proceeding with the ordinary service and engaged in prayer, when Jesus rose and began to question us about the furniture and uncoined silver'" (295; Thackeray's translation). The simplest conclusion is that there are no such "spheres of life."

Confusion about these matters leads to fundamental problems in historical interpretation. Thus a very recent scholar on the Maccabean revolt, Sylvie Honigman, starts out really well, in my humble opinion, writing, "First and second Maccabees have too often been, and still are, read as though their accounts were shaped by the same semantic categories as our own, as if certain words and concepts had the same connotations for their original audience as they do for us. In particular, a recurrent source of misinterpretation is the projection of the present-day categories of 'religion' and 'politics' on these texts." So far, so good, but the power of this observation is immediately undermined in the sequel in which she precisely *accepts* the present-day categories of "religion" and "politics," just reversing their application to the temple situation, arguing that it is *not* religion but politics (dropping those necessary quotation marks): "But whereas according to modern Western semantic categories, 2 Maccabees' high interest in the temple is taken as evidence for it author's religiousness, according to ancient Judean criteria it is actually a token of political side-taking."[114] Put in this way, I'm afraid, the statement seems outrageous (and has aroused outrage). The correct generalization, of course, would be that there were no such categories at all in antiquity, neither "religion" nor "politics." So vis-à-vis concern for the Temple, one simply cannot ask whether it was "religious" or "political." To use Honigman's own language in a different context, "in my view, . . . the very terms of the debate need modification."[115] (I will come back to Honigman and the question of terms in the next chapter.)

A statement about a putative religion, "Judaism" in the Second-Temple period could only mean either that there was a meaningful term in their language semantically cognate with our "Judaism/Jewish religion" or that there is something in our form of life for which we want to claim an ancestry in antiquity even though they did not recognize its existence. Since, as we have seen, the former is simply not the case, then the sentence "Judaism of the Second-Temple period" could only mean that we wish to claim that something in our concept world is the same as something that existed then and to claim that sameness as "Judaism," even though it had no meaning in their language.[116] That is, it didn't exist then on Wittgenstein's account. It can be seen that this would be a normative and not a descriptive practice. The relation of concept to word remains philosophically fraught, of course. There could certainly be ways of expressing a concept that are not tied to a particular single word and, almost necessarily, concepts have to be (at least) developing *before* there are words to name them.[117]

I shall rely here on some very helpful comments of Quentin Skinner:

> What then is the relationship between concepts and words? We can scarcely hope to capture the answer in a single formula, but I think we can at least say this: the surest sign that a group or society has entered into the self-conscious possession of a new concept is that a corresponding vocabulary will be developed, a vocabulary which can then be used to pick out and discuss the concept with consistency. This suggests that, while we certainly need to exercise more caution than [Raymond] Williams does in making inferences from the use of words to the understanding of concepts and back again, there is nevertheless a systematic relationship between words and concepts to be explored. For the possession of a concept will at least standardly be signalled by the employment of a corresponding term. As long as we bear in mind that "standardly" means neither necessarily nor sufficiently, I think we may legitimately proceed.[118]

It follows from this point that scholars would do well to avoid using such anachronistic terms as "Judaism" in describing Jewish/Judean forms of life before the modern period when such usages became current in Jewry and Jewish parlance. We should be neither ascribing nor implying the personal soteriological aspects of Christianities to a putative "Judaism," even though many Jews may have been involved in such doings as well, nor should we be implying the separation of spheres that a word meaning "Jewish religion" would insinuate before Jews en masse—or for that matter, nearly anyone else—made such distinctions and separations between law, politics, religion. Our attempts to translate in this fashion only produce more bank checks without cashing them.

PART II

THE STATE OF THE LEXICON

Questioning the Archive

2 Jewry without Judaism

In search of the question that motivates this book and as an illustration of the virtues of clarity on this question, I will begin by discussing Philip Davies's *On the Origins of Judaism*. I begin with the title, which, in accord with accepted practice, assumes the existence of something called "Judaism" and then searches for its origins. Of course, the title could be construed in a different way also—namely, the search for the moment in which the construct "Judaism" became salient within an episteme, rendering it closer theoretically to the project of this book. Davies's book is exciting to me when it approaches the latter question; troubling when it seems mired in the former one.

Let me begin with Davies's opening statement: "Ancient Judaism is the religious matrix of the three world religions of monotheism (or, if you prefer, monarchic theism) and one of the two parents, along with the classical Greco-Roman culture, that shaped Western civilization."[1] My problems grow from the matrix of this sentence itself, the concept of "ancient Judaism." Red flags with questions went up when I read it first: Does Davies mean here the cult of ancient Israel as carried out in the Second Temple—that is, the cult of the Temple state called Yahud (it quickly transpires that this is indeed what he means)? If that is indeed "Judaism," how could it be that "Judaism" is the matrix for "Judaism" as well as a couple of entities that are not named "Judaism"? Are we speaking of one legitimate and two bastard children (a position that Davies clearly does *not* endorse), as he himself says in the very next paragraph, "whilst Judaism retained the name of the mother; it is not for that reason typologically closer to its parent"? (Samaritanism is, on his view, closest to the parent.) In that case, what reason is there to name the "mother" Judaism at all, since that name does not appear in any of the sources that refer to ancient Israel and the very attempt to call its alleged "religion" Judaism is precisely a project for insisting that rabbinic, medieval, and modern Judaisms (themselves a modern construct) are the direct and correct (typologically closest) descendants of this parent? Finally, applying the name "ancient Judaism" to an alleged ancestress of Samaritanism also seems troubling, since Samaritans themselves, to the best of my knowledge, do not even call themselves *Ioudaioi* but *Israelites*. Of course, Davies is way too sophisticated (and I will take further measure of his sophistication presently) to imagine a single entity to be called ancient Judaism (by page 3 he is speaking of "kinds of Judaism" with reference to 1 Enoch), but the question remains, Why speak of "Judaism" at all?

Indeed, the confusion entailed by this search results in such statements as "The problem of defining 'early Judaism' means asking 'who was a Jew'?"[2] But surely then the term "Judaism" has shifted in meaning within Davies's text (in just four pages) from the name of an alleged "religion" from which other alleged "religions" are derived to the condition of being a member of a collective—however that membership might be defined. In the end, Davies (reflecting indeed the cutting edge) writes, "The outcome of these . . . developments is the now widely shared (though admittedly not unanimous) perception that what is called 'Judaism' in the period before the fall of the Second Temple (and in effect a good deal later) was in reality a set of cultural and religious options. Sometimes these overlapped, sometimes they competed, and they ranged from what sociologists might nowadays call 'civic religion' to quite exclusive sects."[3] So "Judaism" is in scare quotes, or maybe just an allusion to someone else's usage, but then whose? If in antiquity this congeries was not called "Judaism" (and it was not: As we shall presently see, *Ioudaismos* means something quite different in both Maccabees and Paul, the only two ancient literary contexts in which it appears), then who is calling it "Judaism"? If only modern scholars—that is, those who are following the latest "developments" in scholarship, are calling it (the "set of overlapping options") "Judaism," what is gained by using this term, bound to be confused with the "folk" usage that sees one unbroken stream from Abraham Our Father to Abraham Heschel? The very question of when a "set of cultural and religious options" began presents a further analytic conundrum, particularly if at least some of these options are contending with each other.

Davies is well aware of these problems, truly on top of them, as it were. He remarks of modern scholars who certainly de-essentialize a one true eternal Judaism and speak of "Judaisms" as being part and parcel of a system in which the different "Judaisms" contend or a genus of which the different "Judaisms" are species but criticizes these same scholars for not troubling to say what a "Judaism" is. As Davies notes, the implication that Judaism is a genus in which different Judaisms are species is itself logically problematic, as is, also, the implication that once there was a single Judaism from which the individual species descended, producing the congeries. With respect to another scholar who distinguishes sharply between Judaism as an unbroken "religious tradition" and so-called Hellenizers, Davies correctly observes, "Are the Judaisms of Philo or of 2 or 4 Maccabees, traditional or Hellenistic? If such mixtures are possible in Egypt, then why not in Palestine?"[4]

After such effective critique, Davies goes on, however, to make some remarks that raise questions for me. Inquiring into the question whether "'Judaism' is the religion of the 'Jewish people' or are the 'Jewish people' those who adhere to the religion?," he goes on to remark that many Jews in antiquity were converts—free or forced—to "a religion that previously existed."[5] I will try to disentangle this knot, a potential logic-bomb, in fact. First of all, there is a serious question as to the premises of the remark itself. As has been shown in a recent book, the question of conversion was not at all settled during the Second-Temple period and even for a while later.[6] Certainly for important groups (including, for instance, the author of Jubilees), neither of the aforementioned propositions is the case: Jews are those who are born Jews, nothing more or less (although, according to some of these groups, no male uncircumcised by the eighth day could ever be or become a Jew!). Second, what is or could be "a religion that previously existed," if it has no name among any of the people? The very fact that one can become a *Ioudaios* is hardly probative of the existence of a "religion." Else we would have to assume that Hellenicity was a "religion" as far back as the fourth century BC, since Isocrates wrote then, "Those who are called 'Hellenes' are those who share our culture (*paideusis*) rather than a common biological inheritance (*koine physis*)."[7] The implication of this statement is quite clear. It was possible in antiquity to become a member of another *ethnos* or *genos* without that becoming in itself being understood as a "religious" conversion, a term for which there was no analog in antiquity at all.

Surely Steve Mason must be correct in his view that so-called conversion to so-called Judaism was a process of naturalization—free or forced—into something analogous to a nation—that is, a *genos* or an *ethnos*. What's religion got to do with it? Thus Mason writes the following:

> There is a simple model of ethnicity (Athenians are Athenians, Tyrians are Tyrians, etc.), but in this case—as Josephus also emphasizes in the Apion—the Judaeans are unlike Athenians and Spartans, who jealously guard their citizenship. Moses, by contrast, welcomed any who wished to come and live under Judaean laws. Philo makes the same point: those who abandon their family and polis and laws and customs to take up ours should be welcomed as our own flesh and blood. Others comment

on how the Idumaeans, because they adopted Judaean law, *became* Judaeans. Epictetus comments on the same from the outside, as does Tacitus, as does Juvenal: people of other ethnicity, oddly enough, become Judaeans—abandoning their whole set of normal identity markers. (This is not good, from Tacitus' point of view.) It's not about *religious conversion*. It's about a change of ethnicity, which is indeed a remarkable thing (you could do that by becoming Roman, except that Roman citizenship did not diminish your original one in the same way as becoming a Judaean required you to give up your ancestral traditions).

While I am somewhat less inclined than Mason to utilize the term "ethnicity" as itself a modern construction and one that does not quite fit any ancient category of which I know, the point is well taken. Again, as Paula Fredriksen has remarked with her usual precise pithiness, "Jews may be one of the few Western groups now for whom ethnicity and religion closely coincide, [but in antiquity] it was the least odd thing about them." All I would add is that once ethnicity and religion so completely coincide for all ancient societies, then the very distinction of these as analytical categories is already an act of cultural Procrusteanism. Ethnicity, once more, is as problematic a category as religion. Mason further points out that the following text from Josephus (*War* 7. 45) indicates that that author also did not conceive of conversion in the Christian sense:

> Moreover, they attracted to their *thrēskeiai* many Greeks and these had in some fashion become part of them.

> ἀεί τε προσαγόμενοι ταῖς θρησκείαις πολὺ πλῆθος Ἑλλήνων, κἀκείνους τρόπῳ τινὶ μοῖραν αὑτῶν πεποίηντο.

First, the plural *thrēskeiai* makes it absolutely clear that this is not Judaism, not a religion that we have here but cultic practices of various sorts (including conceivably such things as kashruth, Sabbath, etc.). But even more to the point, that they "had in some fashion become part of them" certainly precludes any notion of a religious conversion as opposed to an "ethnic" alliance, for in a conversion to a "religion," one becomes entirely a part of the group and institution to which one joins herself. There was, according to Mason, whose view I will soon further support, no "Judaism" to which to convert.

One of the significant texts that has been cited by scholars to support the contention that Judaism was a "religion" as distinct from an "ethnicity" or "race" in antiquity is the following text from the Roman historian Dio Cassius. Dio (160 AD–230 AD) writes the following:

This was the course of events at that time in Palestine; for this is the name that has been given from of old to the whole country [*ethnos*] extending from Phoenicia to Egypt along the inner sea. They have also another name that they have acquired: the country has been named Judaea, and the people themselves Jews. I do not know how this title came to be given to them, but it applies also to all the rest of mankind, although of *alien races* [*allouethneis*], who affect their customs. This people [*genos*] exists even among the Romans, and though often repressed has increased to a very great extent and has won its way to the right of freedom in its observances. They are distinguished from the rest of mankind in practically every detail of life, and especially by the fact that they do not honour any of the usual gods, but show extreme reverence for one particular divinity. They never had any statue of him even in Jerusalem itself, but believing him to be unnamable and invisible, they devote themselves to him in the most extravagant fashion on earth. (37,16,5–37,17,2)

This text has been frequently understood as implying, as this standard translation [Loeb] does, that Dio is claiming that there are people of different "races" who are called Jews owing to their following of Jewish customs, ergo there is a religion called "Judaism." The translation given, however, is erroneous. Dio has identified the *ethnos* of Palestina, otherwise known as *Ioudaia*, as stretching along the coast from Egypt to Phoenicia. It is clear that this refers to the people of the province (as correctly translated in the Loeb). Therefore, when one sentence later he refers to people of other *ethnoi*, he does not mean people of an alien race but people who live in other lands than *Ioudaia* and are called *Ioudaioi* nonetheless, since they follow the customs of the *Ioudaioi*. He is simply recording the well-known fact that there was a Jewish diaspora, nothing more.[8] Immediately after this sentence, Dio refers to the Jews as a *genos*, hardly supporting a conclusion that he has a concept of "religion" as a separate sphere of existence or identity.[9] According to Michael Satlow's exhaustive and closely argued study, *ethnos* never means something like race, ethnic group, or the like in Greek, but, as in this context, where Dio has clearly used it as a designation of place, that is how we should take it in the very next sentence as well. This matches up, moreover, with his usage at 36.41, where he uses *ethnesi* to refer to lands or provinces.[10] This yields the most coherent reading of Dio's passage: *Ioudaia* is the name of the place; the people who live there are called *Ioudaioi*; there are people in other places who are also called *Ioudaioi*, since they have the same practices.

Davies is well aware of the problem of claiming the existence of a cultural entity if such alleged entity is not recognized at all in the language, directly or indirectly, of the folk in question: "It is only when such a concept as 'Judaism' comes into consciousness, that is, becomes conceptualized, that there is a need to argue about what the concept denotes. . . . But the conscious '-ism' is a prerequisite, or at least a symptom of the emergence of 'Judaism' into historical consciousness." I couldn't agree more; the question becomes, then, a philological one. Davies claims that this conscious concept had been developed and attested in the work known as 2 Maccabees. Therefore, he holds, from the time and place of that attestation, we can speak of an entity called "Judaism." But here's the rub: it is at best highly questionable (in my opinion, in fact, entirely unsupportable) to conclude or suggest that the extremely rare Hellenistic term—*very rarely* attested—*Ioudaismos* means "Judaism" as opposed to loyalty to the polity and practices of the people of Judea.

What Does *Ioudaismos* Mean?

In determining the interpretation of *Ioudaismos* in Hellenistic Judeo-Greek, we must keep certain methodological principles, both general and specific to this case, in mind:

1. An interpretation that locates *Ioudaismos* in the lexical and grammatical system of Greek is to be preferred if it doesn't require "fancy exegesis" or special pleading to maintain it in context.
2. An interpretation that explains why the word is used in these specific literary contexts and not others is to be preferred.
3. The simplest explanation is to be preferred if it suits well the contexts (Ockham's razor).

What then of *Ioudaismos* in 2 Maccabees (and its reflex 4 Maccabees), *the only literary context in which this word appears in ancient Judeo-Greek?* The debate over the meaning of the rare Hellenistic Jewish word *Ioudaismos*, which again only appears in one context, is critical because Davies builds his entire, highly sophisticated apparatus of searching for the origins of "Judaism" on that very *Ioudaismos*. Thus for Daniel Schwartz, before *Ioudaismos* appears on the scene, "being Jewish was basically a matter of place or race [*ethnos* or *genos*, DB], there was no reason to assume that all should agree about belief or practice, any more than all French or all women do."[11] But after this alleged shift, there was, according to Schwartz, every reason to assume precisely that. From this Davies derives three stages in the development of "Judaism": (1) a prereflective time in which "Judean culture . . . is not homogeneous and has not been conceptualized"; (2) "'Juda-ism,' the culture of Judea conceptualized"; and (3) "'Judaism,' the redefinition of 'Juda-ism' as a religion or a cult or a philosophy—a system of belief and practice rather than custom" (13). He thus solves the logical conundrum that I posed about his work, for now we see that it is Juda-ism that is the ancestor of the unhyphenated Judaisms, including Samaritanism—which is closer to hyphenated Juda-ism than Judaism is—as well as Christianity and Islam.

Mason, however, has argued that *Ioudaismos* simply does not connote in any sense the alleged religion or even more generally cultural practices of the Jews. As follows, I will support his view while modifying it—that is, I will accept his negative conclusion as just stated while modifying his own interpretation. If *Ioudaismos* does *not* mean "Juda-ism" as Mason has already concluded, let alone Judaism, and as I will argue at length, then on Davies's own methodological insight, there is no "Judaism" to speak of before some time in modernity (at least among Jews!),[12] for it is only then, I argue in this book, that "such a concept as 'Judaism' comes into consciousness, that is, becomes conceptualized," and "the conscious '-ism' is a prerequisite, or at least a symptom of the emergence of 'Judaism' into historical consciousness." Davies and I are in complete theoretical agreement: there is no Judaism before it is conceptualized and named. This leaves us only the empirical usage over which to contend with the tools of philology. Does *Ioudaismos* name "Judaism"?

Does *Ioudaismos* Mean Judaism?

2 Maccabees and Josephus

In an article published in Hebrew some years ago, Yehoshua Amir gathered the material on the word *Ioudaismos* as it appears in the pens of Jews. Considering all of it together (a total of seven attestations, four of which are found in one context), Amir opines, "Following the first survey of the material, it is possible to sum up that the word Ιουδαϊσμός represents the complex of behavior that is obligated by the fact that someone is a Jew and that this behavior is considered a value for which it is worthy to fight and even to die."[13] As Amir shows, and the point is well known indeed, nouns in *ismos* are the verbal nouns formed from verbs in *izō* quite regularly in Greek (he claims more than a thousand examples). The important question then is, What does the verb from which the noun is derived mean? There are quite a number of *izō* verbs derived from proper nouns in which the verb means acting like a member of a group, or identifying with a group, so *mēdizō* would mean acting like a Mede or taking the side of the Medes. Amir points out that this is usually assigned to someone who is not a Mede himself, and it is frequently a pejorative term.[14] *Hellēnismos*, on the other hand, is something to which Greeks aspire—namely, the proper usage of the Greek language in writing—while *barbarismos* is the opposite of that (a usage still current in English where an error can be called a "barbarism"). In the Jewish usage, however, in 2 Maccabees, the term *Hellēnismos* is used by Jews with reference to other Jews who act like Greeks and are loyal to the Greek cause, thus similar to *Medismos* in the mouths of Greeks.[15] Here is where I part company with Amir. Amir regards the development of this usage of *Hellēnismos* as issuing from the need for the Jewish writer to have a word that means "all of the signs of Hellenistic culture as one entity," because he wants *Ioudaismos* to function as such for Judaeans, and he requires a word that is opposite to *Ioudaismos*. *Ioudaismos* is, according to Amir, a unique term marking the fact that it was only the Judaeans of all the peoples in the Mediterranean world who deemed it necessary to have a name for all the signs of their own culture as one entity. In other words, according to Amir, first came the desire for a word that means "Judaism" and thence *Hellēnismos* as its opposite.[16]

Disagreeing with Amir as to the uniqueness in sense of *Ioudaismos*, Mason insists that *Ioudaismos* is no different in sense from the other ethnic verbal nouns in *ismos* and remarks that Amir's argument of a unique status for *Ioudaismos* as the only noun in the entire ancient world that represents an entire culture or religion "seems a lot to claim for a word that is absent from all Hellenistic-Judaean texts but 2 and 4 Maccabees, completely passed over by Graeco-Roman observers of the *Ioudaioi*, and unparalleled even in contemporaneous Hebrew or Aramaic. A better explanation of this rarity, in light of the usage of parallel forms (above), seems to be that the particular circumstances calling for the usage of this word, which always risked negative connotations, rarely occurred."[17] So far so good. Mason sees *Ioudaismos* as back-formed from *Hellēnismos*, which I will presently suggest is more plausible than the opposite. In my opinion, however, Mason overstates the case, insisting that *Ioudaismos* consists of a countermovement against *Hellēnismos* engaged in bringing back, Judaizing (in the transitive sense), the Judean defectors to *Hellēnismos*: "Judas' antidote to this Hellenizing (Ἑλληνισμός) was a counter-movement, a bringing back of those who had gone over to foreign ways: a 'Judaizing' or Judaization, which the author of 2 Maccabees programmatically labels Ἰουδαϊσμός. The noun appears only in such contexts as these, evidently, because of its inherent sense of (re)alignment. This programme of Judas Maccabeus and his Asidaeans in 2 Maccabees (cf. 14.6) is not then 'Judaism' as a system of life, but a newly coined counter-measure against Ἑλληνισμός."[18]

Let us review the argument. In pre-Christian antiquity, the term *Ioudaismos* appears essentially in only one literary context—namely, the accounts of the resistance of the Maccabees to *Hellēnismos*. Expanding implicitly but significantly on an argument that had been made earlier,[19] Mason argues that the word *Ioudaismos* appears only in this particular literary and historical context because it precisely fits that context and perhaps no other in Jewish antiquity.[20] It fits, moreover, into a paradigm of other terms formed the same way in Greek as a verbal noun from a particular kind of verb, neither of which has the slightest bit to do with the naming of a religion.[21] *Ioudaizō* would mean in the same way "to act like a Judaean," and the verbal noun formed from it, *Ioudaismos*, would simply be the nominal form of that verb, "acting like a Judaean." No more, no less, just like *Hellēnismos*, acting, talking, writing like a Greek.[22] To get a sense of how active this kind of formation was in Greek, it should be enough to cite the following humorous example: Kenneth Dover cites the appearance of the word "euripidaristophanizein" ("to act like Euripides and Aristophanes"), penned by a rival comic poet who considered Aristophanes entirely too intellectual by half.[23] The hypothetical verbal noun from the verb would be exactly *euripidaristophanismos*, hardly the name of an institution, an abstraction, a religion, or even an entire cultural pattern. Hence Mason is on good comparative lexical grounds in denial of such an idiosyncratic interpretation to the one single form from this highly productive Greek paradigm, *Ioudaismos*.

To be sure, as Seth Schwartz has well remarked, Mason's reading will work fine perhaps for such contexts as 14:37 (although I disagree with Daniel Schwartz's interpretation of this passage at a key point, I shall nonetheless cite here his excellent translation, only exchanging *Ioudaismos*—the term in question—for Schwartz's "Judaism"):

> Someone informed to Nicanor about Raziz, one of the elders of Jerusalem—a man who loved his fellow-citizens and had a very good reputation, who due to the goodwill toward him was called "Father of the Jews." In the foregoing times of strife he had brought in a decision for *Ioudaismos* and with complete intensity had risked body and soul for *Ioudaismos*.[24]

In this passage, it is indeed quite easy to see how having decided for *Ioudaismos* means deciding for loyalty to the Judean ways and polity and even for a revival movement meant to reinvigorate such feelings in the backsliders. However, regarding a passage such as 8:1, the case is much harder to make:

> Judas Maccabaeus and those with him, on the other hand, had been going in and out and around secretly to the villages, summoning their kinsmen and those who remained in *Ioudaismos*.[25]

As Seth Schwartz has correctly observed, it is much more difficult to understand the term here as referring to this recovery operation.[26] We need not, however, go from there to taking *Ioudaismos* here as meaning "something very much like Judaism,"[27] as that would presuppose a lexically and grammatically sui generis development of the vocable and the paradigm it belongs to in this and only this context out of all of Greek literature. If we translate in both cases simply as fealty to the ways and cause of the Jews, then I think there is no difficulty. In the first instance, we find Razis jeopardizing life and limb for the Jewish way of life, while in the second case, those who had remained "in *Ioudaismos*" means those who had remained loyal to the historical practices—the *nomoi* or the *ethe* of the *patrie*—of the Judeans. *Ioudaismos* means the practice of such loyalty. The correct translation would be "had remained in Judaizing" or perhaps better "Jewing!"

As Mason correctly notes, it is only in Christian usage that *ioudaizō* has religious moment, per se. See his note on the cognate grammatical form *romaizō* in Josephus *War* 2:562 as well:

> This is the only occurrence of ῥωμαΐζω in Josephus, and the first attestation in Greek literature, though from now on the verb begins to be used heavily by others: Dio Chrysostom (Or. 37.4), Appian (Annib. 177–78; Lib. 304–5; Mac. 7.1; Illyr. 40; Mithr. 5, 107, 109, 182; Bell. civ. 1.5.41; 2.13.91), Philostratus (Vit. Apoll. 5.36), Cassius Dio (50.6.4; 51.1.5). Once again (see Introduction) Josephus stands at the beginning of a trend. In form the verb belongs to a class that had gained prominence during the Persian and then Peloponnesian wars, half a millennium earlier: μηδίζω, περσίζω, λακωνίζω, ἀττικίζω—indicating political alignment with another (normally greater) city or power, usually a forced choice for weaker states in times of crisis (e.g., "Atticize or Laconize?"); cf. Thucydides 3.61.2; Xenophon, Hell. 6.3.14. Even if it was unavoidable, the identification with foreign states implied by the verb carried less-than-noble connotations. In the 2nd century BCE the author of 2 Maccabees ironically adjusted ἑλληνίζω, which had meant simply "to express oneself in Greek" and its condition Ἑλληνισμός for the same purpose: to indicate the shameful adoption of a Greek cultural program by Judean élites, to which he contrasted (with another neologism) the noble counter-measure of Ἰουδαϊσμός—the ongoing condition of the verb ἰουδαΐζω (cf. Mason 2007c). The appearance of ῥωμαΐζω in Josephus and his later Greek contemporaries may result from their reappropriation of the older Greek style that marked this period. Judaizing (*Ioudaismos*) is no more a religion than Atticizing is and, once again I emphasize that we do not have here an abstract

noun for an institution but a verbal noun for an activity or set of activities (such as driving out the "barbarians" for instance or remaining steadfast in the commandments.)

Since *Ioudaismos* is formed grammatically from the verb *ioudaizō*, observing how that verb appears in a crucial Greek source—Josephus—ought to help us sort its meaning as the verbal noun as well. There are two occurrences of this verb in Josephus's corpus, both close to each other in the Jewish war: The first is at 2:454:

> And thus were all these men barbarously murdered, excepting Metilius;
> for when he entreated for mercy, and promised that he would *ioudaizō*,
> and be circumcised, they saved him alive, but none else.[28]

The second is found only a few sentences later at 2:463:

> So the day time was spent in shedding of blood, and the night in fear,
> which was of the two the more terrible; for when the Syrians thought
> they had ruined the Jews, they had the *ioudaizontas* in suspicion also;
> and as each side did not care to slay those whom they only suspected
> on the other, so did they greatly fear them when they were mingled
> with the other, as if they were certainly foreigners.[29]

As Mason has remarked in his commentary ad loc, the only earlier usage of *ioudaizō* is to be found in the Septuagint to Esther, where it translates *mityahedim*, acting like Jews, even pretending to be Jews, in order to save their skins. Josephus's usage seems consistent, if not modeled, on that instance and incident. Although Josephus, as pointed out already, never uses *Ioudaismos*, his (rare) usage of the verb from which this gerund is derived suggests a similar meaning to that which I have argued for in 2 Maccabees (with almost the opposite moral evaluation, however).

I, therefore, like Mason, disagree with Amir and maintain that *Hellēnismos* comes first with *Ioudaismos* a back formation but disagree with Mason somewhat about the semantic effect of the coinage. If we think of *Hellēnismos* in the mouths of Judaeans about other Judaeans as exactly analogous to the use of *Medismos* by Greeks about other Greeks, we can see easily that it is the primary term in this binary opposition. *Hellēnismos*, on this account, means acting like a Greek and being loyal to the Greek cause (thus answering to aforementioned principle 1). *Ioudaismos* would be then seen as a natural back-formed opposite to indicate acting loyally to the Jewish way of life and polity. Goldstein has made substantially the same point, arguing that "Greeks never forgot the history of the Persian wars of the sixth and fifth centuries B.C.E., in which one who deserted the cause of the Greeks to collaborate with their enemies was said to 'Medize,' . . . The implied antonyms of 'Medize' and 'Medism' were 'Hellenize' and 'Hellenism,' which would mean 'be loyal to the Greek cause.'" I am suggesting precisely the same origin and semantics for *Ioudaismos*. This usage is, it would seem, initially unique to Judaeans, but it is a natural development in the particular circumstances of the Maccabean conflicts (thus answering to aforementioned principle 2). The positive sense of *Ioudaismos*, acting like a Judaean, is analogous to the positive sense of *Hellēnismos*, writing like a Greek, even though the latter is more restricted in its scope.[30] In other words, rather than seeing *Hellēnismos* as coined by Jews in order to have an opposition to *Ioudaismos*, I argue for the opposite: *Ioudaismos* was formed as the opposite to Hellenizing disloyalty to mean Judaizing loyalty. It certainly does not attest, pace Amir and from Amir to Schwartz and thence to Davies, to an alleged new consciousness on the part of the Jews that they have a thing, an institution, a "Judaism." I believe that this will fit all the ancient (pre-Christian) contexts well, avoiding Seth Schwartz's strictures, in that it does not involve "fancy exegesis" and that loyalty and adherence to Jewish (or Judean) ways is not reducible to being a member of a religion that we (now) call Judaism. Since all the members of the paradigm of nouns of this form—the aforesaid *Medismos*, siding with Athens and the Persians, *Attikismos*—are gerunds and not abstract nouns, there is no justification to read *Ioudaismos* as other than such a gerund as well. To be sure, in Greek, as far as I know, only *Ioudaismos* and *Hellēnismos* (in that sense of writing like a Greek) have positive valence; nonetheless, it seems by far best to understand and translate it as "Judaizing" in the sense of acting like a Judean without going so far as Mason and asserting that it is a transitive verb always meaning "returning other Jews to the fold." (I speculate that had we Persian "loyalists" writing Greek, for them too *Hellēnismos* would be pejorative and *Medismos* a term of praise). Thus by somewhat softening up Mason's interpretation, I think that the major outlines of his argument can be strongly maintained.

If we examine, moreover, the last-to-be-considered of the usages of the word in 2 Maccabees, we will see this suggestion borne out (or at the very least, uncontradicted). Thus the very first time the word appears (in the world to the best of our knowledge), we find it at 2:21:

> And the heavenly apparitions which occurred for those who nobly with manly valor strived for *Ioudaismos*.[31]

There were heavenly apparitions in honor of those who strived with one another for *Ioudaismos*.[32] There is no reason in the world here not to imagine that *Ioudaismos* means exactly what it ought to—namely, vied with one another in the activity, the doing of acts of dedication to the ways of the Judeans and partisanship for their cause against their oppressors, the "barbarians."[33] Only an a priori and anachronistic idea of *Ioudaismos* as an abstract name for a "religion" or the name of an institution would lead one to imagine "Judaism" here.

An important argument against the notion that *Ioudaismos* was conceived of as a "religion"—even avant la lettre—can be found in the text itself, in the letter of Antiochus V in 2 Maccabees 11:

> 22 The king's letter was as follows: "King Antiochus to his brother Lysias: greetings.
>
> 23 Now that our father has passed over to the gods, in our desire that the people of the kingdom be untroubled and take care of their own affairs, 24 and having heard that the Jews did not willingly concur in their change[34] to Greek ways by my father, but rather, preferring their own way of life, ask that their own regulations be allowed to them—25 now then, in our policy that this people too should be untroubled, we have decided to restore the Temple to them and that they should conduct their civic behavior according to the customs of their ancestors. 26 So you will do well if you send to them and give them the right hand, so that in perceiving our policy they will be in good spirits and happily go about taking care of their own affairs."[35]

Now, what must be observed here is that nowhere in this text is there an indication that it was a religion, *Ioudaismos*, that had been under attack and was now being restored to freedom and legitimacy but Judaic customs versus Greek customs—indeed, the "customs of the ancestors"— just as we find in Josephus. To be sure, these are, at least ostensibly, the words of a Greek, not a Judean, but it is at least in part the *imaginaire* of those very Greeks that is in question here. We have here, in effect, an implicit interpretation of the terms *Ioudaismos* and *Hellēnismos*, the former being glossed as "preferring their own way of life" and "conducting their civic behavior according to the customs of their ancestors," while *Hellēnismos*, we may take it, is "changing to Greek ways." In that sense, it is perfectly intelligible that there would have been a party among the Judeans who rejected every possible accommodation to Greek culture, whether or not it involved a specific violation of the Torah.[36]

A very recent scholarly controversy will help us understand the intervention being made in *this* book as well as get a further glimpse at the stakes of the question. The controversy is around an interpretation of the Hasmonean revolt published by Sylvie Honigman in 2014 and already mentioned in the first chapter.[37] I am not interested, nor competent, to judge the rights and wrongs of her historical reconstruction, which seems to my untutored eye to be both brilliant and flawed, but in how the failure to pursue certain theoretical moves to their logical conclusion undermines certain of the arguments of both Honigman and her opponents, especially Cana Werman.[38] The part of the question that concerns me here is, obviously, the interpretation of *Ioudaismos*. As I have argued already in the first chapter, it is vain to even inquire whether something in the premodern world was "religious" or "political," as neither of these concepts had currency, and any given discourse could be, *in our eyes*, one or the other, or both, while in antiquity the whole distinction is nugatory. Thus, although Honigman explicitly rejects the "instrumentalist" view whereby so-called religion is a smoke screen for so-called political objectives, she forgets the "so-called" too often and feels called upon to write, "From this perspective, the contrasted pairing of *Ioudaismos* and *Hellēnismos* in 2 Maccabees can be seen to have a political connotation."[39] What Honigman seems to miss is that by asserting that the persecution of the Judeans by the Seleucids was *not* a "religious persecution," she is asserting the existence and reality of the category "religion" just as much as her adversaries do. Honigman takes an important step forward in realizing that the category of "religion" is anachronistic applied to 2 Maccabees but undermines this insight by continuing to refer to politics *as an alternative to "religion."*[40]

There certainly are elements of what *we would call* religious persecution related in 2 Maccabees. We need not—particularly, I need not as I am not a positivist historian—dismiss them, explain them away, or account for them as "politics" incognito. The vital point to make is that given that there is not the slightest shred of evidence for "religion" and "politics" as separate spheres in ancient Judaea, it is impossible to engage in an argument of whether something is "religion" or "politics" within that cultural formation, within that form of life. No one, it seems, ever asked themselves whether a given persecution, building a *gymnasion* or eating pig, was a religious persecution or a political one.

The most egregious violation by Honigman of the principle of economy is in her claim that "the concept of proper social order established by the legitimate rule at the foundation (or refoundation) of the temple was captured in the neologism *Ioudaïsmos* by the author of 2 Maccabees."[41] This hypothesis violates principle 1 in that this alleged usage has little or nothing to do with the general usage in Greek of this morphological pattern. It satisfies, however, principle 2 in explaining the usage of this term specifically in *this* literary context as in (nearly) none other in Judeo-Greek but surely violates Ockham's razor in completely adducing an otherwise unknown entity that is unknown paradigmatically and unparalleled in the corpus.

Honigman does not pay adequate attention to *Ioudaismos* as part of a very well-established paradigm in the Greek language. She defines, most succinctly, *Ioudaismos* "to be the righteous social order founded by Judas, the ancestor of the Hasmonean dynasty."[42] There is an a priori category error here. *Ioudaismos* may be the righteous social order indeed, and it may very well be that Judas restored it or refounded it in Jerusalem, but *Ioudaismos* is not the name of what Judas did. *Ioudaismos* is the name for the way Judeans behave (or ought to behave), which Judas and his men fought for, defended, and reestablished as the way of life in Jerusalem. Honigman has confused denotation with the reference. The denotation of *Ioudaismos* is acting as a Judaean acts; its reference in this particular instance is to the order that Judas ostensibly reestablishes and for which he has been fighting. If I were to say that the guerrillas were fighting for freedom, that hardly indicates that "freedom" means the political order that these particular guerrillas have established, even were I to consider it an instance of that. Again, *Ioudaismos* may be the name for a righteous social order, and one of that sort may have been refounded by Judas, but it makes no sense to claim that *Ioudaismos*'s only extension is the order founded by Judas. Similarly, when the text says, "And the heavenly apparitions which occurred for those who nobly fought with manly valor for *Ioudaismos*, so that although they were few in number, they plundered the entire country and chased away the barbarian hordes and retook the temple which was spoken of throughout the entire civilized world and liberated the city, and firmly reestablished the laws that were about to be abolished, the Lord having become merciful toward them in total grace—" [2 Maccabees 2:21–22][43] it indicates that *Ioudaismos* was an existing thing for which these soldiers fought. *Ioudaismos* is, in short, the order that obtained in Judea in the time of Seleukos IV and Onias; it is being fought for and ultimately *re*established by Judas and his followers. This does not constitute a semantic conflation of *Ioudaismos* with the activity of Judas and his men.[44] Here is another analogy: there is a political party in the United States called the Democrats that presumably fights for democracy, but that certainly does not imply that the word/concept "democracy" is only applicable when speaking about the U.S. Democratic party! It, accordingly, strikes me as slightly preposterous to imagine that "the label (*Ioudaismos*) refers to the rules of a particular dynasty."[45] Rather, *Ioudaismos* is an ideal that the author of 2 Maccabees considers realized in his time (or the time he writes about) only in and by the Hasmonean dynasty—quite a different kettle of fish.

By far, then, the most compelling interpretation of *Ioudaismos* in accord with all three of (my own) principles laid out previously is that it follows the semantic/grammatical pattern so well attested in Greek

(Amir's one thousand examples) of acting in a certain way (generally "ethnic" but not by any means always). That is, it means to behave as a Judean, sincerely or not as the case may be. It is indeed, if not the opposite, a member of the paradigm that includes *Hellēnismos* and in contrast with it, as well. As such, 2 Maccabees [4:11–14a] writes the following:

> Indeed, [Jason] abrogating the benevolent royal privileges which had been fixed for the Jews through the agency of Johanan and abolishing the regular civic usages, he innovated lawless practices. With relish he laid the foundations for a gymnasium directly beneath the acropolis, making the strongest of the ephebes submit to (wearing) sun-hats. There was such an apex of *Hellēnismos* and inroad of foreignism due to the extreme impurity of that impious and unhighpriestly Jason that the priests were no longer enthusiastic about the altar ministries. Rather, in their disdain for the Temple, and in their lack of concern for sacrifices, they hurried to participate in the lawless distributions in the palaestra which followed upon the call of the discus; Considering the ancestral values to be worthless, he considered the Greek honors to be the best.[46]

Once again, we have a fairly clear set of glosses on *Hellēnismos*, wearing funny Greek-style hats, exercising in a gymnasium, losing interest in the Temple and sacrifices, and preferring sporting competitions. On the other hand, we may with a fair degree of confidence conclude that continuing "the regular civic usages" is what is known in this book as *Ioudaismos*. In neither this nor the aforementioned such catalogs discussed are specifically "religious" violations singled out as such, as a separate category and a separate semantic field. The argument is not, of course, that the issue is secular as opposed to religious or political as opposed to religious but that those very distinctions do not obtain for this text and for this form of life. From the previous discussion I conclude that by far the best way of interpreting *Ioudaismos* is *doing* the Judean doings, a verbal noun that comprises sacrificing, going to temples, obeying kings, paying taxes, eating certain foods (not just kashruth), wearing certain hats, speaking Judean, everything one does as a Judean, with no distinctions made between what we in our culture would call "religion," "law," "manners," "customs," or "politics," all that which Josephus (as we shall presently see) refers to as the *nomoi* of the fathers and the practices of the *politeuma*.

The Pauline Moment

This interpretation explains well the usage of *Ioudaismos* in the Pauline epistles as well. When the apostle says that formerly he was very advanced in *Ioudaismos*, he is surely not referring to an abstract category or an institution but the practicing of Jewish ways of loyalty to the traditional practices of Jews, described by his contemporary Josephus as "the ancestral [traditions] of the *Ioudaioi*" (τὰ πάτρια τῶν Ἰουδαίων; *Ant.* 20.41 and passim). Now again one might be tempted simply to gloss this as well as the Jewish religion were it not for the fact that this is exactly the usage that we find in Thucydides describing the Plataeans Medizing— namely, that they are accused of "forsaking *their* ancestral traditions" (παραβαίνοντες τὰ πάτρια; Thucydides 3.61.2).[47]

Other attestations of *Ioudaismos* seem also to bear out the interpretation of *Ioudaismos* as a verbal noun, a practice and not an institution. Paradoxically, Paul's usage in Galatians has typically been taking as evidencing the exact opposite. The most important passage is Galatians 1:13–14, where we read (words to be discussed untranslated), "For you have heard of my *anastrophe* then in *Ioudaismos*, how I persecuted the congregation of God and tried to destroy it. And I had advanced in *Ioudaismos* beyond many of my own age among my people, so extravagantly zealous was I for the traditions of my ancestors." Let us begin with the word *anastrophe*, usually translated as "life," as in "former life." Mason has argued, that given the "The accompanying noun ἀναστροφή is stronger than '[my former] life,' as often translated (e.g., NRSV, ASV). It should indicate some sort of 'bent, inclination' or 'turning toward' something, 'a going back' to it, or a 'preoccupation' with it (cf. LSJ s. v.). The zeal mentioned in 1:14 confirms this sense."[48] Mason is right, in my opinion, that "former life" rather prejudices the case and does not correspond to the most frequent usages of this work in Greek. However, once again, I think we need not go quite as far as he does, and I would prefer to translate "conduct" as we find it in Tobias 4:14—πρόσεχε σεαυτῷ, παιδίον, ἐν πᾶσι τοῖς ἔργοις σου καὶ ἴσθι πεπαιδευμένος ἐν πάσῃ ἀναστροφῇ σου—where the last phrase translates well as "be well instructed in all of your conduct," paralleling the first clause, which would read "be careful in all of your works." Paul, then, would be referring to his former conduct in Judaizing—namely, his persecution of the Congregation of God. The use of *Ioudaismos* in the second verse makes this point even stronger. One does not advance in an institution—for instance, an alleged "religion" (except, perhaps, by being promoted within it, obviously inapplicable here)—but in a practice: the practice of Judaizing, in which Paul was more advanced because he was more learned and zealous than the others. Finally, Paul's usage of the verbal noun *Ioudaismos* must be interpreted with reference to his use of the verb as well. As remarked earlier in Galatians 2:14, Paul inveighs, "But when I saw that they were not straightforward about the truth of the gospel, I said to Cephas before them all, 'If you, though a *Ioudaios*, live like a Gentile (*ethnikōs*) and not like a *Ioudaios* (*Ioudaikōs*), how do you force the Gentiles to *Ioudaizein*?'"[49] which clearly means to live according to Judean ways as the opposite of living in the Gentile manner. *Ioudaismos*, the noun derived from this verb, clearly means Judaizing, living according to Judean/Jewish ways and not to be a member of an institution called "Judaism." That this is the case is shown by Mason's observation that "Paul denounces Peter because, though Peter allegedly lives as a foreigner [lit. ethnically DB] and not as a Judaean [Judaically, DB] (ἐθνικῶς καὶ οὐχὶ Ἰουδαϊκῶς, 'you compel the foreigners to Judaize' (τὰ ἔθνη ἀναγκάζεις ἰουδαΐζειν; Gal. 2:14)—a cultural movement that Paul connects tightly with circumcision and observance of Judaean law (2:12, 21)."[50] Since ethnicizing is surely not observing a religion, neither is Judaizing here and hence certainly also not the noun derived quite regularly from this verb, *Ioudaismos*.

A final argument that *Ioudaismos*, in Paul, is not the name for the Jewish religion is the following: Paul never considered himself anything other than a Jew. Were *Ioudaismos* to mean the entirety of Judaic practice and belief, or the religion of the Jews, this verse would constitute a reading of himself out of it. It follows that *Ioudaismos*, if Paul is out of it, *simply cannot* be read as the alleged Jewish religion or even as a name for all that Jews do! It must mean, in his work, perhaps, study and keeping of the rejected Pharisaic *paradosis* (see Mark 7:3). Once again, I arrive at results very similar—if not identical—to those of Mason but by slightly different routes of interpretation. *Ioudaismos*, "Judaizing," seems in all these cases to mean hanging on (zealously) to the customs (traditions of the ancestors) of the Judeans. Any other interpretation (and there are some that seem possible within the context alone) involves importing the later sense of -ism words as the names of institutions or, at least, movements and applying them anachronistically to *Ioudaismos*. Nonetheless, it will be seen in chapter 4 that Paul's intervention had highly significant historical implications.

The epigraphic evidence (very little of it indeed) seems also to support this way of looking at the matter (contra Amir 264). In one case from Stobi (late third to fourth century AD),[51] the inscription refers to someone (or rather, the someone refers to himself in the inscription) as "πολιτευσάμενος πᾶσαν πολιτείαν κατὰ τὸν *Ἰουδαοσμον." (Hengel 146). Amir, as would be expected, translates "behaved in all of his public life according to Judaism," glossing this, "and its meaning is seemingly simple, that he was careful in the performance of the commandments." I agree with Amir's gloss but think his translation misleads at best. Once again, "Judaizing," acting like a Judean, conducting oneself as a Judean conducts oneself (falsely or truly, in this case the latter), is much closer to the sense desired than "Judaism," which implies the modern notion of an -ism. Hengel, for his part, translates "jüdischen Sitte" (Hengel 178), which seems much closer to the mark.[52] Moreover, even if one would want to argue that in this inscription something like "Judaism" is more plausible, the probable late date of the inscription is itself telling and could easily be a usage under Christian "auspices," as it were.

Similarly, for the final extant (to the best of my knowledge) inscriptional example: In an inscription from Porto (Italy), we find the following: καλῶς βιώσασα ἐν το Ἰουδϊσμῷ, "living [with her husband] pleasantly in Judaizing"—that is, in performing/fulfilling the commandments (just as in the Stobi inscription), not surely inside the institution latterly called "Judaism." It is important to note that these two epigraphic instances would raise some minor difficulty for Mason's interpretation, but I believe, on my emendation of that interpretation, they stand very well and do not in any way suggest or imply the sort of semantic development that I will document in the last chapter from (only) Christian sources and the Jews that they affected from the eighteenth century on in Europe. Of course, if these two are indeed under Christian influence, then they don't bear at all on Mason's arguments whatsoever.[53] They do, however, represent the only instances of the use of *Ioudaismos* by Jews (looking from the inside, as it were) outside of Maccabees until modernity.

It seems fair to conclude that the exceedingly rare word *Ioudaismos* does not function as an abstraction for the entire Jewish way of life, still less as a name for its alleged "religion," but refers to the doing (especially the zealous conduct) of a life committed to keeping the Mitzvot or commandments, this designated as "Judaizing" in much the same way that writing Greek properly might be designated as "Hellenizing!" As Amir himself remarks regarding *Hellēnismos*, "In this sense, it is a desired ideal for the sake of which the man of spirit strives all of his life, for the linguistic 'Hellenism' demands careful observance of a thousand small and large rules." Substitute the ancestors' (or the Torah's) way of life for the linguistic, and one arrives at a perfect sense for *Ioudaismos*, a sense that fits both the paradigmatic context of the grammatical and lexical system of Greek and the syntagmatic contexts of its occurrences within Judeo-Greek. We need assume no Judean exceptionalism to make sense of these data.

The Sound of Silence

I can thus, in fine, but agree with Mason's overall conclusion:

> That the five occurrences of Ἰουδαϊσμός in Jewish-Judaean writings owe so much to one creative author, either Jason of Cyrene or his

epitomizer, who seems to coin the word as an ironic counter-measure to Ελληνισμός, should caution us against adopting the word as if it were generally understood to mean the entire culture, legal system, and "religion" of the Judaeans. Outside the Hellenizing emergency and later Christian circles, ancient authors found no occasion for its use— partly, it seems, because of the pejorative resonance of the *Medismos* family, which might obtain also if Ἰουδαϊσμός were used outside of the contrast with a clearly repugnant Ελληνισμός.[54]

The most powerfully convincing of all of Mason's arguments seems to me the argument from scarcity. Were there such a widespread name for all of the Judean "complex of behavior that is obligated by the fact that someone is a Jew and that this behavior is considered a value for which it is worthy to fight and even to die," it seems hardly plausible that it would appear in so few and idiosyncratic contexts as 2 Maccabees and the very few and very specific other contexts in which it shows. Whatever one might say about *Ioudaismos*, it clearly is *not* a key word in the culture of Greek-speaking Judeans.[55]

It is possible, moreover, to add a kind of positive reinforcement to this strong argument from silence. In a recent article, (my new colleague) Roman historian Duncan MacRae has pursued a similar (or at any rate analogical) problem in Roman historiography—namely, the ascription of a tradition of alleged antiquarianism to some Roman Republican writers, especially Varro, as opposed to a putative ancient historiography. After showing that there is no term in ancient Latin that refers to antiquarian-ism and that this term only appears in the fifteenth century among early modern scholars, MacRae remarks, "But the idea that there was no Roman antiquarianism is not just a terminological question—the-Roman s-didn't-have-a-word-for-it argument—instead, this essay will suggest that they did not have the concept either."[56] That is precisely what I would like to suggest for "Judaism" in the next section of this analysis. Even though it cannot be taken as a matter of logical necessity, the difficulty of estab-lishing the existence of a concept in a form of life that shows no word or phrase for it in the language is utmost. Moreover, as MacRae has shown, there are methods available for demonstrating the nonexistence of a con-cept as well (if not of proving it unequivocally). I want to pick up on MacRae's point and argue, mutatis mutandis, that it is possible to show that not only the word but the concept of "religion," and thus of "Judaism," does not exist for Greek-Jewish writers.

Josephus without "Judaism"

Martin Buber notoriously accused the translators of the Septuagint of having invented Christianity by "mistranslating" Torah as *nomos* and argued that it was the "Greek narrowing of the concept of Torah into law that makes possible Paul's opposition of law and faith. 'Without the change of meaning in the Greek, objective sense,' Buber writes, 'the Pauline dualism of law and faith, life from works and life from grace, would miss its most important conceptual presupposition.'"[57] Whatever Paul did or did not understand, I would exonerate the translators of the Septuagint from having perpetrated a "Greek narrowing" of Torah, suggesting rather that they engaged in a Hebraic broadening of the concept of *nomos* into Torah and so were understood by Judean readers. To speak in terms of my first chapter, they were translating Greek into Hebrew, not Hebrew into Greek.

Josephus, the first-century Palestinian priest, general, and eventually historian dwelling in Rome, will provide my evidence here. Without any covering term such as *Ioudaismos* and without a term that means "religion,"[58] how did a Greek-writing Jew (or for that matter, a Hebrew or Aramaic-writing Jew) such as Josephus refer to the Judean way of life? To begin to answer this question, I undertake a look at a very charged word in Josephus (and in Judeo-Greek generally)—namely, *nomos* and its plural *nomoi*. These terms are usually translated into English as "law" and "laws," but I will try to show that that translation also significantly misses the point in Josephus. In his remarkable defense of the Jewish way of life in *Against Apion*, the only term used to describe that way of life is *nomos*. The section will begin, therefore, with an examination of what Josephus means by *nomos*, a task easily and profitably accomplished, since he tells us exactly all that it comprises for him. In Josephus, as I dare say, in ancient writers in general, the abstractions and categories of law, politics, and religion are not useful analytic categories. The following narrative will begin to show how what we call "law," *nomos* in Greek, is imbricated in these complex lexical usages and thus conceptual fields. I submit that the term for Josephus that embraced the Book and the entire Judean way of life was *nomos* and that it was equivalent to Hebrew *Torah* and Aramaic *'orayta*. On one level, this point is trivial, since already in the LXX the regular translation of Torah is *nomos*, but the point here again is not that the Greek translators misunderstood the import of Torah with this translation but that rather the word *nomos* in Greek was broadened in meaning in Judeo-Greek by being used among Jews as the equivalent of Torah. Louis Ginzberg got this right more than a century ago when he wrote, "More than eighteen centuries ago the Jewish historian Josephus observed that 'though we be deprived of our wealth, of our cities, or of the other advantages we have, our law continues immortal.' The word he meant to use was not law, but Torah, only he could not find an equivalent for it in Greek."[59]

The best way to see this is to follow his description and defense of the Judean *nomos* in his *Against Apion*, a text in which Josephus explicitly defends the Judean *nomos* from attacks on the part of several "pagan" authors, including one Apion.[60] Here he gives as full and explicit an account as one could wish for of what *nomos/Torah* means for him:

> But since Apollonius Molon and Lysimachus and certain others, partly out of ignorance, but mostly from ill-will, have made statements about our legislator Moses and the laws [*nomoi*] that are neither just nor true—libeling Moses as a charlatan and fraudster, and claiming that the laws are our teachers in vice and not a single virtue—I wish to speak briefly, as best I can, about the whole structure of our constitution [*politeuma*] and about its individual parts.
>
> For I think it will become clear that we possess laws that are extremely well designed with a view to piety, fellowship with one another, and universal benevolence, as well as justice, endurance in labors and contempt for death.
>
> I appeal to those who will peruse this text to conduct their reading without envy. For I did not choose to write an encomium of ourselves, but I consider this to be the most just form of defense against the many false accusations against us—a defense derived from the laws in accordance with which we continue to live. [2:145–147]

Although, to be sure, Josephus uses here *politeuma*, something like constitution, and thus a term that we would use to refer to politics, government, to refer to the Torah of Moses, the *nomoi* are that which makes up the *politeuma*. Moreover, as shall be demonstrated, he frequently uses *nomos* in this very sense of the whole unified object, the *politeuma*. Within the *politeuma*, there are laws, but let us note of what the laws consist: laws regarding piety, fellowship, universal love of humans, justice, perseverance in labor, and contempt for death. Unpacking this, we see that the whole—by whatever name he refers to it, and he has several—consists of what we might call ritual laws, structures of governance that lead to fellowship and benevolence, but also laws in the strict sense (justice) as well as prescribed practices to inculcate personal moral characteristics. Neither could we extract one piece of this whole and call it law, politics, or religion nor could the whole be nominated with such a covering term. Note that the term *nomoi* includes all these categories and practices and even more, as we shall presently see.

In a lengthy passage, Josephus argues for the totality of the Judean code of *nomoi* as well as its accessibility to all Judeans. Referring to Greek philosophers, including Plato and the Stoics, who are all recognized by Josephus as followers of the true God, he writes the following:

> These, however, confined their philosophy to a few and did not dare to disclose the truth of their doctrine to the masses, who were in the grip of opinions. But our legislator, by putting deeds in harmony with words, not only won consent from his contemporaries but also implanted this belief about God in their descendants of all future generations, [such that it is] unchangeable.
>
> The reason is that, by the very shape of the legislation, it is always employable by everyone, and has lasted long. For he did not make piety a part of virtue, but recognized and established the others as parts of it—that is, justice, moderation, endurance, and harmony among citizens in relation to one another in all matters.
>
> For all practices and occupations, and all speech, have reference to our piety towards God; he did not leave any of these unscrutinized or imprecise. [2:169–171]

I note several things: First of all, the ideas of Plato and the Stoics are designated as "philosophies," not in contrast to the Torah of Moses but as members of the same class. The legislation of the Torah, as opposed to that of the worthy Greeks, is so perfectly designed as to inculcate in all its receivers correct doctrine about God as well, which the others fail to do owing to their esotericism (not their "secularity"). In this passage, Josephus begins a wide-ranging comparison of the Torah of Moses with the practices of other peoples with regard to inculcating merit according to their lights. Josephus has already designated the form of Judean government (*politeuma*), via an apparent neologism, as a theocracy (*theokratia*), rule by God (2:165)—that is, God as he has expressed himself in the Torah. This is not rule by priests, as has been shown by Barclay.[61] Indeed, Josephus's *theokratia* is, as shown recently by David Flatto, nearly the exact opposite of our current usage of the term "theocracy."[62] Josephus here explains how the theocracy works by elaborating a theory in which virtues are inculcated by the Torah via a combination of "words" and "practices," thus rendering it superior to those cultures that seek to transmit their values either by words alone (Athens) or deeds alone (Sparta). Josephus makes the point as well that for the Judeans, *eusebeia* toward God is not a virtue among the other virtues but is the master virtue that incorporates and inculcates all the others. "Words," here, it should be emphasized, means precisely the written "laws" that one studies, as it is glossed in the next sentence,[63] while "deeds" is glossed in the next

Josephan sentence as "instructing through customs, not words" (ἔθεσιν ἐπαίδευον, οὐ λόγοις, 2:172). Josephus is clearly relating to the dual practice, so characteristic of later rabbinism, of lives dedicated both to the study of the Torah, *logoi*, and to the practice of the commandments, *erga*.[64]

As Barclay points out, Josephus here is mobilizing ancient topoi and stereotypes. Thus with respect to Roman virtue, Dionysius of Halicarnassus writes, "Not by words is it taught but inculcated through deeds."[65] Josephus goes on in the next sentences to write explicitly:

> But our legislator combined both forms with great care: he neither left character-training mute nor allowed the words from the law to go unpracticed. Rather, starting right from the beginning of their nurture and from the mode of life practiced by each individual in the household, he did not leave anything, even the minutest detail, free to be determined by the wishes of those who would make use of [the laws], but even in relation to food, what they should refrain from and what they should eat, the company they keep in their daily lives, as well as their intensity in work and, conversely, rest, he set the law as their boundary and rule, so that, living under this as a father and master, we might commit no sin either willfully or from ignorance.
>
> He left no pretext for ignorance, but instituted the law as the finest and most essential teaching-material; so that it would be heard not just once or twice or a number of times, he ordered that every seven days they should abandon their other activities and gather to hear the law, and to learn it thoroughly and in detail. That is something that all [other] legislators seem to have neglected. [2. 173–175]

So far is Josephus here from identifying the Torah with "religion" that Moses is described as a law-giver (*nomothetēs*).[66] (Of course, Josephus has not forgotten his description of the polity as a *theokratia*; indeed, the fact that he was the giver of God's law raises him to a status of divine man [*theion andra*]). Even more striking, the primary purpose for the Sabbath rest here is precisely the opportunity for study of the Torah. Moses combined into a perfect whole the instruction of Israelites in virtue by not leaving any required practices unexpressed (so correctly, Barclay) nor by leaving any words to be theoretical or unpracticed. The *nomos* is thus the perfect expression and teaching mechanism for all Judean merit. The combination of constant hearing of the words and practicing the deeds inscribed in those words achieve excellence: "For us, who are convinced that the law was originally laid down in accordance with God's will, it would not be pious to fail to maintain it [2:184]."[67] Josephus goes on at this point to detail the merits and virtues inculcated by the *nomos*. Among the values and orders inculcated by the *nomos* are some that we in our modern thought world might identify as "politics," "religious," or "legal," without any distinction of these three latter-day abstractions being made by Josephus. Thus the *nomos* has led to concord among all Judeans (hah!) in their conception of God. Moreover, their commonly held lifestyle (*bios*) leads them to concord, as well.

The *nomos* organizes the world with God at the top, as governor of the universe, who designates the priests as managers, as overseers, and judges in disputes (187). Josephus follows this with what might appear as a non sequitur—namely, that one of the merits of the Judean people is the ability to maintain life at the level of a rite or a mystery at every moment of existence (188–189).

> For the whole constitution is organized like a mystic rite [*telete*].

> ὥσπερ δὲ τελετῆς τινος τῆς ὅλης πολιτείας οἰκονομουμένης (188)

Everything in the Torah, including the civil law, the rules for government, the rituals, the morals and ethics, the whole "constitution" (*politeia*) is organized like an initiation ritual into the Mysteries. This passage requires some exegesis. The Mysteries were a vitally important part of Athenian and, more generally, Hellenic life. While we do not know a great deal about the details of the initiation (precisely for this reason—they are, after all Mysteries), we do indeed know that these rituals consisted of doings and sayings together, precisely that which Josephus is vaunting as the special characteristic of the Torah, the Judean constitution over those of Hellenic *poleis*. What Josephus seems to be saying is that while the Athenians in their Mysteries (especially the Eleusinian, in which great numbers of Athenians participated) teach and transform by a practice which involves saying and doing, the Athenian constitution as a whole does not (the point made earlier by Josephus). The Judean constitution, however, incorporates such doings and sayings at every point in its existence; it is, therefore, organized like a Mystery initiation (but for all).

The details are then given: there are the commandments that speak about God and prohibit other gods and make it illegal to make images of him. Following them, Josephus talks about sacrifices and the rules of sacrifice, prayer, and purification rites. Josephus completes this section by emphasizing that all of this is part and parcel of the *nomos* (198). There follows a discussion of sexual practices and marriage rules, funerary rites, and honor of parents. Then we are informed (2:207) that the law prescribes how we ought to behave with friends and the requirements for judges. Next, laws having to do with the treatment of enemies in battle (212) and animal welfare (213) are explored. There follows a description of honest business practice (216), and the list goes on. By the time Josephus is done, he has certainly encompassed what we call government, ritual, religion, politics, and law under the one rubric, *nomos*. As a noted archaeologist writing of an entirely different culture has remarked, "Many things Chacoan [having to do with the ancient culture of Chaco Canyon in the Southwest United States] fascinate us, however, precisely because they resist political, economic, or religious categories."[68] I could not nail this point down better than by citing Josephus's own summary:

> Concerning the laws, there was no need of further comment. For they themselves have been seen, through their own content, teaching not impiety but the truest piety, exhorting not to misanthropy but to the sharing of possessions, opposing injustice, attending to justice, banishing laziness and extravagance, teaching people to be self-sufficient and hard working, deterring from wars of self-aggrandizement, but equipping them to be courageous on their behalf, inexorable in punishment, unsophisticated in verbal tricks, but confirmed always by action; for this we offer [as evidence] clearer than documents.
>
> Thus, I would be bold enough to say that we have introduced others to an enormous number of ideals that are, at the same time, extremely fine. For what could be finer than unswerving piety? What could be more just than to obey the laws?
>
> What could be more profitable than concord with one another, and neither to fall out in adverse circumstances, nor in favorable ones to become violent and split into factions [*staseis*], but in war to despise death, and in peace to be diligent in crafts and agriculture, and to be convinced that God is in control, watching over everything everywhere?
> [2:291–294]

Contrary to the frequent stereotype that Greek Jewish writers reduced the Torah to "law," it is clear from Josephus that he, at any rate, understood *nomos* in a way far more expansive than our notion of "law" would predict. For him, it incorporates civil and criminal law, the organization of government, plus cultic practice including Temple and private observance, and also beliefs about God, much more than "law," "politics," or "religion," incorporating, one might fairly say, all of them and thus demonstrating the falseness of all these terms as categories for describing his world. Robert Cover has explored this point with respect to the Bible itself in a famous essay.[69]

One might be tempted to ask at this point, What's in a name? Even if Josephus uses entirely different lexical items to describe the whole of the Judean way of life, he still recognizes it as an entity, so why not call it "Judaism?" What's at stake, however, is the question of if Josephus interprets that Judean way of life, and if so, how; as a species of the genus that includes the Greeks, the Syrians, the Romans, the Scythians, or as something unique, sui generis.

As was previously discussed in this chapter, historian Yehoshua Amir has asserted that "in the entire Hellenistic-Roman cultural realm, to the extent of our present knowledge, not a single nation, ethnic, or other group saw the need of creating a general term for all the practical and ideological consequences entailed by belonging to that group, with the exception of the Jewish people [scil. in Ἰουδαϊσμός]."[70] I believe that Josephus's lack of use of *Ioudaismos* confirms the point made that Amir is precisely wrong: the Jews/Judeans do not have a unique way of referring to themselves that marks them off from all the other species of Peoples in the world as a genus unto themselves (perhaps as a genius unto themselves, but that is quite a different matter). Precisely on Josephus's witness and in accord with the view of Mason, they regard themselves as one of the "family of nations," so to speak. Translators and historians in their wake go on blithely referring to Josephus's Judaism, thus inventing an entity that I would claim is a chimera borne of looking backward through a telescope from our time to theirs. (Full confession: until quite recently, I was in the category of the blithe as well.) Mason is exactly right, in my view: there won't be any Judaism or any word for it in a Jewish language for many centuries. How many exactly? We are about to see an answer to this question in the next section of this book, but first, an extended detour into Semitism is in order.

3   Getting Medieval *Yahadut*

In contrast to ancient Hebrew and Judeo-Greek, from the Middle Ages on, Hebrew shows a term, *Yahadut*, which as an abstract noun seems at first glance roughly parallel with modern "Judaism." In modern Hebrew, the semantic range of *yahadut* is quite closely cognate to German *Judentum*—namely, that it covers the ranges of English "Judaism," "Jewishness," and "Jewry" (in fact, I will suggest in this chapter and demonstrate in chapter 5 that there is good reason to suspect that modern Israeli *yahadut* is simply a calque on German *Judentum*). Shall we then claim that already in medieval times, the idea of "Judaism" had entered the doings of Jewry? I will perform two philological investigations in this chapter. The first is concerned with showing how an important text of Jewish apologetic of the twelfth century, which ought to have used a term for "Judaism" if there were one, knows of no such term nor even one that means "religion." The second (together with its sequel in chapter 5) will trace the history of the medieval term *yahadut* from its beginnings to its final semantic resting place in modern Hebrew as the Hebrew equivalent of *Judentum*, to wit, the just mentioned "Judaism, Jewishness, Jewry" in English.

The Kuzari without *Yahadut*

The book from twelfth-century Sefardic Spain, known in Hebrew as the Kuzari and regarded as one of Spanish Jewry's iconic texts, was written by Rabbi Yehuda Halevi (c. 1075–1141) in Judeo-Arabic under the title, כתאב אלרד ואלדליל פי אלדין אלד׳ליל: "The Book of Refutation and Defense of the Despised *Din*." Hebrew translators from the time of Yehuda Halevi's slightly junior contemporary Yehuda ibn Tibbon to the present usually give *dat* for Arabic *din*.[1] But we must not hasten to translate *dat* or *din*, especially not as "religion" or "faith," or we shall have proposed as a premise precisely what we are trying to interrogate (begging the question). In the following text, I shall refer to this work simply as the Kuzari. What did the author of the Kuzari and his contemporaneous translator, Rabbi Yehuda ibn Tibbon (1120–1190), mean when *they* used the Arabic term *dīn* or medieval Hebrew *dat*, or better put, how did they use those words? Did either of them understand *dīn* or *dat* in the way modern

English means "religion" or "faith"? We simply dare not read back from modern usages to interpret these medieval texts without risking burying their linguistic-cultural world under the rubble of a modern one, the very opposite of an archaeology. My hypothesis to be developed in the rest of this chapter is that Judeo-Arabic *dīn* corresponds best to *nomos* as used by Josephus and (with a very important *mutatis mutandis* qualification) to *Torah* as well. This would render it untranslatable into English, for *nomos*, as we have just seen, covers both more and less territory than "religion" or "law," as does *Torah* itself as well. Some powerful evidence for this claim comes from ibn Tibbon's translation of Halevi's Arabic into Hebrew.[2] Let me emphasize again a crucial point: the argument is not that these words don't mean "religion" but that they mean something else—"law," "custom," and so on—which would still presuppose that in the medieval Judeo-Arabic and Hebrew, there was "religion" but that it wasn't called *dat* or *dīn*. Nor am I suggesting that these words *sometimes* mean "religion" and at other times "law" or "custom." I remind of the very useful formulation of C. P. Jones, already cited in chapter 1 to the effect that when we say that a given word has two meanings in some foreign language, all we are saying is that English has no word that matches the semantic range of that foreign tongue.[3] In this case, turnabout is fair play, and it means as well that the "foreign" tongue has no word that matches English "religion" either, even if parts of things that we call "religion" are embedded in the usage of the given word along with many other things that we don't call "religion" or even call "not religion."

Is **dīn** "Religion"?

Dīn (plural *adyān*, generally equal to Hebrew *dat* because the words have evolved semantically together) is one of the words in Arabic most often translated as "religion." As shown by recent research, however, its usage in late-ancient and early medieval Islamic texts suggests rather normative customs or traditions (which may or may not be conceived as divine in origin). The term is loosely associated with religion, but in the Qur'an, it means the way of life that righteous Muslims must adopt to comply with divine law (Qur'an and *sunnah*), or *shari'a*, and to the divine judgment or recompense to which all humanity must inevitably face without intercessors before God.[4] Note that as with *nomos* for Josephus, *dīn* incorporates the whole of prescribed human practice, including what we might divide into ritual prescriptions and civil law. Its usage in the Kuzari and in ibn Tibbon's Hebrew rendering of same also indicate a much more complex semantics than the reduction to "religion" or "law" would betoken. One term that I will introduce in this discussion is "doings," a term that certain archaeologists are using to indicate all the practices, verbal and corporeal, that mark the form of life of a given human collective.[5] The virtue of this term is its relative colorlessness and oddness with respect to contemporary categories, as opposed to terms like "religion," "ethnicity," and the like.

Let us begin the semantic investigation (I am giving ibn Tibbon's text with Arabic *Vorlage* where I deemed it necessary or helpful):

> They have asked me what I have to say to refute and answer those who dissent from us of the philosophers and the men of the *torot* [Arabic אלאדיאן (*al-adyān*)] and the *minim* who dissent from the majority of Israel. And I remembered that which I had heard of the arguments that the sage offered, who was with the King of the Khazars, who entered the *dat* [Ar. *dīn*] of the Jews four-hundred years ago today, as is recorded and known from the Chronicles (1:1).

Ibn Tibbon's translation here is fascinating. For אלאדיאן, (*al-adyān*), the plural of *dīn*, ibn Tibbon translates in the first instance *torot*. My suggestion is that when Halevi contrasts philosophers to adherents of *al-adyān*, ibn Tibbon understands him to mean the adherents of revealed *dīn* or Scriptures, thus *torot*. *Torot* must, at least, mean revealed Scriptures in this context. Moreover, at Kuzari IV, 3, ibn Tibbon gives once again *torot* for this word, when Halevi refers to the philosophers among the adherents of *al-adyān*. When Halevi is referring specifically to Christians and Muslims (*al-naṣārá wa al-muslimūn*), then ibn Tibbon translates this word as the People of *Torot*. On the other hand, when the king enters into דין אליהוד (*dīn al-yahud*), where even ibn Tibbon translates as *dat*, it seems most plausible to suggest that for ibn Tibbon *dat* means what *dīn* means in the Qur'an, referring to the entire way of life, the "doings" of a people, of a sort that all peoples have whether right or wrong. In other words, I suggest that for ibn Tibbon, since both *dat* and *torah* can translate *dīn*, they are close to being synonyms in his language with the proviso that Torah must be used when contrasting a *dat* that is revealed to a *dat* that purports to be the product of reason. The translation "religion" from either the Arabic or the Hebrew of ibn Tibbon quite obscures this point.

There is further an absolutely determining text for the meaning of "People of *Torot*." In response to the Kuzari's claim that the Indians have buildings that are hundreds of thousands of years old and that, therefore, the claim of the Jews to a recent creation is falsified, the rabbi remarks:

> This would damage my belief if this were founded on reliable opinion or in a book [Ar. *kitāb*] that has won general agreement without

controversy according to an agreed-upon chronology, but this is not the case. This [The Indians] is an undisciplined people and they have no clear chronicles and they anger the people of *Torot* [Ar. אהל אלאדיאן *ahl al-adyān*] with such matters, just as they anger them with their statues, their idols, and their tricks. And they claim that they aid them and they ridicule those who say they have a book from God. They have written on this few books; individuals wrote them. The feeble minded will be seduced by them like a few astrological books that claim dates going back ten-thousand years [and other nonsensical books of the Nabateans]. (1:61)

Here the sense of ibn Tibbon's "people of *Torot*" for Halevi's *ahl al-adyān* is absolutely clear, since we have its precise antonym, the "pagans" of India. It must mean, therefore, at least in extension, something like *Ahl al-Kitāb*.

The next text here rather complicates this suggestion, however.

For he had the same dream many times, as if an angel spoke to him and said to him: "Your intention is pleasing to the creator but your deed is not." And he was very devoted to the liturgy of the *Torah* [Ar. *dīn*] of the Khazars, to the extent that he used to serve in the temple himself and serve the sacrifices himself with a whole heart.

It is quite mysterious to me why suddenly here ibn Tibbon has given *Torah* for *dīn* rather than *dat*. In contrast to the texts that we have observed until now where the plural of *Torah* seems always to have referred to Christians and Muslims as opposed to "pagans," here the devotion of the king of Khazars is also to a Torah (once again, in Arabic, *dīn*). Being perhaps overly subtle, I am tempted to claim that this is a sign of respect for the Khazar king who, although nominally a pagan as well, certainly seems to be a monotheist, one who listens to the words of God as communicated to him in dreams, where the message he has received is that his intentions are desirable but not his actions, so perhaps those intentions are dignified with the name *Torah* by the translator.

In the sequel to this passage, we read:

And however he used to devote himself in those acts, the angel would come to him at night and say "Your intention is pleasing to the creator but your deed is not." And this caused him to investigate the *'emunot* and the *datot* [Arabic *al-adyān wa'al-nihāl*] and in the end he *Judaized* [Ar. *wa tahwwad*],* he and most of the nation of the Khazars. (1:1)

---

* ותהוד.

Perhaps, as I suggest, this text provides some support for the notion that when ibn Tibbon wrote "Torah" for the Kuzari's former devotion, it is this very simultaneous devotion to the Creator and desire to find out the truth of the desired practice that, paradoxically perhaps, renders it a Torah. An illuminating point here is ibn Tibbon's translation of Halevi's אלאדיאן ואלנחל [al-adyān wa'al-niḥāl] as "the 'emunot and the datot." It seems clear that datot here is a rendering, as it is most frequently, of adyān, while 'emunot is niḥāl [the change in the order of the terms from the Arabic to the Hebrew is a mystery to me], which normally means something like "sects" in Arabic and presumably in Halevi here as well. It can only mean here the doings of Jews, Christians, and Muslims. ibn Tibbon, it would seem, did not wish to use (or lacked in his Hebrew lexicon) a word meaning "sects" and chose, therefore, 'emunot, not to be understood here as individual tenets, as in, say Sa'dya Gaon, but systems of belief that form groups, oddly analogous to modern English "faiths." I'm not sure what to make of this, but it suggests perhaps a somewhat Christianizing understanding of division by dogma on the part of ibn Tibbon, which may have further significance as we continue our study (see below).

In any case, in the next passage, the semantics of *Torah* for ibn Tibbon seem again quite clear, since he, quite typically for Jewish writers of Arabic and translators from Arabic into Hebrew, uses *Torah* for Arabic *shari'ah* as well:

> The [Ishma'elite] sage responded: "There have indeed appeared by his [the Prophet] agency miracles, but they are not a necessary sign for acceptance of his *Torah*. [*shari'ateh*]."*

The Kuzari responds that it is not logical that people would accept the words of a prophet as genuinely from God without miracles, to which the Ishma'elite Sage replies:

> Behold, the book of our *Torah* [Ar. *kitābana*] is full of the words of Moses and the Children of Israel, and no one denies what He did to Pharaoh and that he split the sea and rescued his chosen ones and drowned those with whom he was angry and brought down for them the Manna and the quail which he fed them for forty years in the desert and that he spoke with Moses at Mt. Sinai . . . , all of this is well known and famous, and no one imagines that this was done with tricks or that it was imaginary. (1:9)

---

*   It is interesting to observe that when Halevi actually cites a verse from the Torah, he refers to it in his Arabic as אלתוראה [al-tawrah] (1:99).

To which the Kuzari replies:

> I see that I need to ask the *Yehudim* for they are the remnant of the
> Children of Israel, because I see that they are the argument and the proof
> for any *baʿal dat** that the creator has a *Torah [shariʿah]* in the world. (1:10)

Ibn Tibbon translates two different Arabic terms here as "Torah":
שריעה and כתאבנא (*shariʿa, kitābana*), "our Torah [in the mouth of the
Islamic sage]"—namely, the Qur'an. Even though the Kuzari quite logically comes to the conclusion that if the evidence for the divine nature of
the Qur'an comes from the fact that it refers to Moses and his miracles,
which no one denies, then he should go straight to the source, the
Yehudim and their Torah directly; nonetheless, ibn Tibbon has translated
both of these Muslim Arabic terms as *Torah* in his Hebrew, suggesting
that they are close to being synonyms for him. His translation of *dīn* as
Torah when it refers to the revealed Scripture of the Peoples of the Book
suggests strongly that that word too belongs to the widest meaning of
Torah as *nomos*, the whole way of life of a people, in the case of *Torah*,
specifically, for ibn Tibbon, a way of life revealed by Allah.

The expectations of the Kuzari to be richly rewarded for his pains in
asking a *Yehudi* seem, however, to be quickly dashed:

> When one of the Sages of the *Yehudim* came, the Kuzari asked him
> about his *'emuna* [אעתקאדה *itikādah*]. The Sage began, "We believe
> in the God of Abraham, Isaac, and Jacob [אסראיל] who took the
> Children of Israel out of Egypt with wonders and signs and journeys
> fed them in the desert and gave them the Land of Canaan after pass-
> ing them through the Sea and the Jordan with great miracles and sent
> Moses with his Torah [*shariʿateh*] and thousands of prophets after him
> who warned them about his Torah [*shariʿateh*] and the good reward for
> him who keeps it and the harsh punishment for him who denies it, and
> we believe everything that is written in the Torah, and the matters are
> lengthy."

> Then the Kuzari replies: "I was right when I decided not to ask a
> *Yehudi*, because I knew that their memory [tradition] was lost and their
> wisdom diminished, for the degradation and poverty have not left them
> any good character. You should have said, O *Yehudi* that you believe in
> the creator of the world who organizes and conducts it, and who cre-
> ated you and sustains you and discourses similar to this which are com-
> mon to anyone who has *dat*, and for which he pursues truth and the

---

*   This seems to lack an Arabic *Vorlage*, according to Qafih's text at any rate, but probably
    attests to a variant reading. The term seems to mean "possessor of a divine law" or
    something of that sort.

desire to emulate the creator in his righteousness and wisdom."
(1:11–12)

The shift from אעתקאדה (itikādah) in the Arabic, "opinions," to the singular 'emuna in the Hebrew seems again to signify a notion for ibn Tibbon—who spent the bulk of his life in Southern France and hence among Christians—that tends toward the Christian usage of a "faith." The Arabic term here translated by ibn Tibbon as *dat* is again *dīn*, which seems here to be semantically marked as distinct from שריעה, *Torah*, as perhaps the particular(ist) *Torah* over against the genus/universal *dīn* (Hebrew *dat*). The rabbi is using the latter term clearly to refer to the Torah revealed by Moses, and the Kuzari seems to consider this some kind of particularism that actually contradicts that which a possessor of *dat* has, a kind of universal desire for truth and *imitatio dei*. The rabbi immediately rejoins in the name of the revealed Torah:

> What you speak of is the logical *dat* ['al-dīn 'al-qiāsī 'al-siāsī]* to which speculation leads and into which enter many ambiguities. For if you ask the philosophers about it, you will find that they do not agree on one practice and one opinion (1:13)

---

* Kogan: "the syllogistic, governmental religion." One wonders why ibn Tibbon did not translate 'al-siāsi at all, unless it was a simple error, a kind of homoteleuton. The editor of this series, Andy Bush, has contributed what I take to be a brilliant (unassimilably brilliant, in fact) remark at this juncture:

Is there such a thing as a "simple error," especially from a Wittgensteinian-philological point of view? If ibn Tibbon translates "logical" (Kogan's "syllogistic") for one of the Arabic terms—I don't know which, al-qiasi or al-siasi—but not the other, does that mean that he doesn't have a word, i.e., a concept, that would correspond to Kogan's "governmental," and not in general, but specifically in relation to al-din? Of course, it is the Haver [Rabbi] who is speaking, so for Halevi in Judeo-Arabic, there is a term available, but only (at least in this context) as the way of characterizing al-din from what the Haver sees as the life-form of the philosopher (so you can have the concept without playing the game!). But it would seem to reinforce your argument—that is to say I would not have been able to make these observations without your argument—to note, against the "Judaism" thesis, that when ibn Tibbon tries to convey the philosophical distinction, he can't quite get there in Hebrew, because, it would seem, 85 pages into your book, if he could recognize, conceptualize and say "governmental" din/dat/torot, then he would likewise be able to say "religion."

Brilliant indeed but, as I say, perhaps unassimilable.

and, therefore, are clearly in need of revelation, Torah. *Torah* is, then, a special case of *dat*.

The next text that I cite illustrates this interplay between *dat* and *Torah* [*dīn* and *shariʿa*] even more complexly from the point of those philosophers:

> The philosopher said: Once you have internalized this kind of *'emuna*,* do not worry which *Torah* [*shariʿah*] you should observe [שרע תשרעת] or which *dat* [*dīn*] or which practice or in which speech or which language you exalt; or invent for yourself a *dat* [*dīn*] for the sake of submission, and to exalt and to praise and for conduct of your personal behaviors and those of your family and those of your city, provided they trust you and listen to you. Or take for yourself as a *dat* the rational *nimmusim which* the philosophers invented. But put your direction and intention on the purity of your soul. (1:1)

From the ibn Tibbon text alone, it would seem as if *Torah* (*shariʿah*) and *dat* (*dīn*) were indeed two different things: the first seems again to refer to revealed Scripture (although the philosopher would apparently reject this claim on the very grounds that he is advancing here) and the second to that which is logical, for you can invent for yourself a *dat* or take the one that the philosophers have already invented.[6] Now *dat* in all of these cases is the Hebrew rendering of ibn Tibbon of *dīn* in Arabic. I would argue that this paragraph precludes the translation of *dat* as "religion," for whatever we mean by "religion," it is not understood (except in the New Age) as something that one simply makes for oneself or derives from philosophical logic. Even a philosopher must use language that his interlocutors understand. A discipline or set of practices seems a much more plausible rendering here.

An interesting further semantic riddle has been introduced here—namely, the term *nimmusim* (representing the Greek *nomos* in the Hebrew plural) that has been used here in the philosopher's jargon to indicate rules, manners, ways of living. This is, of course, a word with a past, cognate, as it is with *nomos* as used in both the Septuagint and Josephus (as well as other writers of Judeo-Greek, e.g., Paul) to translate *Torah* into Greek. The word has now returned from Greek into Hebrew and (Christian and Jewish) Arabic as well. In contrast to its use in Judeo-Greek as Torah, in its Judeo-Arabic echoes it seems most often to mean norms of conduct established by human beings (as, incidentally, it does in modern Hebrew) and stands in contrast to Torah.

---

* Once again, the Arabic has אעתקאדה (*itikādah*).

We find this word again several times in the Kuzari and inter alia in the language of our rabbi himself. Let's try now to get a sense of its usage:

> Said the Rabbi: "This is how people were before Moses. Except for a very few, they were seduced by the *nimmusim* [Ar. *nawāmis*] of the stars and natures, and went from *nimmus* to *nimmus* [*min nāmūs ilā nāmūs*], and from god to god, and it is even possible that they held many of them [the *nimmusim*], and they forgot their leader and manager who had put those [*nimmusim*] as a cause for their benefit, but they believed that themselves (the *nimmusim*) cause benefit, but in fact they cause harm depending on the preparation and the timing. The benefit comes from the Word of God, and the damage from its absence." (1:79)

Halevi (or rather his character, the rabbi) is trying to persuade that without revelation, sacrifice and other cultic acts are useless. At the beginning of the section, he produces an elaborate parable about a fool who breaks into a doctor's medicine cabinet and proceeds to distribute drugs to various and sundry without knowing which drugs are for which disease, how much to give, and so on, so that in the end, many of the patients die. Some, moreover, observing that a certain drug is very efficacious to a particular patient now want it for themselves, little knowing how specific its efficacy is. Halevi then compares the folks before revelation to these patients and their foolish priests. They, observing that certain folks succeeded, thought it must be their *nawāmis* (Hebrew *nimmusim*) that caused their prosperity and were accordingly seduced to follow it but then transferred their loyalties from one *nimmus* to another and even from one god to another, and forgetting the creator of these *nimmusim*, the user of them (the doctor), they thought the practices themselves were the cause of the benefits, but they themselves (the *nimmusim*) cause damage when they are misapplied. The benefit comes from the Word of God, not from the practices alone, and the damage from its absence.

This analogy, as opposed to certain others that Halevi invents, is very strong and revealing. He is arguing that the sincerity of the Kuzari in his cult, in many particulars seemingly identical to Israelite cult, can, nonetheless have inimical effects, just as efficacious medicaments, when not prescribed correctly, can cause great damage to the body. While in the beginning of the passage, it seems as if he is referring to institutions, call them "religions" if you like, by the end it is absolutely clear that *nimmusim* are not institutions but particular practices, analogous to individual drugs and therapies. *Nimmusim* will clearly not map its usage onto "religions" either.

The next passage both expands and somewhat complicates this usage:

Said the Kuzari: "Let's go back to our main subject. Instruct me, how did your *Torah* [*dīnukum* in the Arabic] begin and spread and become accepted, and how did the opinions which were initially divided become unified? And how many years did it take for the *'emuna* [*al-dīn*]ʸ to become founded and built up until it became completely strong? For the beginnings of *datot*,* without doubt, are by individuals, who fortify themselves to disseminate that which God wants to be shown; they get bigger, either helped by their own power or because a king arises who helps them and forces the masses with respect to that matter."

Said the *Rabbi*: "Only the rational *nimmusim* [*al-nawāmis*] which began with people have arisen and grown in this fashion, and when it is a success, he will say that he was helped and taught by the creator and such like that, but the *nimmus* [*al-nāmūs*] whose beginning is from the creator arises suddenly, when he says 'Be!,' as he said 'Let there be!' at the creation of the world." (1:80–81)

The Kuzari himself gives a perfectly rational, historical—one might say nearly modern—account of the origin and development of *datot*. Note again that ibn Tibbon is reluctant (not more than that, apparently) to translate Arabic *dīn* as anything but Torah, when referring to that of the Jews. The rabbi, predictably enough by now, argues that that narrative of how a *dīn* comes into being, becomes widespread and powerful, only applies to the sort of logically derived, rational form of a *nimmus*, but revealed *nimmus* simply comes into being with the very creation itself. It is neither invented by a human being nor does it require any historical processes to explain its advent or success. Whatever way we would wish to gloss נאמוס\נימוס here, since it refers once to the rationally derived practices of the philosophers and once to the Torah, it does not seem to match in usage any modern European term, including "religion." It seems rather to be the covering term that includes both *nimussim* on the one hand and *Torah* on the other for the entire way of life, the doings, of a given people with the former generally marked as logically derived by humans and the latter as revealed by God.

The final example of the usage of *nimmusim* in this work will further illumine its usage. After an elaborate (and not particularly illuminating) parable about a group of people lost in the desert, one of whose number finds his way to India where he is recognized by the king and the rest of

---

*   לאן מבאדי אלמלל (*leanna mabādi'a al-milal*), which means something like "the beginnings of communities." Qafiḥ gives here Hebrew עמים, something like "peoples" or "nations." It is significant that ibn Tibbon chose *datot* for this, but I don't yet have all the implications clear.

the folk are invited to come as well on condition that they all observe the king of India's rules, the rabbi goes on to say:

> The (people of the) other *nimmusim** didn't see any of this but they said to them: "Receive the service of the King of India just as those associates had, and after death you will arrive to the King, and if you don't do it, he will distance you and torture you after your death." Some of them said, "No one has ever come to us to tell us that after his death he has been to Paradise or Hell," but most of them preferred an orderly and harmonious society and accepted the service. Their hope of the reward was secretly weak but outwardly strong and faithful, and they magnify and glorify themselves over the ignorant among them with their faith. (1:109)

In the solution to the parable, such as it is, we are informed that the king of India is God, the wanderer who found him Moses, and the associates the Hebrew prophets. Those associates come to other folks and tell them the story, which upon hearing they accept the *nimmus* of the Israelites and abandon their other *nimmusim*. It is fascinating to note that, according to Halevi, their acceptance does not mean a turn of faith in the sense of transferring from one set of beliefs to another such as we would expect under the western regime of "religion" but rather a preference for the orderly society that the Torah presages. All of this surely militates against the anachronistic translation, endemic in the literature, of any of these terms as "religion." I feel, without being able to prove it, that Hebrew *dat* here is closer to its meaning in the book of Esther, where we are informed of the Judeans that "their *datim*[8] are different from all peoples, and they do not do/perform the *datim* of the king" (Esther 3:8)—that is, the rules and regulations or laws of the king,[9] not very close indeed to any version of the usage of the word "religion" today.

The Naming of the Peoples

A further way of getting at the question of whether Halevi/ibn Tibbon possess a "religion"-like concept or a concept of "Judaism" (without a name) is to observe closely the terminologies they use to refer to different human collectives in their world.[10] In the following passage, we will observe a gap between the terminology of the Arabic and that of ibn Tibbon's Hebrew, a gap that is instructive:

> Said the Kuzari [to the philosopher]: I find your words compelling, but they don't really answer my question, as I know of myself that my soul

---

*   The Arabic has only ותלך אלנואמיס אלאכר (*wa tilka al-nawāmis al-akar*). Ibn Tibbon translates this quite naturally as "the possessors of the other *nimmusim*."

is pure and my practices are appropriate according to the desire of the Creator. And with all this, I still was told [by an angel in a dream] that my intention is desirable and not my practice. It follows ineluctably that there is action that is desirable in itself and not by logical deduction.

If this were not the case, why are Edom and Ishma'el who divided the world between them fighting with each other? Each one of them is pure in soul and his intention is towards God, and they are modest and ascetic and fast and pray, yet each goes on killing each other and believes that his killing is great righteousness and coming close to the Creator, may he be blessed. And each one believes that he will go to Paradise, and to believe both of them is logically impossible. (1:2–3)

The Kuzari argues that the philosopher cannot possibly be correct that actions are a matter of indifference and only "character" matters, since, although he himself knows that his heart is pure, he nonetheless has repeatedly been informed in a dream that there is something deficient in his practice and that he must discover what it is. Clearly there is some desirable practice, desirable in itself but not discoverable through logic or philosophy. If the correct way to practice, moreover, were indifferent or could be logically derived (and not from revelation), why would Christians and Muslims be fighting to the death over it? The significance of this passage is that ibn Tibbon seems to have no Hebrew terminology to name Christians and Muslims and uses the ethnonyms "Edom" and "Ishma'el" instead.[11] This is all the more striking since in the Arabic text that he translated, we find *al-naṣārá wa al-muslimūn* = "Christians and Muslims!"

The significance of this point is underlined when we find the gesture precisely repeated in the sequel with a further addition:

Afterwards the Kuzari said to himself, "I will ask Edom and Ishma'el, for one of the two practices must doubtlessly be the desired one. But as for the *Yehudim*, sufficient is what is obvious me from their down-trodden state and small number and the fact that everyone despises them" (1:4).

Once again, the Arabic has "the Christians and the Muslims [*al-naṣārá wa al-muslimūn*]," which would entitle one to see the *Yehudim* as the name of a religious group, but once again, ibn Tibbon has only the ethnonyms for the two other groups, suggesting that for him, *Yehudim* is an ethnonym as well. It is even more surprising to find ibn Tibbon not using the term "Islam" when it is given in Halevi's text. At 1:5, we read, "Afterwards he called upon a certain scholar of *Islam*" (Ar. *al-Islam*), but ibn Tibbon's

Hebrew gives us "one of the Sages of Ishma'el!" ibn Tibbon seems to be resisting (or rather, his language resists) an abstraction that seems, even inchoately, to name what will even potentially issue in a name for a "religion."

In the next passage, ibn Tibbon seems satisfied to refer to the Christians as *Notzrim*, after, once again, identifying their sage as a Sage of Edom. I reckon that this is owing to the fact that here, even Halevi refers to the Christians as the *'umma* of the Christians, following the Muslim fashion of styling themselves also, as well as other collectives, as an *'umma*, a people or political society. As remarked to me by Dr. Lena Salaymeh, "When the Prophet moved to Medina, he entered into a non-belligerency agreement (a document that is often called the 'Constitution of Medina') with the Jewish and other tribes and this document identified all the signers as one *ummah*. This implies that *ummah* refers to a political community."[12] This makes it all the more striking, in my opinion, that Halevi here refers to Christians and Jews, as well as Muslims, as *'ummot*:

> [The Edomite Sage said]: And even though we are not of the Children of Israel, we are more worthy to be called "The Children of Israel," for we follow the words of the Messiah, and his friends from among the Children of Israel were twelve, in place of the tribes. And afterwards a large number of the Children of Israel followed after those twelve, and they were like yeast for the *'umma* of the *Notzrim*.
>
> We have become worthy of the greatness of The Children of Israel, and there came to us, strength and might in the lands, and all of the *'ummot* [*wa gamī' al-'umam*] are called to this *'emuna* [*al-dīn*] and commanded to cleave to it, to exalt the Messiah, and to elevate the tree upon which he was hung and all that is similar to this. (1:4)

On the face of it, if all the *'ummot* are called to this *'emuna* ("faith"), Christianity—the Arabic has *dīn*—then the "faith" itself can hardly be called an *'umma*, and yet it is. It is the *'umma* made up of all the other *'ummot* who join it in belief; hence it is an *'umma* for ibn Tibbon and also an *'emuna*. The "Christian" speaker speaks against ethnicity and insists that it is faith that justifies the name "Children of Israel." It is just possible that ibn Tibbon here reveals greater awareness of the peculiarities of "Christianity" over against Judaic or Islamic thought—namely, that Christians consider themselves a "faith," so this particular *'umma* can be defined as an *'emuna*, a faith. In the Christian context, where it is the explicit ideology that right belief is what constitutes both membership and salvation, one must struggle for a distinction between something like "religion" and "nation," but this distinction is so unnatural for the Jewish writer(s) that they enter into self-contradiction and incoherence to represent it.

I will close my discussion in this section (without claiming completeness of treatment), perhaps appropriately, with a short text on heaven and hell:

> "As for the coming rewards which are so pleasant to you, Our sages already preceded to describe Paradise and Hell, and measured them in breadth and length, and narrated the pleasures and the tortures, more than the other *'ummot qrovot* [Arabic *al-milal al-qarībah*]* have narrated" (1:115).

The terminology adopted here by Halevi leaves, it seems, little room for doubt. The Jews, the Christians, and the Muslims are all considered by him folks who belong to *'ummot*, not to *datot*. They have *datot*, but as we have just seen, that hardly adds up to "religion" either; actually the best translation for *datot*, as well as *nimmusim*, might be "doings," after all. One must conclude that not only is there no word in Halevi's Arabic or ibn Tibbon's Hebrew that means "Judaism," the very concept is also absent from their conceptual frameworks, which are much more complex and nuanced than that term would indicate, and this is the payoff of this research, not the negative result of the denial of the existence of "Judaism." As hard as Halevi is reaching for some ways to name that which he is talking about, the vacillations between *dat, shari'a, nimmus* (and the even more complex nuances of usage in ibn Tibbon) do not allow for simplex ways of speaking about Jews, Christians, Muslims, philosophers, and Indians; sometimes ethnic groups, sometimes groups characterized by certain "doings." Although I am not in a position here to conduct a full and complete study of Arabic and Judeo-Arabic—and such will have to remain a desideratum—the evidence presented here from the analysis of the Kuzari suggests strongly that the concept of "Judaism" remained foreign at least to this key Judeo-Arabic writer of the high Middle Ages.

The Semantics of No Judaism

Without our modern abstractions and one for one translation possibilities, the picture is indeed a muddy one, as muddy as any set of human doings, but there are certain traces of perspicuity in the mud. Tracking our way through the following fairly lengthy citation may help us see these spoors:

---

* Here ibn Tibbon gives *'ummot* for Halevi's *milal*, while elsewhere he gave *datot*. The terminology is not solidified at all.

Said the *Rabbi*: "I see that you condemn us owing to our poverty and lowliness, but it is precisely with that that the great ones of those *'ummot* [*al-milal*] glorified themselves [Ar. *wa bihimā yatafākhar afdal hadhihe al-milal*], for the *Notzrim* pride themselves on the one who said: 'If one has slapped you on the right cheek, turn your left cheek to him, and if someone takes your cloak, give him your shift.' This one and his followers for hundreds of years received calumny, torture, and killing in sensational ways, and this is what they gloried in. And similarly those who hold the *Torah* of *Ishma'el* [*shar' al-Islam*] and his associates until they triumphed, and they glorified and exalted themselves because of those people and not because of the kings who became powerful and whose kingdoms became enormous and carriages were wonderful. It follows that we as well our closeness to God is greater than were we to have greatness in this world."

I first recapitulate a point that has been made earlier, noting that Christians and Muslims are both referred to as *'ummot* and not *datot*. Interestingly, however, here the Christians are referred to by what seems to be a marker of their affective allegiance and not as a nation, *Edom*, as we have seen in other places. On the other hand, members of the collective of Islam (which certainly, for instance, at the time of Halevi included Persians) are referred to by the ethnonym *Ishma'el* (which ought properly, it would seem, to designate Arabs, not Muslims.) The same *Ishma'el*, moreover, is designated as having a *Torah* (in the Hebrew, see the following text) which seemingly refers to the Qur'an but also to the set of practices, the doings that it enjoins. It is important to note that neither name occurs in the Arabic here as in the Hebrew. For the latter, Halevi does use *Islam* and its *shari'a*, and for the former only refers indirectly to Christians by citing the Gospel without naming the folks who hold that Gospel. The names are thus significant for our evaluation of the Hebrew of ibn Tibbon.

At this point, the Kuzari interjects and remarks that it would be the case that the Jews would have been praiseworthy for their humiliation as the Christians are, had the Children of Israel accepted their lowliness voluntarily, but he knows that the moment they have power, they will kill their enemies. The same terms are used immediately following referring to Israel and its Torah in both the Arabic and Hebrew respectively that were used with respect to Islam/Ishma'el earlier, suggesting that a *shari'a*, a *Torah*, is something that, according to Halevi, different *'ummot* may have and hold (at any rate, "the adherents of the book"). *Shari'a* is, however, not the totality of Islam; is Torah the totality of the doings of Jewry? The rabbi goes on:

You have found my most shameful point, King Kuzar. It is true: if most of us had received from our poverty submission to God and his *Torah* [*šariʿateh*], the divine word would never have left us alone for so long. But only a minority of us are of this opinion. But there is, nonetheless, reward for the majority as well, because they maintain the exile whether voluntary or involuntary—for if they wanted to, they could become a comrade of that oppressor, just by saying a word without any effort, and this is not forgotten by the Just Judge. But if we had been suffering this exile and this poverty for the sake of God as is fit, we would have been the glory of the generation and waiting for the Messiah, and we would have been bringing near the future salvation that we await.

As for us, we do not accept anyone who comes into our *Torah* with only a word, but with practices that carry with them much effort, purification and study and circumcision and many *Torah* practices [*wa aʿmāl shariʿa kathira*] and that he should follow our way of life [*wa al-aḥrā an yasīr sīratanā*].*

Here it does seem as if "our Torah" means entering into Jewry (Hebrew *giyyur*).

The finale of this passage bears out this ambiguity:

And one who has conjoined himself in this fashion he and his progeny will have a great portion of closeness to the Blessed God. But withal the *ger* [untranslatable word that means something on the order of convert but also naturalized citizen, one not born in the territory in which she currently lives] who comes into our Torah [אלדכיל פי דין ישראל *al-dākhil fi dīn Israʾel*]† will not be equal to the indigene, for only the indigenes are worthy of prophecy, and the others, the zenith of their possibility is to receive the prophetic words, and they may be sages and saints but not prophets. (1:113–115)

Here, quite pointedly, Halevi does *not* use *shariʿah*, still less *Torah*, but *dīn*. This translation by ibn Tibbon strongly suggests, as we have seen earlier, that he prefers not to use *dat* when referring specifically and exclusively to Jewish tradition and substitutes *Torah* in such instances, not, however, entirely consistently. Once again, this suggests that for him *dīn* is at least roughly equivalent to *Torah* but translated as such only

---

* מנהג כמנהגינו. The Arabic here has ואלאחרי אן יסיר סירתנא (*wa al-aḥrā an yasīr sīratanā*), translated by Kogan as "the best way of putting it is that he should follow our way of life," which, were one minded as I am, one might translate as "do our doings."

† The Arabic does not have a match for *ger*, only the paraphrase, "one who enters the *dīn* of Israel." The term is ibn Tibbon's addition.

(with one exception) when it refers to the Torah of the Jews (or even the other Peoples of the Book) but with a strong preference for *dat* when the followers of forms of life not deemed given by God are in question. Halevi, it must be noted, makes his infamous distinction between Jews of the blood and "converts" as not being quite worthy of the same distinction.

Altogether, we have as many questions as answers here, perhaps more, but these questions would not have been raised or even suspected had we been content to foreclose them by using words like "religion" or "Judaism," words that are foreign to the vocabulary of both of our twelfth-century Jewish writers. The abstractions are imposed by translators—nearly all of us, nearly all the time, present author not excepted—filtering ancient and medieval experience through the lenses of our own highly marked symbolic structures with their sharp distinctions between religion and the secular, between law and religion. Premodern folk simply did not perceive human activities in terms of a distinction between the things people do and the abstractions that explain them, such as "religion," "culture," and "economy." It is important to emphasize, however, since I do not wish to be misunderstood: When I speak of the premodern or extra–Euro-American, I am *not* claiming that they were incapable of making abstractions, that modern Europe represents an advance over all other cultures. As clearly shown by Fitzgerald[13] and others, the abstracting and distinguishing of separate categories in modernity served colonial and capitalist ends and does not represent progressing mental or cultural competence.

At the same time, and this is crucial to my overall historiographical claims, we can observe the beginnings of a shift between the overall semantics of Halevi's Judeo-Arabic and ibn Tibbon's Hebrew in the latter's usage of *'emuna* in reference to a particular human collective, at the same time as ibn Tibbon uses only the ethnonyms to refer to these groups as well. Indeed, it is the refusal to begin our investigation by assuming the term/concept "religion" that will empower this observation that enables us to ask the as-yet-unanswered question. The most interesting two facts referring to this distinction between the two Jewish writers in the previous discussion are that ibn Tibbon has available in his lexicon the word *'emuna* as meaning a group of people who hold a certain set of opinions or dogmas and that he translated *dīn* sometimes as *dat* and sometimes as *Torah*. Is there any explanatory framework that might help us make sense of this diversity? Without being able to articulate this here in any detail at all, let me tentatively suggest, for the sake of future argument, that it might be defensible to suggest in the most tentative way that the difference of Halevi's Arabic, written, of course, for Arab Jews in the dar al-Islam, and ibn Tibbon's Hebrew, written for the Jews of Christendom, respond to real cultural difference that grows out of these disparate situations.

A Christian Kuzari: For Comparison's Sake

A marvelous text from tenth-century Old Church Slavonic about the Christianization of Kievan Russ has surprising affinities with the Kuzari and affords some measure of support for my very tentative aforementioned suggestion.[14] I will do it just enough justice to show how its differences from the Kuzari are telling of Christian and Jewish difference in respect to our inquiry and thus, perhaps, provide a partial explanation for the differences in semantic fields between Halevi and ibn Tibbon. The text begins with an account of the Russ as pagans and their king as a plunderer and waster. At a certain point, after failing to defeat the Bulgars, he makes peace with them:

> [In the year 6494 (986)] Vladimir was visited by Bulgars of Mohammedan faith [вра], who said, "Though you are a wise and prudent prince, you are ignorant of [lit. do not know/you] the covenant / law / testament / tenet [закон]. But believe in our covenant / law / testament / tenet [закон], and revere Mahomet." Vladimir inquired: "What is [the nature of] your faith [вра]?" They replied: "We believe in God, and Mahomet instructs us the following: we ought to cut our private parts, and we should eat no pork, and drink no wine; however, reportedly, after death, one may indulge in carnal desires [lit. fornication / commit adultery] with women. Mahomet will give each man seventy beautiful women and, having chosen the most beautiful among them, he will confer upon her the charms of them all, and she shall be this man's wife. Reportedly, every carnal desire will be permitted, but whoever is poor in this world will be no different in the next." They also spoke other false things which out of modesty may not be written down. Vladimir listened to them, for he was fond of women and all kind of carnal indulgence [lit. fornication]; this is why he listened with pleasure. But cutting off the genitals and abstinence from pork and wine were disagreeable to him. "Drinking," said he, "is the joy of the Russians. We cannot exist without this."

The conceptual split between "ethnic" and "religious" identity is dramatized by this delineation of these proselytizers as being Bulgars by ethnicity and Muslims by "faith." Indeed, the Bulgars had only been converted to Islam (according to yet another such legend) two years or so before the events told here.[15]

The next visit presents us with another surprising ligature of ethnicity and "faith":

> After that Germans from Rome came and said: "We came, since we are sent by the Pope," and said to Vladimir: "This is what the Pope said: 'Your land is the same like ours, yet our faith is not similar to yours, since our faith is light; we bow before the God who created heaven and earth, stars and the Moon and every breathing being, while your gods are but wood."
>
> Vladimir asked them: "What is your covenant?" [заповд, lit. order, law].
>
> And they reply: "Fasting depends upon one's strength. If one eats or drinks, all this is in the glory of God, as our teacher Paul said."
>
> Then Vladimir said to the Germans: "Return to wherever you came from, since our forefathers would not have accepted this."

For some reason, the author does not wish to use the term "Catholic," but it remains fascinating that his example of Catholics and name for them is "Germans." Perhaps in his world, the most proximate Catholics were, indeed, in and from Germany, just as, perhaps, his proximate Muslims were Bulgars. This guess is somewhat borne out by the sequel, for following this visit from the "Germans" attempting to make him Catholic, the narrative continues with a visit from a Jewish proselytizer but with a bit of a surprise as to who he is:

> Having heard of this came Khazarian Jews [жидове козарьстии], saying, "We have learned that Bulgars and Christians came hither to instruct you in their faiths [в?ра].
>
> The Christians believe in him whom we crucified, but we believe in the one God of Abraham, Isaac, and Jacob."
>
> Then Vladimir inquired: "what is your covenant?"
>
> They replied: "circumcision, not eating pork or hare, and observing the Sabbath."
>
> The Prince then asked: "where is your native land?" and they replied: "in Jerusalem."
>
> Then Vladimir inquired: "Is it indeed there?"
>
> They answered, "God became angry at our forefathers, and on account of our sins scattered us to [all] corners / locations [around the world], and our land was then given to the Christians."
>
> The Prince then said, "How can you teach others while you yourselves are cast out and scattered abroad by God?
>
> If God loved you and your covenant [закон], you would not be thus dispersed in foreign lands. Do you wish the same to happen to us?"[16]

Once again, the representatives of the "faith" in question are marked by an ethnic identity separate from the marking by "faith." Fascinatingly, these Kazar Jews are precisely the converts or their descendants spoken of in the later Kuzari. Just as Bulgars and Germans represent their respective "faiths," so these Kazars represent the Jews. Once again, they fail to persuade.

Needless to say, this failure too is followed by the final and successful visit of a Greek Orthodox scholar who succeeds in converting the Pagan Russ to Orthodox Christianity. As with the Kuzari, the "winning" side has the lion's share of the text. What is important for the present inquiry—and there is so much more to be said about this text in addition to what has already been written about it—is the terms in which the alternatives are named. Even absent a philological study of the words being translated as "faith" and "covenant" here, one can see from features of the text itself that something different is happening here discursively from what we find in the Kuzari—namely, that geographic and ethnic origin and "faith" are being explicitly sundered here: these Catholics are Germans, these Bulgars are Muslims, these Jews are Khazars [!], and the Orthodox Christians are Greeks. Contrast this with the identifications of Jews as Israel, Christians as Edom, and Muslims as Ishma'el in the Kuzari and one can see the point of the difference that nonidentification by "religion" makes; hence the Kuzari's nonneed to use a term anywhere cognate to "Judaism," an abstraction that would name a putative "religion" that clearly does not exist in his cultural world, even though, as we are about to see, there was a word that is a candidate for such usage within the Hebrew of his time, making it even more telling that he does not use it. We shall see why in the next part of this chapter.

The Meanings of *Yahadut*

Medieval and modern Hebrew have a word, *yahadut*, which is most often given as the equivalent of "Judaism." The modern usage, however, does not match the English word "Judaism," which comes closest—and this is no accident—to the usage of German *Judentum* and covering senses divided in English into "Judaism," the religion or sometimes the culture of the Jews, "Jewishness," the condition or state of being a Jew, and "Jewry," the corporate body of the Jews. This multiple sense of *yahadut* is not attested, however, before modernity, as I shall establish now. Indeed, I would go so far as to say that it is only in the early modern period that *yahadut* begins to be used in any sense other than "Jewishness," implying both senses available in English usage for that vocable—namely, the juridical state of being a Jew—and (very rarely and perhaps dubiously; see the following section) the alleged distinguishing characteristics of being a Jew.

The Medieval Usages

The word *yahadut* is found most often in the Middle Ages in contexts of status, including especially *gerut* (entering into the status of *yahadut*). It is apparently—see what follows here for possible arguments against its primacy—found first in a very late midrash, Midrash Sekhel Tov (Rabbi Menahem ben Shlomo, 1138), where we read:

שכל טוב (בובר) בראשית פרשת לך לך פרק יז
ואין מטבילין את הגרים לא בלילה ולא בשבת, וגר שטבל לשם קרייו. או גיורת
שטבלה לשם נידתה, לא עלתה להן טבילה זאת, וחוזרין וטובלין לשם יהדות.
ומברכין על הטבילה

> We do not immerse the *ger* neither at night or on the Sabbath, and a convert who immersed because of an emission or a female *ger* who immersed because of her menstrual period, these immersions are not valid [for *gerut*] and they must immerse again for the sake of *yahadut*.[17]

There are many reasons in Jewish doings for one to immerse in a *mikva* (ritual bath); only one use of the bath is *gerut*, becoming a Jew.[18] Be that as it may, "for the sake of *yahadut*" here means simply immersing in the *mikva* in order to become a Jew, to enter into the juridical status of *yahadut*.

We find a further usage from about the same time found in the anthology of commentaries on the Torah from the Tosafists of twelfth-to fourteenth-century Rhineland and northern France (and it seems at first that we cannot specify the origin of this particular source more closely than that):

הדר זקנים בראשית פרק לה
שאלה מטרוניתא לר׳ עקיבא שאחר שקראו הקדוש ברוך הוא אברהם שוב לא
נקרא אברם. ויעקב נקרא בשמו יעקב אע״פ שקראו הקדוש ברוך הוא ישראל.
אמר לה אברהם שהיה לו שם גיות כשנולד שהרי עדיין לא נתגייר אברהם
וכיון שקראו הקדוש ברוך הוא שם יהדות אין דין לקרותו שם גיות. אבל יעקב
שמתחלה נמי קראו הקדוש ברוך הוא יעקב ולא נשתנה שמו אלא על שם כי
שרית עם אלהים ליכא חששא לקרותו בשמו הראשון. והא דכתיב לא יקרא
עוד שמך יעקב הכי פירושה כלומר לא יאמר עוד
שלקחת הברכות ברמאות אלא ישראל יהיה שמך:

> A certain matron asked Rabbi Akiva: [How come is it] that after the Holy Blessed One called him Abraham, he was not ever called Abram, whereas Jacob was called by his name Jacob even though the Holy Blessed One called him Israel?! He said to her Abraham who had a name of *goyut*, for when he was born Abraham had not yet become a *ger*, once the Holy Blessed One called him by a name of *yahadut*, there

is no logic to calling him by his name of *goyut*. But Jacob who from the beginning was called Jacob by the Holy Blessed One, he remains Jacob and his name was not changed but only owing to "For you have fought with God," there is no reason not to call him by his original name. And as for that which is written, "Your name shall not be called Jacob any more," this is its meaning: It will no longer be said of you that you took the blessings by swindling but rather your name will be called "Israel."

This is an intriguing text that both adds a nuance to the usage of *yahadut* and raises—at least seemingly—serious issues with regard to the chronology of the developments. The text ostensibly records a conversation between the great Palestinian Rabbi of the second century, Rabbi Akiva, and a Roman lady (this lady appears frequently in rabbinic literature asking tough questions of Rabbis). The woman, who must have been a Christian Roman lady given her knowledge of Bible, asks why, after God tells Abram that his name is no longer Abram but Abraham, he is never referred to by his former name, whereas Jacob, who gets a similar message from God about changing his name to Israel, continues to be referred to by his former name as well. The answer is that Abraham's former name was his name in *goyut*, the state of being a *goy*, non-Jew, so upon his *gerut*, that name is no longer valid at all, and his name belonging to *yahadut*, the state of being a Jew, replaces it completely, whereas Jacob, of course, never underwent *gerut*, and his new name reflects his meritorious act but did not cancel out the old name. If this is, as it purports to be, a citation from classical rabbinic literature, it would predate the usage of *yahadut* by centuries, but this text has absolutely no parallel nor hint of a parallel anywhere. It occurs only here, rendering it highly suspicious. Fortunately, we are consoled, once more, by philology. In other manuscripts of this same medieval tradition, the text reads שאל הגמון לר״ת, "a certain governor asked Rabbenu Tam (1100–1171)," none other than the founder and greatest of the Tosafists of the twelfth century in France (and grandson of Rashi), so the medieval origins of this usage remain uncontested.[19] This is a highly plausible conclusion since the entire text here comes from those same Tosafists.[20] Once again, it is clear that we have a medieval and not a late-ancient word, used consistently with what we have seen so far. Note that both of these early medieval usages are in the context of *gerut*; the first uses the term *yahadut* as the object of *gerut*—"He immerses for the sake of *yahadut*"—and it is clear from the context that *yahadut* refers to the juridical state of being a member of Jewry, not an abstraction referring to a state of conviction nor even collection of practices (both of which attend it, of course) but the inness or outness of the person. As such, and as we see from the second text in particular, the opposite of *yahadut* is *goyut*, the state of being a gentile. I judge, therefore, on the basis of the evidence I have seen and cited here that *yahadut*, a word first appearing in Hebrew at the beginning of the medieval period, is closest in usage to the English "Jewishness," the state or character of being a member of Jewry. No abstraction naming the Jewish religion but only the concrete term Torah and its equivalents and no abstraction naming the Jewish people but only Israel can be adduced for the premodern world.

INCURSUS; OR, SPECIAL PLEADINGS?

Oddly enough, there are three apparent earlier attestations of the word *yahadut* that I have discovered in the literature, but all three appear to be anomalous vis-à-vis the tradition of usage that I have just asserted. All these anomalous usages, however, are highly suspect, as they are each philologically very uncertain. The seemingly most telling instance found in the literature is in Rashi (1040–1105) to Sanhedrin 74b. The context is one in which Jews are instructed by the Mishna that they must be willing to die as martyrs even for a "light *mitzva*." The Talmud glosses the "light *mitzva*" with the Aramaic term ʿarqəta demesana, on which Rashi comments:

רש״י מסכת סנהדרין דף עד עמוד ב

ערקתא דמסאנא—שרוך הנעל, שאם דרך הנכרים לקשור כך ודרך ישראל בענין אחר, כגון שיש צד יהדות בדבר ודרך ישראל להיות צנועים אפילו שנוי זה שאין כאן מצוה אלא מנהג בעלמא יקדש את השם בפני חביריו ישראל.

ʿarqəta demesana—the shoe lace, for if it is the way of the Gentiles to tie like so and of Israel to do it differently, for example if there is an aspect of *yahadut* in the matter, and it is the way of Israel to be modest, even this difference where there is no *mitzva* at all but just a customary practice, he ought to be martyred in front of other Israel.

This passage, otherwise quite straightforward, constitutes a rather puzzling use of the term "aspect of *yahadut*." As it is, it must refer to "the way of Israel to be modest"; in other words, the *yahadut* here is the modesty and thus by adopting the practice of the Gentiles in lacing his shoes, which is allegedly immodest, he would be showing himself as abandoning Israel under the pressure of threatened martyrdom, and he must, therefore, allow himself to suffer it. This Rashi text is cited as such by several later writers without further comment. The text of Rashi, as it stands, however, is barely construable and I, very gingerly, suggest that the text of Rashi that has come down to us is corrupt and should read, צד

יהירות "an aspect of *yehirut*": arrogance, pride, or showing off *in the alleged Gentile practice*. This fits the context perfectly as it is a direct contrast to the alleged "modesty" of the Israelite practice. Without this emendation, moreover, the text makes no sense, leaving out the crucial point—namely, that the Gentile practice is show-offy, while Jews are allegedly modest. With "an aspect of *yehirut*," the text makes perfect sense. This emendation is perfectly plausible graphically as the difference between *d* and *r* is minimal in Hebrew script and frequently mistaken in manuscripts. A further support for this suggestion is found in a slightly later commentator on the Talmud, the RI"D (1165–1240), who has written here:

פסקי רי"ד מסכת סנהדרין גמרא דף עד עמוד ב אפי' לשנויי ערקתא דמסאני,
פי' שינוי היה בקשירת שרוך הנעל במקומם בין יש' לגוים, ואם יעשה יש'
כדרכי הגוים היה נראה להם פריצות ויוהרא

> Even to change the lace of the shoe, its meaning is a difference between Jews and Gentiles in the tying of the shoes in certain places, and if an Israel will do in the fashion of the Gentiles, it would appear to them as wantonness and pride [*yohara*].

Hardly an absolute proof, but this writer who has read Rashi and frequently glosses him and cites him uses the noun-form that corresponds to my suggested emendation. *Yohara* and *yehirut* are virtual synonyms constructed of the same root: YHR. The collocation ṣad *yahadut* only appears in much later rabbinic literature and almost always in contexts that demonstrate that this single text of Rashi is its source. Of course, if my emendation of the text be accepted, then we do not have any instance of *yahadut* here at all, but absent manuscript proof, it cannot be entirely ruled out either, in which case we would mark down "aspect of *yahadut*" as a very early example of *yahadut* as a certain quality of Israel—namely, modesty and such it was certainly read and understood by both early modern (such as R. Yosef Karo in the sixteenth century)[21] and modern authors. I cannot summarily dismiss, therefore, the possibility that Rashi did write here *yahadut*, and it is the very modesty to which he refers that he calls by that name, anticipating much later attested usages of the term—including in Yiddish—to refer to a characteristic of the Jew. In any case, to be sure, such usage appears possible to those early modern writers even if unprecedented before them and unique even for them in this particular context and only here.

The earliest attestation of *yahadut* is from Rav Sherira Gaon (906–1006):

ששאלתם. ישראל שנשתמד. ויש לו אשה ישראלית. ונולד לו בן ממנה. מותר
למולו בשבת או לא. כך הראונו מן השמים. שמותר למולו בשבת. מאי טעמ'.

זרעו של אברהם ותולעת יעקב הוא. ואיפשר שתוהה ועוזב את בנו בתורת
יהדות. ולא עוד אלא שהרי אמו ישראלית ואיפשר שילך אחריה

As for that which you asked: An Israelite who apostasized who has an
Israelite wife and a son was born to him from her, is it permitted to
circumcise him [the baby] on the Sabbath or not? They showed me
from heaven that it is permitted to circumcise him on the Sabbath.
What is the reason: He is of the seed of Abraham, the worm of Jacob
[Is. 51:14], and it is possible that he will leave his son in the Torah of
yahadut. And not only that but behold his mother is an Israelite and it
is possible that he will follow after her.[22]

The explanation of our crucial term in this text is not easy. The most
obvious meaning would precisely gloss *torat hayahadut* as the Torah of
Judaism, as opposed to the Torah of Islam or the Torah of Christianity,
to whichever of these the father had apostasized. We have seen earlier in
the somewhat later period of the Kuzari, the usage of Torah in this sense
as the doctrine or book of any of the so-called Abrahamic collectives,
none of them named there, however, *yahadut*. This attractive and simple
interpretation would render this earliest apparent usage of the vocable
quite anomalous, however, in view of the fact that the usage that is most
prevalent, perhaps ubiquitous, throughout medieval Hebrew is the one I
have documented here: *Yahadut* means the state of being a Jew, not an
entity that could have a Torah. The word *torat* would seem to be a problem for my interpretation. There is, however, another not-at-all obscure
sense for the word *torah* when in the collocation *betorat* nn.—namely, "in
the category of." This is a very well attested usage, for which one
example will do here: "These [moneys] came into his hands *betorat* a
deposit"—that is, these moneys came into his position under the category of a deposit (and not a gift or a loan; Babylonian Talmud, Baba
Metsia 61b).[23] We could, therefore, remain consistent with nearly all the
rest of medieval Hebrew usage and translate, "The father will leave him
in the category/state of *yahadut*"—that is, "Jewishness." If we circumcise
the baby, there is a possibility that the apostasizing father will leave him
in that state, the category of *yahadut*, "Jewishness." Moreover, since his
mother remains an Israelite, there is a chance that he, the child, will follow her in that. This interpretation is supported as well by the fact that
yahadut is used here with respect to a matter of personal status.
Nonetheless, this interpretation cannot be proven; the text must, therefore, remain somewhat ambiguous and could certainly represent a very
early usage that will after many centuries become dominant.

A final example of an allegedly early use of *yahadut* has already been
disposed of philologically decades ago. In Esther Rabba 7:11, the *textus*

receptus reads that the Jews had "held onto their *yahadut*," leading several lexicographers to mark this as the earliest appearance of the word in Hebrew literature. As early as 1961, however, E. E. Urbach demonstrated that this reading is an artifact of early modern prints and all witnesses have *yiḥudan*, their special status.[24]

INCURSUS 2: ABRAHAM ABULAFIA'S *YAHADUT*

In the writings of the prophet/mystic/Messiah Abraham Abulafia (1240–c. 1291), we find a seemingly startling occurrence of the term *yahadut*. Abulafia has conceived a plan (dictated to him by God) to go see the pope in Rome, apparently with Messianic intent.[25] In his account of the events, Abulafia writes, וצוה האפיפיור לשוערי ביתו . . . שאם יבא שם רזיאל לדבר אתו בשם היהדות לא יראה פניו כלל, "and the Pope commanded the guards of his house . . . that if Raziel [Abulafia's self-designation] to speak to him *beshem hayahadut*, he will not receive him at all."[26] As Idel shows, anticipated by other scholars as he notes, there was a notion circulating at that time that the Messiah would have to meet with the pope and that that meeting would signify his advent (בוא) as the Messiah. Since, in other parallel texts, what the Messiah is to do on that occasion is to request Mosaically of the pope that he let the people go, Scholem reasoned that this must be what speaking *beshem* (= in the name of) *yahadut* must mean here—that is, *yahadut* is equivalent in usage here to English "Jewry." A second scholarly opinion reads *yahadut* here as the "Jewish religion," to which supposedly Abulafia meant to "convert" the pope. Idel argues that for Abulafia, *yahadut* refers to a particular characteristic of Jewish spirituality, the quality of confession, confession connected with various names of God. *Yahadut*, for Abulafia, is derived from the root YDH, to confess. Idel ties this, moreover, to the context of Abulafia's spiritual writing in general.[27] Much of Abulafia's writing in these passages as cited by Idel, however, is allegorical, and it is, accordingly, difficult to determine to what exactly Abulafia refers in "ordinary" language, but suffice it to say that it seems that for him, *yahadut* indicates a particular character ascribed especially to Jews.[28] As Elliot Wolfson remarks, "Thus, in the continuation of the passage, he notes that the Jews, who are from the seed of Judah, are called yehudim, for they 'admit the truth and say "More than all the goods of this world, it is sufficient for us to have knowledge of the name."'" The inimitable destiny of the Jews is to cultivate and propagate this soterial knowledge—the letters of the word yehudim (יהודים) are rearranged as Yh"w dayam (יהו דים)—that is, it is sufficient (*dayam*) for them to call upon the name (*Yh"w*)."[29] In other words, the name *Yehudim* borne by Jews—I agree with Wolfson here; this is not universalism—indicates almost allegorically the true destined character of the Jews, and *yahadut*, interpreted allegorically, would then be the name of that character.

This interpretation is confirmed by another quite difficult passage, in which we find use of the word *yahadut* in Abulafia's corpus, as cited again by Idel:

איש יהודה שמעו—זו היא תשובת השכל שהשיב לשואלים וזכר איש יהודה
בעבור היות שמו מיוחד להוראה היהודית והודיענו שתכלית הנחמה אינה
לרעיונים לבד השואלים עד שיושלמו שלימות יהדות כלומר הודאת ידיעת
האמת והוצאה מן המבוכה.

Man of Judah: hear [Jeremiah 11:2?]! This is the response of the Intellect who responded to those who asked and he mentioned "Man of Judah" because this is the special name for the Judean instruction [teaching concerning Jewishness] and it has informed us that the telos of consolation is not only intellectual until the questioners will be completed in a complete *yahadut*, that is confession [*hoda'ah*] of the knowledge of the Truth and exit from confusion.

On this confounding passage, Wolfson has again helpfully remarked,

It is a typical Abulafian text which is not completely transparent, but the gist of it is that the intellect—I presume the reference is to the active intellect—is imparting knowledge of the name (YHWH), which is encoded in the expression *ish yehudah*, since for Abulafia the name instructs about the teaching concerning Jewishness, בעבור היות שמו מיוחד להוראה היהודית, and thus ultimate comfort (or salvation) is tied to what he calls שלמות יהדות, the fulfillment of *yahadut*. In the previous paragraph Abulafia goes to great length to establish the connection between the name and the matter of praise הודו is equal to אהיה which is equal to הודאה and this is transposed into הודאי as well as הוא די. I just cannot see any other way to render this except by assuming that Abulafia wanted to establish an inherent connection between the name and what he considered to be the essence of Judaism, the knowledge of the truth, ידיעת האמת.

Now whatever the precise meaning here of Abulafia's argument, in any case, the explanation of *yahadut* is explicit. The fulfillment of *yahadut* is the *hoda'a*, the confession of the knowledge of the truth.

There are two more crucial passages (both of which have been pointed out to me by Wolfson). In the first, we find the following:

והוא הנביא היושב על כסא יי כשלמה ומשה ואברהם ואהרן שנכתרו הם
והדומים להם בכתר המילה וגלו העטרה ופרסמו מלכות היהדות ובכתר
התורה במשה ובכתר כהונה באהרן ובכתר מלכות העשר והממשלה בשלמה

וְעַל הָאִישׁ הַזֶּה נֶאֱמַר וְעַל דְּמוּת הַכִּסֵּא דְּמוּת כְּמַרְאֵה אָדָם עָלָיו מִלְמַעְלָה וְהוּא
בִּדְמוּת וּמִתְדַּמֶּה לוֹ וּמַרְאֵהוּ הוּא מַרְאֵה דְּמוּת כָּבוֹד יְיָ[30]

And he is the prophet who sits on the throne of God as Solomon and
Moses and Abraham and Aaron who have been crowned—they and
those like them—with the crown of circumcision and revealed the
corona and made known the kingship of *yahadut* and with the crown
of Torah with Moses and the crown of the priesthood with Aaron and
the crown of kingship of the ten and the rulership with Solomon and
with respect to this man it is said and on the image on the throne, the
image of a man on it from above and it is an image which is identical
to him, and *his appearance is the appearance of the Glory of Y'.*

This is, indeed, another mysterious passage in Abulafia's writing. I
will not go into its deep meanings but only observe that it seems most
likely to me that *yahadut* here is parallel to priesthood, and Torah, as a
status of human beings. The crown of circumcision, revealing the
corona, reveals the kingship of Jewishness. The notion, however, that it
anomalously means "Judaism" cannot be excluded (which could potentially support its very rare usage as such in the passage from R. Sherira
Gaon discussed earlier as well).

In the second passage, however, the meaning is crystal clear, and only
"Jewishness" will do for English:

וְאָמְנָם אֲנַחְנוּ הַיּוֹם הַנִּקְרָאִים עַם אֱלֹהֵי יִשְׂרָאֵל בְּתוֹרָתֵנוּ, הִנֵּה אֲנַחְנוּ יֵשׁ בְּיָדֵינוּ
רְאָיוֹת חֲזָקוֹת מִכָּל צַד שֶׁאֲנַחְנוּ נֶחְלָקִים לִשְׁלֹשֶׁת מַעֲלוֹת אֱנוֹשִׁיּוֹת. וְהֵן מַעֲלַת
כְּהֻנָּה וּמַעֲלַת לְוִיָּה וּמַעֲלַת יַהֲדוּת[31]

And although we are called today the people of the God of Israel in our
Torah, we have strong proofs from many passages that we are divided
into three human degrees, the degree of the priesthood, the degree of
the Levitehood, and the degree of *yahadut.*

In this passage, it is quite clear what *yahadut* means. Just as the priesthood and the Levitehood are states of human being, so is *yahadut* here.
As in other medieval Hebrew literature previously surveyed, it simply
means the state of being Israel, a Jew. Israel is divided into three higher
statuses: the highest is the priesthood, the next highest is the status of
being a Levite, and the next is simply being a Jew. The usage is entirely
parallel to the much more common locution—priest, Levite, Israel—where
Israel means a Jew who is neither a priest nor a Levite. The solution to
this crux in Abulafia seems to me quite different than Idel's. Where Idel
saw the very meaning of the word *yahadut* in the special practices and
interpretations ascribed to Jews by Abulafia, I wish to suggest that

yahadut is used essentially in its ordinary sense of the state of being a Jew, of being Israel, and the explanations cited and discussed by Idel of this name are just that; they are etymological, allegorical explanations of why Jews are called *Yehuda* and *yahadut*. On this interpretation, we have not learned from Abulafia much more than we already knew about the semantics of *yahadut* in the Middle Ages.

Passage to Early Modernity: The Fifteenth Century

In the fifteenth century, we continue to find significant uses of *yahadut* that follow and develop its earlier significance. One of the more fascinating ones is the following text from the collected sermons of Rabbi Yitzhaq Arama (1420–1494, Aqedat Yitzhaq). Arama returns to the perennial problem of the difference between the treatment of Abraham's old name, Abram, and that of Israel's old name, Jacob. His usage is slightly different, however:

עקידת יצחק בראשית שער יח (פרשת לך לך)

ומ"מ שנוי השם הזה הוא צורך המילה אשר יצוהו כי בשתים יתחתן לו היום
להיות לפניו גר צדק באמת. והנה המעלות האחרונות פוסלות את הראשונות
בלי ספק. כי השם הראשון היה שם ערליותו ואין ראוי לזכרו עתה. (ט) ולזה
היה הקורא אותו בו עובר בלאו ועשה (ברכות י"ג א) מה שאינו כן ביעקב
שעם ששם ישראל היה עקר לא נעקר הראשון ממקומו כי שניהם כאחד טובים
ושוים ביהדות אלא שהשני מורה על השררה הנוספת

And in any case the changing of [Abram's name to Abraham] was deeply connected to his circumcision which God had commanded him, for with these two [signs] God married him that day to be before him a *ger* of righteousness and truth. And the latter status cancels the earlier one without a doubt, for the first name was the name of his uncircumcision and it is not appropriate for it to be mentioned now. And this is the reason that one who refers to him now by it [the old name] is violating a negative and positive commandment [TB Berakhot 13a], which is not the case with Jacob for even though the name "Israel" is his main name, the first name has not been uprooted from its place, for both of them are equally good and equal in *yahadut*, while the second one only refers to additional sovereignty.[32]

Once again, an argument that the changing of Abram's name to Abraham was of much greater significance than the changing of Jacob's to Israel but with a twist in the language. The point is essentially the same as what we have seen—namely, that Abraham's name change represented an entire ontological shift in his being, and therefore, it is inappropriate to refer to him later on by his former name, especially, as

Arama points out, as the name change and the circumcision come together and—hardly aleatorily—with the image of God marrying Abraham, the wedding ring being the circumcised penis and the ketuba the name change. With Jacob, however, the name change is not so fraught, as we have already seen. Abraham's name change is from his name "in uncircumcision" to his name in *yahadut*, while Jacob's two names are equal in their *yahadut*—that is, in their status of being Jewish names and not the names of uncircumcision. *Yahadut* is clearly here, as earlier, the state of being in Jewry and not among the ranks of the uncircumcised.

Another later fifteenth-century writer provides a further wrinkle in the usage. Rabbi Isaac Karo (Toledo, 1458–Jerusalem, 1535), uncle and guardian of the more famous R. Yosef Karo, author of the Shulkhan Arukh, wrote a very popular (to this day) commentary on the Torah. In it, we find the following apparently—but actually not so—telling usage of *yahadut*:

תולדות יצחק בראשית פרק לא

ויש אומרים ופחד יצחק יראת אבי יצחק לשי״ת הועילה אותי שזכות אב תועיל
לבן, ולפי זה הפי׳ וישבע יעקב בפחד אביו הוא שנשבע ביהדות אביו ויראתו
את הש״י.

And there are those who say, *The Fear of Isaac*, means Isaac's fear of Y', may he be blessed, was effective for me, for the virtue of the father will be effective for the son, and according to this, the interpretation of *and Jacob swore by the fear of his father* is that he swore by the *yahadut* of his father and his fear of Y', may he be blessed.[33]

The difficult verse in question is when Jacob swears by "the Fear of Isaac my father." Since, of course, it is impossible for traditional commentators to understand this as referring to a tribal god of Isaac, the verse is puzzling. After offering several interpretations given by various commentators, Karo proffers this one, that the fear of Isaac means his fear of Y', and since the virtue of the father is of use for the son in his dealings with God, Jacob can refer to the fear of Y' manifested by his father, Isaac. What is interesting here for our investigation is the glossing of Isaac's fear of Y' by the term *yahadut*, which would seem clearly to identify *yahadut* in a personal commitment within and not only in an external status as we have generally observed in the earlier rabbinic texts discussed here. This is not so unequivocal as might seem, however, for swearing by one's *yahadut* was quite a common turn of phrase, as can easily be shown. This usage is well known, in fact, and appears in most lexica of Hebrew usage. What Karo seems to be trying to do here is to make sense of how one might swear by one's father's fear of heaven and glossing it, therefore, with the common Jewish oath, "by my *yahadut*," my "Jewishness."[34] Nonetheless, it would seem that even in this equivocal context, we can see hints at *yahadut* being used to refer to a "religious"— and I use the term advisedly here—disposition.

The only other usage of *yahadut* in this author resolves the ambiguity, if not of the just-discussed text, of the possibilities for usage by this author in this time and place:

תולדות יצחק במדבר פרק יז

שמעו נא בני לוי המעט מכם כי הבדיל אלהי ישראל אתכם מעדת ישראל
להקריב אתכם אליו וגו', ובקשתם גם כהונה רב לכם בני לוי, ואם נאמר
שכלם לויים, אי אפשר שחמשים ומאתים אנשים כלם משבט לוי שלעולם נהגו
בקדושה ויהדות מבעטים במשה רבן,

Hear then, O sons of Levi: Is it but a small thing unto you, that the God of Israel hath separated you from the congregation of Israel, to bring you near to Himself, to do the service of the tabernacle of the LORD, and to stand before the congregation to minister unto them? And you requested also the priesthood [v. 10]!? It is too much for you O sons of Levi, but if we will say that all of them were Levites, it is impossible that two-hundred and fifty, all of them from the Tribe of Levi which always behaved in holiness and yahadut are rebuffing Moses their leader![35]

Rabbi Isaac's argument is that it is impossible that all the rebels in Korach's rebellion were from the tribe of Levi, since it is unimaginable that 250 of that tribe exemplary for its holiness and *yahadut* would behave in such fashion. It is absolutely unequivocal and explicit here that *yahadut* is a quality deemed characteristic of Israel. Given what we know already, it might well be "modesty." In any case, we can see how entirely different Karo's usage here is from that Abulafia, where *yahadut* was not Levi-hood, while here it is the very characteristic of Levi-hood.

In another fifteenth-century Jewish author, we begin to detect a shift in the usage of *yahadut*. Don Isaac Abarbanel (sometimes Abravanel) was born in Spain in 1437, expelled (with all the Spanish Jews who refused conversion to Christianity) in 1492, and escaped to the Kingdom of Naples. After suffering several more expulsions, he died finally in Venice. Well-known as a financial genius, he served several Spanish and Portuguese potentates in distinguished positions and became fabulously wealthy several times over. He is well-known as the author of many Hebrew books but especially of a great commentary on the Bible, known today among Jewish scholars, as "The Abarbanel." This background may shed some light on his usages of the term *yahadut*:

אברבנאל דברים פרק ל

כל הגוי' אשר הדיחך ה' אלהיך שמה ר"ל שהם מעורבי' בהם ונחשבים כמוהם
ובלבם ישובו אל ה'. ועל החלק האחרון מהיהודים המפורסמים אמר ושבת
עד ה' אלהיך ושמעת בקולו ככל אשר אנכי מצוך היום אתה ובניך. ר"ל שהם
ישובו ויעשו המצות וישמעו בקול ה' הם ובניהם בפרסום לפי שלא עזבו שם
אלהיהם. וכאשר ישובו אל ה' וילכו אחריו וירוצו אלו ואלו כל אחד כפי מצבו
ועניינו הבטיח שהש"י יקרבם אליו וזהו ושב ה' אלהיך את שבותך ורחמך
ושב וקבצך וגומ'. הנה אמר ושב ה' אלהיך את שבותך ורחמך על כל החלק
היהודים המפורסמי' ומחזיקים ביהדותם ועליהם אמר את שבותך לפי שהם
בשביה ועבדות.

All the nations to which Y' drove you [Deut. 30:1–3]. It means to say that
they are mixed with them and thought of like them, but in their
hearts, they will return to Y'. And on the last body of the famous (i.e.,
open and identifiable) *Yehudim*, he said *and you will return to Y' your god
and obey him as I command you this day, you and your children.* It means to
say that they will return and do the commandments and obey the voice
of Y', they and their children openly, for they had not left the name of
their God. And when they return to Y' and go after him and run, these
and these, each one according to his situation and his personality, Y',
may he be blessed, has promised them that he will bring them near to
him, and this is [the meaning of] *And Y' your god will return to you in your
captivity and have compassion for you and gather you etc.* Behold he said:
*And Y' your god will return to you in your captivity and have compassion for
you* about the entire portion of the identifiable *Yehudim* who had held
onto their *yahadut.* And of them, he said *your captivity,* as they are in
captivity and slavery.[36]

Although this text is a bit cryptic, fortunately Abarbanel himself (in
Deuteronomy 28:65) has given us more explicit information about his
view that is necessary to interpret our citation. According to Abarbanel,
Deuteronomy 30:1–3 speaks of two groups of Jews. Abarbanel writes that
the Israel in Exile is divided into two groups: a very small one that continues to hold onto the *dat* and continue in the Torah of Y' and be called
Israel, and a much larger group, owing to the troubles and persecutions
transgress the *dat*, as the verse says, "And they worship other gods."

It is absolutely clear that Abarbanel refers the Torah text here to his
own situation in Christian Spain with a large group of Jews having
Christianized as *conversos* and a smaller group to which he himself
belonged remaining open in their Jewish identity and doings. Based on
this division of Israel into two groups, Abarbanel interprets our verses,
and we can understand his interpretation. For those who have left the *dat*,
God commands, *And you shall return to your heart*, for their repentance

will be in their hearts but not in their mouths. As Abarbanel says here, these are those who are so assimilated to the people that they are among that they are indistinguishable from them. But of those who never left the fold, it is said that God will bring them closer to him and have compassion on them, and so on. Now what is crucial for my philology here is the usage with respect to the latter group—a usage we don't find in the parallel text—of "held onto their *yahadut*" to designate the ones who remained openly faithful to Y', his commandments, and the name Israel. Combined with the distinction between a kind of return to Y' in the heart, we begin to feel that we are in the presence of a *yahadut* that is taking on certain elements of later modern usage as well, but still we are in the range of "Jewishness" here more than "Judaism"—that is, an identity that was tenaciously enacted. Of the larger group, God doesn't say and "will have compassion on them," for they are not suffering, having given up their status as Israel but that they will be gathered and returned to the fold and to the Promised Land if they return in their hearts, while of the smaller group who suffer and are persecuted for their open faithfulness, we hear of God having compassion for them and returning to them and bringing them home. Most further usages of *yahadut* in Abarbanel fit earlier contexts naming the state of being Jews, of being Israel before defecting for something else, and not a quality of Jewish being. But we can certainly detect here the semantic slippage that will help produce the latter-day usages, especially as Hebrew comes increasingly in contact with the semantic systems of modern European (read: Christian) languages.

There is, however, more to be learned from him. In his commentary on Ezekiel (20:37), he writes the following:

אברבנאל יחזקאל פרק כ

... לפי שאני נשבע חי השם אם לא ביד חזקה וזרוע נטויה ובחמה שפוכה אמלוך עליכם, ואמר יד חזקה וזרוע נטויה וחמה שפוכה לכלול כל בני ישראל אם היהודים שעמדו בדתם וטעמם לא נאמ' שהנה ימלוך עליהם ביד חזקה ובכחו הבלתי בעל תכלית ואמר זה על היהודים אשר בארץ אדום, ואמר ובז־רוע נטויה על היהודים שבבארץ ישמעאל שעמדו ביהדותם ושמרו דתם, וכנגד המשומדים והאנוסים שיצאו מכלל הדת אמר ובחמה שפוכה אמלך עליכם שהחמה היא מפני שעברו על דת, ורמז בזה שאף על פי שישתדלו הם וזרעם אחריהם להיות כגוים גמורים הנה לא יהיה כן כי תמיד יקראו אותם משפחות הארצות יהודים ובשם ישראל יכנו בעל כרחם ויחשבו אותם ליהודים ויעלילו עליהם שהם מתיהדים בסתר ובאש שרוף ישרפו אותם על זה

... for I swear to you by the Life of the Holy Name if I will not rule over you with a strong hand and an outstretched arm and with outpoured wrath. And he said: with a strong hand and an outstretched arm and with outpoured wrath in order to include all of the Children of Israel, for with respect to the Jews who remained steadfast in their dat and their opinion, it is not said that he will rule over them with a strong hand . . . , rather it is about the Jews who are in Edom, and an outstretched arm is said of the Jews of Ishma'el who remained in their yahadut and kept their dat. And it is with respect to the apostates and the "forced ones" [those forced to apostasize] who exited from the dat that he says with outpoured wrath who transgressed the dat, and the proof of this is that even though they and their children after them will strive to be as complete Gentiles, it will not be so, for the peoples of the lands will always call them Jews, and by the name Israel, they shall be called against their wills, and they shall be thought of as Jews, and they will slander them saying that they behave as Jews [mityahadim] in secret and they will be burned in fire. (Abarbanel Ezekiel 20)

The prophet has just referred to the Jews' idea that once they arrive in foreign lands, they will be able with impunity to worship foreign gods and completely forget that they are/were Jews. It is on this that Abarbanel comments and paraphrases Ezekiel. It is riveting to see that once again Abarbanel uses *yahadut* in this sense in a context where he is clearly attacking (reads the prophet as attacking) the *conversos* of his day. Note here how Israel of the Bible and most Jewish parlance is glossed here as *Yehudim*, Jews, once quite a rare usage. I begin, very tentatively, very pendulously, to suggest a pattern—namely, that as Jewish authors become more and more involved with Christians, the likelihood that *yahadut* will at least tend partly, and later fully, to match the usage of *Iudaismus* (and its cognates) in Christian usage becomes more pronounced.

We next meet *yahadut* again in the sixteenth century, where it seems to have continued the usage and development in the Abarbanel and taken on at least some of the connotations of conversion to a "religion" not out of keeping with the general shifts in the senses not only of the word but of the conceptualizing of that aspect of life in Europe at about that time. The text is, once again, in the context of a *gerut*, and not entirely surprisingly, we find it in a commentary on the book of Ruth, the proto-*ger*, by R. Moshe Alsheikh.

Since we will be spending some time with this extended and crucial text, I will begin by introducing its context. The book of Ruth chapter contains the following famous narrative. A Judean woman with two sons living in the Land of Moab has married them to two local women. The two sons having died and Naomi wishing to return to the Land of Israel, she implores her widowed daughters-in-law to return each to her mother's house:

10 And they said unto her: "Nay, but we will return with thee unto thy people." 11 And Naomi said: "Turn back, my daughters; why will ye go with me? have I yet sons in my womb, that they may be your husbands? 12 Turn back, my daughters, go your way; for I am too old to have a husband. If I should say: I have hope, should I even have an husband to-night, and also bear sons; 13 would ye tarry for them till they were grown? would ye shut yourselves off for them and have no husbands? nay, my daughters; for it grieveth me much for your sakes, for the hand of HaShem is gone forth against me." 14 And they lifted up their voice, and wept again; and Orpah kissed her mother-in-law; but Ruth cleaved unto her. 15 And she said: "Behold, thy sister-in-law is gone back unto her people, and unto her god; return thou after thy sister-in-law." 16 And Ruth said: "Entreat me not to leave thee, and to return from following after thee; for whither thou goest, I will go; and where thou lodgest, I will lodge; thy people shall be my people, and thy G-d my G-d; 17 where thou diest, will I die, and there will I be buried; HaShem do so to me, and more also, if aught but death part thee and me." 18 And when she saw that she was steadfastly minded to go with her, she left off speaking unto her.

It is on these verses that the following passages from Alsheikh comments:

אלשיך רות פרק א

וכן נעמי אמרה להן שבנה בנותי, כלומר שובנה אל ה', אך יהיה בארצכן ולמה תלכנה עמי וכו'. על כן עתה בלכתה מעמה, אמרה אל יעלה על לבה כי בארצה תוכל לעבוד את ה', כאשר הבינה מדבריה, באופן שאחרי כן בעובדה את אלהי נכר תטיל האשם עלי. על כן כמדברת אל רות עודנה ערפה לפניה, אמרה הנה מעתה שבה יבמתך אל עמה ואל אלהיה, כי בשובה אל עמה לא יבצר משוב אל אלהיה, כלומר כי ממוצא דבר תבין ערפה, כי אם תשוב לארצה, אל אלהיה תשוב, למען העיר לה אזן, שאם יהדות בלבה לא תלך

And thus Naomi said to them "return my daughters," that is return to Y', but let it be in your lands and "why will you go with me, etc.?" Now, therefore, with [Orpah] leaving her, she said that she shouldn't let it even occur to her that in her land, she will be able to serve Y', as she had understood from her words, in such fashion that afterwards when she will serve strange gods, she will place the blame on her. When she was speaking to Ruth, Orpah was still present, she said, "Look, your sister-in-law is going back to her people and her gods," for with the return to her people, it would be impossible for her not to return to her gods, that is to say, from the expression of the matter, Orpah should understand that if she returns to her land, she will return to her gods, in order to enlighten her ear, that if *yahadut* is in her heart, she ought not to go. (Alsheikh Ruth 1)

Alsheikh understands the story as a kind of test that Naomi has set for her daughters-in-law. She suggests to them the tempting option of turning to Y' (in Alsheikh's language, as in the language of medieval Hebrew in general, *gerut*) while returning to their family homes and marrying local Moabite men. Orpah seemingly takes the bait, but as she is leaving, Naomi makes sure to clarify to her / for her that if she goes home, she will not be able to worship Y' but will return to her local gods. She does this so that Orpah will be not able to blame her for misleading her in the original statement. Therefore, before Orpah actually left, she emphasized to Ruth in Orpah's hearing that Orpah is going back to her people and her gods so that Orpah will understand clearly the meaning of her action—namely, that if she really has *yahadut* in her heart, she would not go. This is the earliest text of which I know in a Hebrew Jewish text where *yahadut* is not the status or quality of being a Jew but an internal commitment. It belongs clearly in the early modern period.

The next passage in the same context gives us further information of what Alsheikh means by the word *yahadut*:

אלשיך רות פרק א (טז)

ואפשר אמרה, הנך מפצרת זה כמה פעמים שאשוב אל עמי, ואין ספק כי אין זה רק לנסותני, היש ה׳ בקרבי אם אין, ואשובה לי כאשר שבה ערפה על פי דבריך, אך אל תפגעי בי, כלומר כי אין פגיעתך זאת צודקת בי כאשר בערפה, כי אני רוח אחרת עמי למלא אחרי ה׳, כי דעי וראי כי כל פרי דחיותיך לפגוע בי שאשוב אל עמי, אינו אם אעזוב את ה׳ אם אין, רק לעזבך לשוב מאחריך לבד, אך לא מאחרי ה׳, אפילו הייתי שבה מאחריך. כי מה שהוא עתיד שאני מבקשת הוא, באשר תלכי אלך ובאשר תליני אלין שהוא לעתיד, אך מהאמונה והאלהות זה כבר עמך עמי ואלהיך אלהי, ולא כאשר תלית השיבה לאלהי ועמי בשיבה אל ארצי: (יז) ושמא תאמרי אם כן למה זה אפציר ללכת בארצך, אם גם בארצי גם כן יהיה לי יהדות,

It is possible she said: "Behold, you have several times tried to persuade me that I should return to my people, and I have no doubt that that is only to test me as to whether I have Y' in my innards or no, and [then] I would return just as Orpah returned following your words. That is to say, your persuasion is not fair to me as it was for Orpah, for I have a different spirit to obey Y'. You must know and see that all the fruit of you pressure to persuade me that I should return to my people, is not whether or not I will abandon Y', only whether I will abandon you alone, but not abandon Y', even were I to abandon you. For what I ask for in the future is that whither you goest, I shall go and where you

sleep I will sleep; that is for the future, but with respect to divine faithfulness, it is already [the case] that your people are my people and your
god is my god, and not that which you have entailed the return to my
gods and my people were I to return to my country. And perhaps you
will say, if that is the case why do I beg to go to your country, if even in
my country, I will have *yahadut*." (Alsheikh ad loc)

Alsheikh reconstructs Ruth's discourse in her approach to her mother-
in-law, making it clear that for her, the primary commitment is to Y' the
God of Israel and to the People Israel. She is deeply dedicated to her
mother-in-law Naomi as well, but that is epiphenomenal to her first loyalty to Israel's god. So for her, even were she to remain in Moab, she has
no doubt that she would remain faithful to this new god of hers and his
worship. Alsheikh goes on, however, to put into her mouth a further
question—namely, having established that she will be faithful to Y' even
were she to remain in Moab, why does she push so hard to accompany
Naomi back to Canaan? Alsheikh's language, impossible, of course, for a
biblical character, is that since I will have *yahadut* anywhere, why do I beg
to return to Canaan with you? Now, in fact, this usage is equivocal. It
could mean "have Judaism," the internal commitment and practice,
something more like its modern usages, and the collocation *"yahadut* in
the heart" of the last passage would support this reading. On the other
hand, it could mean the status of being a Jew, as in nearly all previous
instantiations of the word. We need not decide between these equivocal
readings, for it is often through such contextual equivocations that
semantic change takes place.

In yet another passage of Alsheikh, we seemingly get even closer to
modern usage (but don't actually):

אלשיך בראשית פרק יז
ויהיה שהוקשה להם, אחר שברית מילה שקולה ככל התורה כולה וגדולה יותר,
שעל התורה נכרתו עליה שלש בריתות, ועל המילה שלש עשרה בריתות,
ולמה כאשר הוזכר פה דרך ה' שהוא גמילות חסדים—כמו שאמרו ז"ל שהוא
צדקה ומשפט—למה לא הוזכרה המילה שבה תלוי כל היהדות.

For it was difficult for them, since the covenant of circumcision is equal
to all of the Torah and even greater, for with regard to the Torah, three
covenants were made and with circumcision thirteen, why is it that
here where he mentioned the way of Y' which is acts of kindness—as
in their saying that it is righteousness and justice—why was not circumcision, since all of *yahadut* is dependent on it?

Without going into unnecessary details for the present context,
the point of the question is that in a passage that seems to mention the

essence of Torah, circumcision—which is frequently mentioned in rabbinic literature as the most important of all commandments—is left out. The answer to this question need not detain us either. What is crucial is that in posing the question, Alsheikh describes circumcision as that on which all of *yahadut* depends. At first glance, it certainly appears that the most attractive way to understand *yahadut* is the whole essence of Jewish doings, a usage very close, it would seem, to modern acceptations of *yahadut* in Hebrew and "Judaism" in English. Since it is so important that all of "Judaism" is dependent on it, why is it not mentioned in a situation where the most important commandments, the way of Y', are being described? However, this would be an inaccurate reading. Alsheikh is saying something entirely different. Alsheikh writes explicitly that a male who is not circumcised is not a Jew. Given that, his usage of *yahadut* is no different here from earlier medieval usages—namely, that the Jewishness (the status as Jew) of the person is dependent on his being circumcised. His very status in *yahadut* is what is crucially dependent on his circumcision, and in that sense, it is fundamental to all of the Torah and all of the commandments (for men).

Once more, I would hypothesize that as the meaning "Judaism," an abstraction that begins to partially replace *Torah* in Jewish parlance in the modern period, grew in strength and breadth through the period, an equivocal passage such as this one in Alsheikh became resignified (giving the latter-day Christianized usage, as will be shown in the next two chapters, a past that it never had). That is the way of semantic shift through ambiguities and equivocations.

Here's one final example of such equivocation in Alsheikh. Of Mordecai, the book of Esther says:

איש יהודי היה לבדו בשושן הבירה כי השאר לא שמרו יהדותם

> There was a Yehudi man along in Susa, the capital, for all the rest did not keep their *yahadut*. (Alsheikh Esther 1)

Why is Mordecai alone called *Yehudi* in the city when there certainly were many more? The answer Alsheikh gives is that the others did not keep their *yahadut*, which can mean they did not keep their Jewish identity or did not keep their Judaism, and so through such equivocations meanings shift. Finally, there are further passages in Alsheikh himself that seem, like his *yahadut* in the heart, to be using the term already in the sense of a commitment, a loyalty, if not as an abstraction or a doctrine. We could at any rate hypothesize that in this sixteenth century, early modern Hebrew writer we find presaged, or even a kind of *preparatio* for the semantic developments that will take place with *yahadut* in the following centuries.[37] Alsheikh remains the first Jewish writer, to the best of my knowledge, who refers even once to *yahadut* as something that is in the heart. It is perhaps in this writer, as well, that for the first time we find *yahadut* as a reference to the whole system of belief and practice that will only become more common throughout the modern period, eventually resulting in these words being used virtually identically to their Christian cognates.

Not entirely surprisingly—to me, at any rate—one of the first attested usages of *yahadut* seemingly as the name of a putative Jewish religion is found in the German-Jewish cultural sphere. Thus we find R. Israel Lifschitz of Danzig (1782–1860) writing in his commentary *Tif'eret Israel* on the Mishna at Shevi'it 10:9, once again in the context of *gerut*, the following:

ונ״ל דר״ל בעבור צערו על איבוד ממונו, ימאס בדת יהדות

> "It seems to me that what it means to say is that owing to his pain at losing his money, he will spurn the *dat yahadut.*"

It is just possible to gloss this still as he will spurn the law of *Jewry*, in which case *yahadut* is not in itself yet the name of a religion, Judaism, but surely *yahadut* is growing very close to its modern senses here—indeed, if, as I suspect, we have here a very early calque on German *Judentum*, then both meanings are equally present, as in German they are indistinguishable. It should be noted that this usage appears several times in the same work and is first attested in this author as far as I can discover.

There is, to be sure, one apparent, somewhat puzzling antecedent to this usage from the fourteenth century (Rabbenu Ya'aqov Ba'al Haturim 1269–1343):

גר קטן מטבילין אותו על דעת ב״ד כישראל לכל דבריו וקטן שנתגייר בין
ע״י ב״ד בין ע״י אביו יכול למחות כל זמן שלא נהג בדת יהדות שעה אחת
[כשנתגדל ואין דינו כישראל מומר אלא כעובד כוכבים גמור ואי נהג בדת שעה
א׳] משהגדיל אינו יכול למחות

A minor *ger* may be immersed on the authority of the court and he is completely an Israelite, and a minor who became a *ger* whether on the authority of the court or on the authority of his father may protest when he attains majority as long as he has not acted in accordance with the *dat yahadut* even for one hour, and his status is not one of an Israelite apostate but a complete Gentile, but if he acted in accordance with the *dat* even for one hour, he may not protest. (Qissur Piskei Harosh, on the Rosh, Ketubbot 12a)

It is virtually impossible for us to imagine here a meaning other than "the law of Judaism" or "the practice of Judaism," at any rate, but this usage would be so anomalous for such an early period that something is suspect. Since we are still in the realm of *gerut* where *yahadut* has mostly appeared until now, perhaps we still need to read here "in accordance with the custom/law of Jewry" and continue to eschew the abstraction. It certainly is the case that this ambiguity would provide an easy semantic model for a later usage such as that of R. Lifschitz, in which the "religion of Judaism" is fully intended and not the "religion of Jewry."[38]

In classical rabbinic texts, by which I mean rabbinic texts of classic genres, of the nineteenth century, for the most part only the older meanings obtain. An excellent example is from the text known as Malbi"m (Meir Leibush ben Yehiel Michel Wisser 1809–1879). Malbi"m writes the following:

מלבי״מ בראשית פרק לה
שמך יעקב. יעקב הוא שם הטבעי מצד הנהגתו הטבעיית, ושם ישראל הוא מצד ההנהגה הנסיית, שיחול עליו הענין האלהי עד שמפניו יגורו אלים ובני אלהים ישרתוהו, אמנם שם יעקב לא נעקר כי היה שם יהדות,

"Thy name is Jacob" "Jacob" is the natural name from the point of view of [God's] natural conduct, and the name "Israel" is his name from the point of view of his miraculous conduct, that the Divine will enter him until angels will fear him and the children of Elohim will serve him, but his name "Jacob" was not uprooted, as it is his name of *yahadut*. (Malbim Genesis 35)

The theological sentiment has changed from the Middle Ages, but the fundamental idea and usage of *yahadut* is entirely the same. Even though the name Israel has been given owing to metaphysical reasons, the name Jacob is still appropriate for him, as it is a name given to him when he was in the state of *yahadut* (again in contrast to Abraham, whose first name Abram was given to him when he was in the state of *goyut* and only Abraham is his name in [the state of] *yahadut*). In the very same author, however, we can also find a usage similar to that of his Northern contemporary, Danzig, whom we have encountered just previously, and even more "modern" than that. In the following citation, Malbim seems to be making a clear distinction between "religion" and the secular, between "religious" and "political" motivations:

מלבי״מ אסתר פרק ג ויהי
העבדים לא משנאה הלשינוהו להמן, רק מאשר הטיל עליהם לשמור מצות המלך ולמחות בעוברי רצונו, וע״כ לא הלשינוהו עד שהתרו בו תחלה, שעז״א

ויהי כאמרם אליו. זאת שנית שהתמידו בהתראה יום יום ולא שמע אליהם, אז
הגידו להמן, לראות היעמדו, ר"ל שמרדכי הגיד להם שלכן אינו משתחוה להמן
בעבור שהוא יהודי ואינו יכול להשתחוות לו מצד דתו. אולם תרוצו זה צודק
שלא ישתחוה לו בעת שהמן הולך מרחוק ואינו רואה, שאז אינו משתחוה רק
מצד שעשה עצמו אלוה, אבל אם משתחוה לו בעת שהמן רואה אותו, שאז אין
זה לשם אלהות רק מצד שררותו, כי לכל שר וגדול הדרך להשתחוות בפניו,
ואם גם בעת שהמן יראה לא ישתחוה לו יודע כי לא מחמת יהדותו ודתו עושה
זאת, רק מצד שמורד במלכות,

It was not from hatred that the servants informed on Mordecai to
Haman. Just because he had enjoined them to guard the command of
the king and to protest against those who violated his desire. And therefore they did not inform on him [Mordecai] until warning him first, and
it is for this reason that it says: "And it was while they were saying to
him." Moreover, they were constant in warning him every day and he
did not listen to them, and only then did they inform to Haman, "to see
if they would stand," that is to say that Mordecai had told them that for
this reason he does not bow down to Haman, "because he is a Yehudi,"
and he may not bow down to him owing to his religion. And indeed,
this justification is correct that he should not bow down to him when
Haman walks at a distance and doesn't see, for then he doesn't bow
down only from the point of view that Haman makes himself a god,
but were he to bow down to him when he [Haman] sees him, for then
it has nothing to do with Haman's godhood but only owing to his
power. For every great prince, it is the custom to bow down before him,
and if also at the time that Haman sees him he doesn't bow down, it
will be known that it is not because of his *Yahadut* and his religion that
he does so but only because he is a rebel against the kingdom. (Malbim
Esther 3)

Mordecai the Yehudi refuses to obey the order of the vizier, Haman
the Wicked, and bow down to him. The servants inform Haman that that
is the case. Now Malbim explains that these servants bore no ill will
toward Mordecai but were just following orders. They even warned
Mordecai that they would have to inform on him were he to continue in
his scofflaw behavior more than once. Mordecai defended himself, saying that he could not bow down since he is a *Yehudi*. Now note the distinction that Malbim (not the book of Esther!) makes. Had Mordecai not
bowed down to Haman from a distance but bowed down in his presence,
then Mordecai would have been blameless, for it would have been
clear that his objection to bowing down to Haman is owing to the implication that he has been deified, something that Mordecai as a *Yehudi*

cannot, of course, countenance. But Mordecai doesn't bow down even when Haman is present. Such bowing down is normal to indicate respect for the authority of the vizier and has nothing to do with him having been deified, but Mordecai doesn't bow down owing to his religion, and it would seem that this is not because of his "religion" but for a *political* reason—namely, that Mordecai is a rebel against the kingdom. Note that although Malbim does not use a word for "political," he certainly seems here to be articulating this opposition having imported, as it were, the opposition from modern Christian thinking.

The Upshot: Premodern *Yahadut* Is Not "Judaism"

The results of this not exhaustive (but perhaps most thorough to date) study of the semantics of *yahadut* in premodern Jewish parlance suggest two sets of usages that sometimes overlap. In juridical or semijuridical contexts, *yahadut* is used to indicate the status of being a Jew, of being a member of the juridical group, Israel, or Jewry. The origins of this usage are hidden in fog, but it is attested fairly early in medieval rabbinic usage in two contexts as we have seen: on the one hand as the designation of the purpose of an immersion in the *mikva*, where immersion for the sake of *yahadut* means simply in order to become a Jew; on the other hand, as the designation of the status itself, so that Abram was Abraham's name in *goyut* and Abraham his name in *yahadut*. The second branch of usages is found primarily, if not entirely, in homiletic contexts, especially in interpretations of the Bible. There, *yahadut* with several nuances is used generally to indicate a practiced commitment to worship of the god of Israel and loyalty to the ancestral practices of the Jews, to the Torah, not, therefore, much different from *Ioudaismos* that we have explored in the preceding chapter. In none of these instances does *yahadut* ever refer to an abstraction on the order of the "Jewish religion" or even "Jewish culture" as it does today. Just perhaps to make this conclusion easier to absorb, let me cite one fact that has revealed itself here that will be developed further in the final chapter: never until the second half of the nineteenth century do we ever find *yahadut* forming the subject of a sentence or of a verb—that is, never is there a *yahadut* that believes anything, demands anything, rejects anything, competes with anything, and so on. This grammatical absence is the clearest proof that something is semantically grossly different about premodern *yahadut*. On the other hand, we do find in the beginnings of the early modern period (R. Y. Karo) indications that other usages are developing (via his citation of what is almost surely a corruption in Rashi's text), and toward the end of what might be called the early modern period of Jewish culture, further indications that some traditionalist Jewish intellectuals are beginning to utilize the distinction religious/secular in a fashion not entirely unlike their Christian and western European contemporaries.

Matters begin to change more drastically in modern times but quite unevenly among the different geocultural centers of Jewry. The last section of this book in two chapters will follow the story of the formation of the idea/word "Judaism" née (Christian Latin) *Iudaismus* in the Ekklesia and its very belated entry into Jewish parlance thus precipitating the existence of Modern Judaism in all its variety.

PART III

A NEW DISPENSATION

The Christian Invention of "Judaism"

4   "Judaism" out of the Entrails of Christianity

Like so much "Judaism" in this book, the Judaism of our Christian poets has much to do with the history of Christian thought.
—David Nirenberg, *Anti-Judaism: The Western Tradition* (New York: W. W. Norton, 2013), 231

In this chapter, I propose quite a new turn of the key word "Judaism" in a combination designed to unlock an important aspect of cultural history. I moot the thesis that "Judaism" as an abstraction (as opposed to the rare Greek verbal noun, "Judaizing") in antiquity is a Christian term of art invented initially for purposes of the formation of Christian orthodoxy. This point is not, of course, by any means entirely new to this book or my innovation. Indeed, it has been anticipated in various and partially overlapping ways by other scholars who could be said to have been sounding keynotes for the new key. I will rehearse their work briefly.

An interesting, if introductory and necessarily cursory, book by Leora Batnitzky sounds one such keynote in her formulation that something called by her "Judaism" became a religion in the nineteenth century as part and parcel of the invention of the nation-state as, in part, a project for incorporating into a polity folks of different "religious" persuasions, "religion" itself having been produced for the purpose as well.[1] There is insight in her analysis and a particular interest in her insight that this development ranges across the board (among German Jews!) from radical reforming thinkers such as Abraham Geiger to the founders of neo-orthodoxy such as Rabbi Shimshon Raphael Hirsch, but two things trouble me: the first is the (granted) nearly exclusive attention to German Jews, while the second is the unquestioned assumption that there simply *is* something called "Judaism" out there, not itself historically bound and determined, and the only question is whether it is, or is perceived as, a religion or something else.

A more sophisticated version of the thesis can be found in the work of David Nirenberg. In his book about anti-Judaism,[2] Nirenberg demonstrates both brilliantly and definitively how the "Judaism" of which western discourse speaks is itself a projection of universal negative tendencies and intractable sociocultural tensions onto Jews. Moreover, he demonstrates as well that exposure and analysis of this projection—and not the *acceptance* by Marx of this projection—was by and large the point of Karl Marx's "On the Jewish Question":

> Marx's fundamental insight here was that the "Jewish question" is as much about the basic tools and concepts through which individuals in a society relate to the world and to each other, as it is about the presence of "real" Judaism and living Jews in that society. He understood that some of these basic tools—such as money and property—were thought of in Christian culture as "Jewish," and that these tools therefore could potentially produce the "Jewishness" of those who used them, whether those users were Jewish or not. *"Judaism," then, is not only the religion of specific people with specific beliefs, but also a category, a set of ideas and attributes with which non-Jews can make sense of and criticize the world.*[3]

This is a stunning reading of Marx's remark that Christians will forever "produce Judaism out of their own entrails." Nirenberg, however, stops short of taking the full measure of Marx's profound insight, to wit that "Judaism" is *always* a product of Christian guts. Just as "the Jew"—as opposed to Jewish individuals—is always/everywhere necessarily a product of non-Jewish discourse, and given the absence of any Jewish talk of "Judaism" until very recently, there is no "really real," no "religion" from within, no Judaism, at all, but only a construction from the outside. "Judaism" following Marx is a projection of non-Jewish discourse, projectile vomiting from their entrails.[4] This is the new and perhaps discordant key that I choose to strike here. If Nirenberg shows throughout his tour de force of a book how "Jews" are a product of a Christian *imaginaire*, one that functions in multiple and repeating patterns,[5] I argue that this is even more the case for the abstraction "Judaism," unknown—as seen in the previous chapters—to Jews until modernity. Nirenberg's "Anti-Judaism" becomes simply "Judaism."

A Palinode

In a much earlier adumbration of the argument that I am making here, I proposed that the invention of "Judaism" by Christian writers was part and parcel of the invention of "religion" in the fourth and fifth centuries. As demonstrated at length by Brent Nongbri in his Yale dissertation,[6] some of my key evidence was simply misconstrued by me, in large part because I committed what I take to be now a cardinal sin, depending on translations for scholarly work.[7] Consequently, I now am convinced that the idea expressed there that "religion" in something close to the modern sense was fabricated in the fourth century is generally invalid.[8] I withdraw, therefore, my claim that "religion" was invented in the fourth century. Nongbri himself, however, forcefully asserts his agreement that this time period "marks a certain epistemic shift."[9] Nongbri's own account of that epistemic shift is of great interest and has much to teach us. I would focus here, however, on the transformations of *Ioudaismos* that I see taking place then. If, in its earlier and very rare usage, as I have argued in chapter 2, *Ioudaismos* in the pens of Palestinian Judeans means only doing Judean doings, now it comes to mean, in Christian parlance, something quite distinct from that. Abandoning the (now clearly perceived as) anachronistic term "religion" in my analysis, I am going to term—without any claim to originality here—the new turn as the invention of "orthodoxy," as well as its concomitant body, the Church, for which here, however, I will use the Greek term *Ekklesia*. The immediate advantage of these terms, "orthodoxy" and *Ekklesia*, over "religion" is evident; they are, in fact, extant terms in the language of the time. Put in other words, the shift in question involves the shift from locative to nonlocative accounts of group boundaries and definitions. According to Rowan Williams, "'Orthodoxy' is a way that a 'religion,' separated from the locativity of ethnic or geocultural self-definition as Christianity was, asks itself: '[H]ow, if at all, is one to identify the "centre" of [our] religious tradition? At what point and why do we start speaking about "a" religion?'"[10] I will modify this only by suggesting that in place of "religion" here and to keep things clear, let us substitute *Ekklesia*, not as the building or as the local community but precisely as the corporate body of orthodox Christianity as well as its supernal homologue. The *Ekklesia*, we might say, invents "Judaism" as an alternate, as the dark double of the true *Ekklesia*, transforming Jews from a People to an *Ekklesia* via the medium of orthodoxy, an *Ekklesia* that it names *Ioudaismos* in Greek.[11]

The Art of the State: *Judaism* in the Theodosian Code

In support of this interpretation, I would adduce the empire-wide Code of Theodosius of 438.[12] In order to more fully appreciate the import of that code, we need first to study the Christian usages over time of *religio* and *superstitio*.[13] In Latin, as has been well documented, in its earliest appearances, *superstitio* was not in binary opposition to *religio*. Indeed, too much *religio* could be *superstitio*. It was not the index of worship of the right gods but of the right or wrong worship of the gods.[14] Maurice Sachot concurs that, in the Latin of the early Empire, *superstitio* was itself not so much the opposite of *religio* as a type of *religio*, simply a dangerous and illegitimate excess of *religio* itself.[15] As Peter Brown puts it, "Outside

Epicurean circles, superstition was not treated as a cognitive aberration—an 'irrational' belief in nonexistent or misperceived beings. Superstition was a social *gaffe* committed in the presence of the gods. It betrayed a lack of the ease and candour that were supposed to characterise a free man's relations with any persons, human or divine. Excessive observance was strictly analogous to flattery and ostentation; and magic was a form of graft and manipulation."[16] Beard, North, and Price write, "[*Superstitio*] was ambiguous between two meanings: excessive forms of behaviour, that is 'irregular' religious practices ('not following the custom of the state') and excessive commitment, an excessive commitment to the gods."

In later Christian Latin, *religio* is no longer used as the practices that are useful and appropriate for maintaining Roman solidarity and social order, as in Cicero,[17] but as the belief in that which is true—that is, as sanctioned by an authoritatively and ultimately legally produced ecumenical orthodoxy. Beard, North, and Price support this point:

> "*Religio* is worship of the true god, *superstitio* of a false,"[18] as the Christian Lactantius remarked in the early fourth century A.D.—so asserting that alien practices and gods were not merely inferior to his own, but actually bogus. The traditional Roman distinction seems to have made no such assumption about truth and falsehood: when Romans in the early empire debated the nature of *religio* and *superstitio* they were discussing instead different *forms* of human relations with the gods. This is captured in Seneca's formulation that "*religio* honours the gods, *superstitio* wrongs them."[19]

In other words, with the shift in *religio* from a Ciceronian set of practices that support order in the state[20] to *religio* as true worship of the true God comes into play a shift in the usage of *superstitio* as well. It no longer means any practices that are useless or excessive for the state but the false worship of wrong gods.

A paradox in the representation of Judaism within the Theodosian Code illustrates these points. Throughout the code we find sometimes *religio* (XVI 8.10) of the Jews and sometimes *secta* (XVI 8.9), used of the Catholic "sect" as well (catholicae sectae XVI 5.44), or *superstitio* (XVI 8.24), but as legal historian Amnon Linder observes, after 416 only *superstitio* is used. In the older Roman usage, this shift to exclusive designation as *superstitio* ought to mark an absolute delegitimation of the *superstitio* of the Jews entirely unlike its prior status as *religio licita*, in Tertullian's famous—if pleonastic—phrase. However, Linder also describes a complex and increasing legislative *legitimation* of "Judaism" through the fourth and fifth centuries. Both Günther Stemberger and Lee Levine have pointed to the paradox engendered by the fact that the Palestinian patriarchate achieved its heyday in the fourth and early fifth centuries[21]—that is, precisely as the Jewish position was otherwise deteriorating drastically.[22]

Moreover, as Seth Schwartz has recently put it, "The legislation incorporated in the Theodosian Code book 16 titles 8 and 9 (and scattered through other books of the Code) constitutes the first more or less systematic exposition in a Roman imperial context of the view that local Jewish communities are fully licit and partly autonomous, and that their leaders are to enjoy the privileges of clergy and the right to rule their constituents in partial accordance with Jewish law."[23] Here, then, is the paradox. How can it be, then, that *Iudaismus* definitively became a *superstitio* precisely when "the Christian Empire—to a far greater extent than the pagan Empire—accepted Judaism as a religion rather than as a nation or a people?"[24] To put the paradox otherwise, if *superstitio* names the practices that are harmful to Roman order, how is it that *Iudaismus* becomes a *superstitio* just as it is legitimized by the state?

The answer I propose is based on my earlier statement that *superstitio* itself has shifted in meaning; indeed, the whole semantic field has shifted. First, however, let me sharpen the apparent paradox. The legitimation of Judaic doings included the Jewish priesthood[25] and the synagogue and went so far as to comprehend recognition of the Jewish Sabbath and festivals, including Purim (XVI 8.18,[26] provided the Jews didn't mock the crucifixion on that occasion,[27] an exemplary instance, perhaps, of mimicry turned mockery). The following has a particularly "modern" ring: "[Buildings] which are known to be used by Jews for their meetings, and which are described as synagogues, let no-one dare to desecrate or occupy; for all shall keep their own with rights undisturbed, without attacks on *religio* or worship" (CTh XVI 8.20) of July 26, 412 (Honorius).[28] Particularly dramatic is the continued, even enhanced, right of the *primates* of the Jews (including probably the Rabbis) to excommunicate (XVI 8.8).[29] This power continued well after 416, and during that time, Jewish autonomy was enhanced by other laws as well.[30] Indeed, "in a law of Justinian from 553 (No. 66), the lawful observance of the Jewish religion and its cult was taken for granted."[31] Furthermore, through the fourth century, the Jewish doings received greater and greater legitimacy in the recognition of the Jewish Patriarch as the virtual Metropolitan of the Jews.[32] As Schwartz writes, "In the late fourth century the patriarchs reached the peak of their power. The Palestinian church father Epiphanius and the Codex Theodosianus both indicate that the *apostole*, or *aurum coronarium* [the Jewish head tax, exacted by the Patriarchs from the Diaspora], was now collected as if it were a conventional tax." In 397, Arcadius and Honorius affirm that "we shall imitate the ancients by

whose sanctions it was determined that those privileges which are con-
ferred upon the first clerics of the venerable Christian *lex* shall continue,
by the consent of Our Imperial Divinity, for those persons who are subject to the power of the Illustrious Patriarchs, for the rulers of the synagogues, the patriarchs, and the priests, and for all the rest who are
occupied in the ceremonial of that *religio*" (XVI 8.13).[33] "Religion" is not
what is lost in translation but what is found(ed) in translation; once *lex*
referring to Christianity and once *religio* referring to the Jews, both translated in the standard Englishes as "religion." This law was reaffirmed in
404.[34] Despite the explicit rhetoric of the law of 397, Schwartz makes the
important point that "the laws about the Jews in the Theodosian Code
are not at all conservative. By their very existence they constitute a significant innovation, because they imply that by the late fourth century
the Roman state consistently regarded the Jews as a discrete category of
humanity. I would suggest that the state had not done so, at least not
consistently, between the first and the fourth centuries."[35] In my reading
of the archives, in addition to providing evidence of the growing importance of the Patriarch, these materials suggest the high importance of the
representation, perhaps a sort of colonial trompe l'oeil, in Bhabha's
terms,[36] of a powerful and prestigious Jewish Patriarch in the discourse
of the orthodox Christian Empire.[37] The best way I can think of to resolve
this paradox is to hypothesize that *Iudaismus* was being produced by
the "True *Ekklesia*" as a "False *Ekklesia*," a sort of mimic-church—not a
heresy: recall that for Justin it has its own internal heresies—with its own
hierarchy and trappings to set off and solidify the identity of the orthodox Christian *Ekklesia*.

With the shift in designation Linder dates to 416, "Judaism," paradoxically, in effect—to coin an oxymoron—became a *superstitio licita*,[38] a
genuine though wrong orthodoxy from which conversion was possible,
leaving a remainder that guaranteed the existence of the Christian herself.[39] In a law variously dated to 412, 418, and 420,[40] we read, "Let no one,
as long as he is innocent, be disparaged and subject to attacks because he
is a Jew, *by whatever religio* [XVI. 8. 21]."[41] "*By whatever religio*" here means
apparently any Christian sect, orthodox or not.[42]

The licit status of the *superstitio*, "Judaism," as opposed to "heresy"—
and consequently the crucial conversion of "Judaism" from heresy to
superstitio or alternative but wrong *Ekklesia*—is beautifully indicated in
the following edict of Honorius and Theodosius:

> We punish with proscription of their goods and exile, Manichaeans and
> those persons who are called Pepyzites [=Montanists]. Likewise those
> persons who are worse than all other heretics in this one belief, namely,

that they disagree with all others as to the venerable day of Easter, shall
be punished with the same penalty if they persist in the aforesaid
madness.

But we especially command those persons who are truly Christians . . .
that they shall not abuse the authority of *religio* and dare to lay violent
hands on Jews and pagans who are living quietly and attempting nothing disorderly or contrary to law. (CT XVI 10.24)[43]

If they do do so, continues the edict, "they shall also be compelled to
restore triple or quadruple that amount which they robbed." As Humfress
remarks on this law of 423, "This vision of peaceful, law-abiding, fifth-
century 'pagans' and Jews legally pursuing hard-line Christians through
the courts of the Roman empire, for the four-fold restitution of their
robbed property, is diametrically opposed to the more usual fifth century
rhetoric of Christian triumphalism. And it provides stimulus and justification for an account of the *evolution* of late paganism as an alternative
to a repetition of the traditional historiographical story of its demise."[44]
Hal Drake has commented on explicit fourth-century discourse that indicates the coexistence of Christians and "pagans," with "heretics" marked
off as the genuine enemy.[45] If that is so for "late paganism," then it is even
more so for "early Judaism." "Judaism" was evolving within the context
of the world that Christianity, Christendom, and the Christian Empire
had made for it.

Christianity needed a Jewish orthodox *Ekklesia*. Everything about
Title 8 of Book XVI suggests that *Ioudaismos* is to be legitimated while
vigorously protecting Christians and Christianity from any temptations
to cross the border. The indictment of the Quartodecimans as worse than
Manichaeans in the passage just read makes this point eloquently.[46] The
trenchant condemnation of the "Caelicolists," by all signs a hybrid of
Jewish and Christian doings, in this Title (8.19) immediately preceding a
law (8.20) enjoining the absolute protection of synagogue and Sabbath
for Jews also argues for this interpretation.[47] It is hybridity that is at
once the threat and the guarantor of the "purity" of Christianity and
Judaism, the whole system necessary for the discursive production of an
orthodoxy that was "one of the primary discursive formations around
which ancient Christian strategies of self-definition coalesced."[48]

The crux of the matter seems to me to be that in order for there to be
a true *Ekklesia*, there had to be a false one too, another member of the
paradigm in which *Ekklesia* functioned semantically. Let us go back, then,
and look at the beginnings of the Christian naming of *Ioudaismos* and
work our way up to the period in question at the end of the fourth century and beyond. What I hope to show is that the development of

Christian orthodoxy involved not only the production of Christian heresies but also the interpellation (hailing into existence) of another self-
imagined "orthodoxy," another *Ekklesia*, as it were, with an imputed
orthodoxy of its own, that of the Jews.[49] This dark double of the true
Ekklesia was frequently, at least later on, named, in fact, *Synagoga*.
Needless to say, this word *never* has such a meaning in Jewish sources, as
it refers in them only to a building and a community that worships in it
and not a corporate body (corporeal or mystical) at all.[50] This latter
orthodoxy, the orthodoxy of the phantasmal *Synagoga*, was named by
Christians *Ioudaismos/Iudaismus*. As we shall observe, this term, originally used by its earliest Christian writers as an internal flaw or tendency
in *Christianismos* through the fifth century becomes the name for that
other (false) orthodoxy, "Judaism." Let us now trace at least a bit of
this history.

Ignatius; or, *Ioudaismos* and *Christianismos*

Ignatius of Antioch has been generally held to be the first Christian
writer to contrast *Christianismos* to *Ioudaismos*. Lately, however, several
scholars have identified a lost text of Marcion, his *Antitheses*, as our first
source for this terminology.[51] This is doubly interesting since that quite
extreme figure preached that there is absolutely no continuity between
the Hebrew Bible and its God and the Father of the Christ, rendering an
absolute break between following Christ and *Ioudaismos* necessary.
Ignatius, who is the earliest directly and well-attested writer to use this
terminology, is no gnostic but also is mightily striving to produce a distance between what he calls *Christianismos* and what he terms *Ioudaismos*
(whether he learned the term from Marcion, which seems to me unlikely,
or borrowed it from Paul who, as we have seen in chapter 2, uses it quite
differently.) The bishop and future martyred saint inveighed mightily
against those who blurred the boundaries between Jew and Christian. His
very inveighings, however, are indicative of the ideological work that he
is performing. For Ignatius, it seems, one can be a follower of Jesus and
(heretically in his eyes) nonetheless engage in *Ioudaismos*: "It is perverse
to talk of Jesus Christ and to Judaize [ἄτοπον ἐστιν Ἰησοῦν Χριστὸν λαλεῖν
καὶ Ιουδαΐζειν]" (Magnesians 10:3),[52] he proclaims, thus making both
points at once, the drive of the nascent orthodoxy—understood as a
particular social location and as a particular form of self-fashioning and
identity making—to normative separation and the actual lack of such
clear separations "on the ground." There is, however, an important, even
crucial, further wrinkle in this verse. The Ignatian verse goes on to say,
"For *Christianismos* did not believe on *Ioudaismos* but *Ioudaismos* believed
on *Christianismos* wherein every tongue believed and was gathered

together unto God. [ὁ γὰρ Χριστιανισμὸς οὐκ εἰς Ἰουδαϊσμὸν ἐπίστευσεν, ἀλλ *Ἰουδαϊσμὸς εἰς Χριστιανισμόν, {ᾧ} πᾶσα γλῶσσα πιστεύσασα εἰς θεὸν συνήχθη]." This sentence is rather puzzling: Does it mean that Judaism has been founded on and derived from a putatively earlier Christianity? Will the Greek suffer such a construal? Given the final clause of the sentence, it would seem that *Ioudaismos* here means the People who have become parts of *Christianismos* (see German *Judenthum* as discussed in the next chapter), as have other peoples. Letting that be as it may, it would seem fair to conclude in any case that *Ioudaismos* for Ignatius is some kind of abstract noun that can serve as the subject of a sentence. Whatever it means for Ignatius, this formal shift is in itself highly significant; we will not see its like among Jews until the end of the nineteenth century!

The question of names and naming, naming Christian, naming Jew, naming *Christianimos*, naming *Ioudaismos*, is central to the Ignatian enterprise. Near the very beginning of his letter to the Ephesians, in a passage the significance of which has been only partly realized in my view, Ignatius writes, "Having received in God your much loved name, which you possess by a just nature according to faith and love in Christ Jesus, our Savior—being imitators of God, enkindled by the blood of God, you accomplished perfectly the task suited to you [Ἀποδεξάμενος ἐν θεῷ τὸ πολυαγάθητόν σου ὄνομα, ὃ κέκτησθε φύσει δικαίᾳ κατὰ πίστιν καὶ ἀγάπην ἐν Χριστῷ Ἰησοῦ, τῷ σωτῆρι ἡμῶν· μιμηταὶ ὄντες θεοῦ, ἀναζωπυρήσαντες ἐν αἵματι θεοῦ τὸ συγγενικὸν ἔργον τελείως ἀπηρτίσατε]" (1:1).[53] Although this interpretation has been spurned by most commentators and scholars of Ignatius,[54] I would make a cornerstone of my construction to read this as a reference to the name "Christians."[55] It was, after all, in Ignatius's Antioch that the people were first called by that name (Acts 11:26). Ignatius is complimenting the church in Ephesus as being worthy to be called by the name of Christ owing to their merits.[56] Indeed, as Schoedel does not fail to point out, in Magnesians 10:1, Ignatius writes, "Therefore let us become his disciples and learn to live according to the Christianizing. For one who is called by any name other than this, is not of God. [μαθηταὶ αὐτου γενόμενοι, μάθωμεν κατὰ Χριστιανισμὸν ζῆν. ὃς γὰρ ἄλλῳ ὀνόματι καλεῖται πλέον τούτου, οὐκ ἔστιν τοῦ θεοῦ.]"[57] Even more to the point, however, is Magnesians 4:1: "It is right, then, not only to be called Christians but also to be. [Πρέπον οὖ*ν ἐστὶν μὴ μόνον καλεῖσθαι Χριστιανούς, ἀλλὰ καὶ ἐ*ιναι]."[58] Ignatius tells the Ephesians, then, that they are not just called Christians but are Christians by nature (φύσει), as it were.[59] Ignatius goes on in verse 2 to write, "For hearing that I was put in bonds from Syria for the common name and hope, hoping by your prayer to attain to fighting with beasts in Rome, that by attaining I may be able to be a disciple, you hastened to see me."[60] Once again, the interpretative tradition seems to have missed an attractively specific interpretation of "name" here that links it to the "name" in the previous verse. It is not, I opine, the name of Christ that is referred to here[61] but the name of "Christian," which equals "disciple" (cf. again Acts 11:26: "And the *disciples* were called Christians first in Antioch"). The "common hope" is Jesus Christ (cf. Eph. 21:1; Trallians 2:2),[62] but the common "name" is "Christian."

I would suggest that Ignatius represents here the martyrological theme of the centrality of martyrdom in establishing the name "Christian" as the legitimate and true name of the disciple; this in accord with the practice whereby "Christianos eimi" were the last words of the martyr, the name for which she died.[63] Similarly in the next passage, Ignatius explicitly connects martyrdom with "the name": "I do not command you as being someone; for even though I have been bound in the name, I have not yet been perfected in Jesus Christ" (3:1). The "name" in which Ignatius has been bound (i.e., imprisoned and sent to Rome for martyrdom) is the name *Christianos*.[64] The nexus between having the right to that name and martyrdom or between martyrdom and identity, and the nexus between them and heresiology, separation from *Judaizing* is also clear.[65] In opening his letters with this declaration, I think, Ignatius is declaring one of his major themes for the corpus entire: the establishment of a new "orthodox" (by his lights) Christian identity, distinguished and distinguishable from *Ioudaismos*, which is manifestly not "Judaism" but a form of what we would call "Christianity" to which Ignatius denies legitimacy. Neither *Christianismos* nor *Ioudaismos* signify Christianity or Judaism. If this is seen as a highly marked moment in his texts, then one can follow this as a dominant theme throughout his letters, and the protoheresiology[66] of Ignatius is profoundly related to this theme as well.

This issue is most directly articulated in Ignatius's letter to the Magnesians. He exhorts, "Be not deceived by *heterodoxiai* nor by old fables, which are useless. For if we continue to live until now according to *Ioudaismos*, we confess that we have not received grace [Μὴ πλανᾶσθε ταῖς ἑτεροδοξίαις μηδὲ μυθεύμασιν τοῖς παλαιοῖς ἀνωφελέσιν οὖσιν· εἰ γὰρ μέχρι νῦν κατὰ Ἰουδαϊσμὸν ζῶμεν, ὁμολογοῦμεν χάριν μὴ εἰληφέναι]" (Magnesians 8:1).[67]

Ioudaismos is defined here by Ignatius as "heterodoxies and old myths," but what precisely does he mean? Let us go back to the beginning of the letter. Once more, Ignatius makes a reference to the "name": "For having been deemed worthy of a most godly name, in the bonds which I bear I sing the churches" (1:1).[68] Here, as Schoedel recognizes, it is almost certain that only the name "Christian" will fit the context. This thought about the name is continued explicitly in Ignatius's famous "It is right, then, not only to be called Christians but to be Christians" (4:1).[69]

On my reading, it is the establishment of that name, giving it definition, "defining . . . policing, the boundaries that separate the name of one entity [*Christianismos*] from the name of another [*Ioudaismos*]," that provides one of the two thematic foci for the letter (and the letters) as a whole, the other—and related—one, being, of course, the establishment of the bishop as sole authority in a given church. But what are these two entities *Ioudaismos* and *Christianismos* for Ignatius?

Ioudaismos, so far for Ignatius does not seem to be what it means in other writers of and before his time—namely, the "false views and misguided practice," or "insisting especially on the ritual requirements of that system."[70] Ignatius troubles to let us know that this is not the case, as we learn from the aforementioned famous and powerful rhetorical paradox in his *Letter to the Philadelphians*: "But if anyone *expounds Ioudaismos* to you, do not listen to him; for it is better to hear *Christianismos* from a man who is circumcised than *Ioudaismos* from a man uncircumcised; both of them, if they do not speak of Jesus Christ, are to me tombstones and graves of the dead on which nothing but the names of men is written [Ἐὰν δέ τις Ἰυδαϊσμὸν ἑρμηνεύῃ ὑμῖν, μὴ ἀκούετε αὐτοῦ. ἄμεινον γάρ ἐστιν παρὰ ἀνδρὸς περιτομὴν ἔχοντος Χριστιανισμὸν ἀκουείν ἢ παρὰ ἀκροβύστου Ἰουδαϊσμόν. ἐὰν δὲ ἀμφότεροι περὶ Ἰησοῦ Χριστοῦ μὴ λαλῶσιν, οὗτοι ἐμοὶ στῆλαί εἰσιν καὶ τάφοι νεκρῶν, ἐφ᾽ οἷς γέγραπται μόνον ὀνόματα ἀνθρώπων]" (Philadelphians 6:1).[71] After considering various options that have been offered for the interpretation of this surprising passage,[72] Schoedel arrives at what seems to me the most compelling interpretation: "Perhaps it was the 'expounding' (exegetical expertise) that was the problem and not the 'Judaism' (observance)."[73] I would go further than Schoedel by making one more seemingly logical exegetical step—namely, to assume that for Ignatius, *Ioudaismos* is the expounding. In Ignatius, I suggest, *Ioudaismos* no longer means observance of laws as it had in Paul but a broader set of Jewish "doings," including verbal ones.[74] In other words, for him, *Christianismos* and *Ioudaismos* are two *doxas*, two theological positions, a wrong one [ἑτεροδοξία, 8:1][75] and a right one, a wrong interpretation of the legacy of the prophets and a right one. The right one is that which is taught by the prophets "inspired by his grace" and called "*Christianismos*" as it is that "revealed through Jesus Christ his Son, who is his Word" (8:1). The words quoted certainly seem to mean that *Christianismos* consists of "speaking of Jesus Christ," Gospel—still oral[76]—while *Ioudaismos* is devoting oneself to the study of Scripture. Although, to be sure in chapter 9 of Magnesians, Ignatius mentions one aspect of practice—namely, the abandonment of the Sabbath for "the Lord's Day," assuming that the plausible translation "Lord's Day" for κυριακή is correct,[77] but the issue there too, as we can see, is not *nomos* versus grace but an insufficient Christocentrism; by keeping the Scriptural Sabbath and not the Lord's day, these Christians belie that they are true "disciples of Jesus Christ, our only teacher."[78] Ignatius explicitly links those who maintain the Sabbath and not the Lord's Day alone as those who deny Christ's death, as well (9:1), a point that will take on greater significance later in this text.

I would emphasize again that this has nothing to do with anything that we would call "Judaism," since for Ignatius, *Christianismos* and *Ioudaismos* both are species of what we would call "Christianity." The argument that for him *Ioudaismos* and *Christianismos* are both versions of what we would call "Christianity"[79] comes from his clear statement that his opponents are those who say, "Unless in the archives I find (it), in the gospel I do not believe (it)" (Philadelphians 8:2).[80] Ignatius's antagonists, real or imagined, are clearly folks for whom Gospel is richly significant but Christians, even uncircumcised ones, who preach some "heterodox" attachment to Christ—on Ignatius's view—or even merely an insistence that everything in Gospel be anchored in Scriptural (the only Scripture they had, the "Old Testament") exegesis.[81] They do not put Christ first, and therefore, they are preaching *Ioudaismos*, and they are "tombstones."

What is this *Ioudaismos*, and how does it define *Christianismos*? A slower reading of the passage will help answer this question:

> I exhort you to do nothing from partisanship but in accordance with Christ's teaching. For I heard some say, "unless in the archives I find (it), in the gospel I do not believe (it),"[82] and when I said, "It is written," they answered me, "That is just the question." But for me the archives are Jesus Christ, the inviolable archives are his cross and death and his resurrection and faith through him—in which, through your prayers, I want to be justified. (8:2)[83]

Once we concede that it is not written, fixed gospel texts that are being referred to here, it makes perfect sense that some would say that if they cannot ground it in the Scripture they do not believe it in the Gospel. These Christian adherents of what Ignatius called *Ioudaismos* simply deny as part of the Gospel itself anything of the story of Jesus that contradicts Scripture or isn't grounded in Scripture. The group in Philadelphia to which the future martyr is objecting so strongly would be, on this reading, Christians who insist that the Gospel can only contain scriptural truth, and this was acceptable to the Philadelphian congregation with whom they were in communion. For Ignatius there is, in contrast, only one source of truth—that is, the Gospel, the narrative of Jesus's actual death and resurrection. That must be the correct interpretation—whether or not Ignatius had some sort of written texts about Jesus—for otherwise the statement that the "Archives are Jesus Christ, his cross and death" makes no sense.

"Gospel," I suggest, for Ignatius, functions semantically very much as it does in Paul, except—and this is critical—for Paul, the opposition is Gospel/Nomos while for Ignatius, the opposition is Gospel/Scripture, accepting the Good News of Jesus's actual physical death and resurrection versus exegeting the Bible.[84] The somewhat confounding moment, however, is Ignatius's statement that "it is written," which seems to counteract this view. There are two possible interpretations that I would suggest: the one is that Ignatius first simply declares that whatever he claims as in the Gospel is / must be already written in the Archives, and when they retort that that is the question, he resorts to his claim that the Gospel *is* the Archives, the only Archives that matter. A second possibility would be that when Ignatius says "it is written," he already means it is written, as it were, in the only Archives that matter to him—Jesus Christ, his death and resurrection in the flesh. They misunderstand, retorting that it is not written, which he then clarifies with his Jesus archive. That is exactly the question that they put to Ignatius: "They answered me, 'That is just the question,'" to wit. Indeed, Ignatius, whether or not the physical death of the Son of Man is written in the Archives is precisely the question. For Ignatius, however, for whom the nonscriptural kerygma is central and who sees, as he insists over and over, such reliance on Scripture as itself *Ioudaismos*, the exegeting of Jewish Scriptures, and not *Christianismos*, the exegeting of Christ's birth, actual death, and resurrection in the flesh. Whether or not Ignatius had access to any written Gospels or pregospel literature, his claim is absolutely clear and unambiguous: the Archives are Jesus Christ, *not what is written in Scripture*. For what seems to be the first time, the tension between holding the sacredness of Scripture for Christians and their rejection in favor of a New Dispensation will be, if not solved, reduced by the expedient of naming that tension "Judaism." As Nirenberg points out, "'Judaism,' [was projected] as a form of interpretation, an attitude toward word and world."[85] Having very little to do with "real Jews," this would have, nonetheless, consequences for Jews going forward.[86]

This opposition between Ignatius and these other Christians, referred to as practicers of *Ioudaismos*, has been symbolized by him already as an opposition between those who keep the Sabbath and those who only observe the Lord's Day. Here Ignatius draws it out further via an epistemological contrast between that which is known from Scripture (= *Ioudaismos*) and that which is known from the knowledge of the very facts of the Lord's death and resurrection (= χριστομαθία). As we have previously seen, for Ignatius, those who observe the Sabbath are implicated as ones who deny the Lord's death as well (Magnesians 9:1). These ostensible Christians who, according to Ignatius, "Judaize" might very well have held a Christology that was too "high" for Ignatius's taste. I have argued elsewhere that Jews who held a version of Logos theology, and perhaps might even have seen in Christ the manifestation of the Logos, might yet have balked at an incarnational Christology[87]—that is, rather than the "low" Christology of which so-called Jewish-Christians are usually accused, these Christians might have insisted on a Docetism that denied that the Logos ever took on flesh, and Ignatius's *Ioudaismos* might then be a doxa that the Christians of Philadelphia had inherited from such a tendency. That which is not found in the Archives, then, is precisely the notion that the Logos could die! That is, exactly that which Ignatius himself claims as the something which the gospel has that is distinctive over against the Old Testament (9:2): "The coming of the Savior, our Lord Jesus Christ, his passion and resurrection." This suggests strongly that, if not precisely the same people—if, indeed, there were such people altogether—it is the same complex of Christian Jewish ideas, accepting Jesus, accepting the Logos, denying actual physical death and resurrection, which Ignatius names as engaging in *Ioudaismos*, Judaizing, the product of overvaluing of Scripture against the claims of the gospel, which alone must be first and foremost for those would have the name Christian, that name for which Ignatius would die.

Schoedel has surely advanced our understanding by showing that "it was Ignatius and not they [the 'heretics'] who polarized the situation."[88] Ignatius produced his *Ioudaismos* in order to more fully define and articulate the new identity for the disciples as true bearers of the new name, *Christianoi*. Ignatius has, in some important sense, taken the first step in the invention of Judaism as a defining other to Christianity. In a pattern to be repeated throughout history ad nauseam, the "Judaism" that he creates has very little to do, it seems, with Jews, not even in his imagining. Similarly, according to an early modern writer, the "Bachelor Marcus of Toledo," Christians who "bind themselves like livestock to the letter" and "have always given and still give false meaning to divine and human scripture" are "in confederation with the synagogue." And as Nirenberg emphasizes, "The targets of his [the bachelor's] accusations of Judaism, were not 'real' Jews." Indeed, they included even the Pope in Rome in their beastly congregation.[89] "Real Jews," however, as shown in the previous chapters, have no such names for themselves or their doings. This "Judaism" is a Christian device.

Jerome and Epiphanius

I wish to suggest here that *Ioudaismos*, the anti-*Ekklesia*, was invented and the word shifted in meaning precisely so that *Christianismos* could have an other (in its semantic paradigm of what sort of thing it is, an orthodox *Ekklesia*). As Nirenberg puts it in another context, the expulsion of Jews from Spain, "These were exhilarating times for a Christian society trained to hear the hoof beats of apocalypse in the retreating footsteps of the Jews. *But they were also highly unsettling to a society used to thinking about Christianity in terms of its difference from Judaism. How would Christianity define itself if the living exemplars of that difference vanished?*"[90] Indeed, it turns out in the end that Christianity would be very capable of defining itself over against that other imaginary "religion," Judaism, and one suspects from reading Nirenberg that the absence of "real" Jews only enhanced that project.

The practice, in any case, of defining "Christianity" as a distinct, different member of a paradigm that includes something called "Judaism" begins quite early among Christian writers, but again it seems almost a rooky error on my part to have identified these as "religions." By the fourth century, Eusebius of Caesarea, the first church historian and an important theologian in his own right,[91] could write, "I have already said before in the *Preparation*[92] how Christianity is something that is neither *Hellēnismos* nor *Ioudaism*, but which has its own particular characteristic god-fearing [ὁ Χριστιανισμὸς οὔτε Ἑλληνισμός τις ἐστιν οὔτε Ἰουδαισμὸς, οἰκεῖον δέ τινα φέρων χαρακτῆρα θεοσεβείας],"[93] the implication being that both *Hellēnismos* and *Ioudaismos* have, as well, their own characteristic forms of god-fearing (however, to be sure, wrong-headed ones). He also writes the following:

> [This compels us to conceive some other ideal of god-fearing (*theosebeia*), by which they (the ancient Patriarchs) must have guided their lives.] Would not this be exactly that third form midway between *Ioudaismos* and *Hellēnismos*, which I have already deduced as the most ancient and venerable of all[94] and which has been preached of late to all nations through our Saviour. . . . The convert from *Hellēnismos* to *Christianismos* does not land in *Ioudaismos*, nor does one who rejects the Jewish worship become ipso facto a Greek. (*Demonstratio* 1.2.9–10)[95]

Here we find in Eusebius a clear articulation of "Judaism, Hellenism, and Christianity" as "ideals of god-fearing." There is something called *theosebeia*, which takes different "forms." Nonetheless, as Nongbri compellingly argues, *theosebeia* does not equal "religion":

Rather, the terminology here concerns τροποι θεοσεβειας (methods of worship) that are associated with ethnicities; Eusebius' rhetoric here is racial, ethnic, and civic. He claims that Jesus "instituted the union of a new nation to be called by his own name" (εις νυν εβαλλετο νειου εθνος επι οικειωι ονοματι συστασιν ποιησασθαι). Far from isolating "religion" as a separate entity from nationality, Eusebius boasts of a new nationality that is the renewal of what he regards as the most ancient race, the Hebrews. For Eusebius, Christianity links together worship practices with ethnic and civic identity.[96]

Nonetheless, as Nongbri recognizes, there *was* a shift in the fourth to the fifth centuries. The new *ethnos* model eventually didn't quite work for the *Ekklesia* in formation. If, then, it wasn't the invention of "religion," how shall we imagine it? The first attempt, in my view, was via heresiology, that great technology for identity founded by Justin Martyr.

The fullest expression of this conceptual shift may be located in the heresiology of Epiphanius (fl. early fifth century). For him, not only "Hellenism" and "Judaism" but also "Scythianism" and even "Barbarianism" are no longer the names of peoples with their places and doings but of "heresies"—that is, institutions other than orthodox Christianity within / outside of Christianity[97]:

> 1.3.11 When error had its beginning history had arrived at the point I have indicated. <Hellenism began with the Egyptians, Babylonians and Phrygians,> and then made a hash of <men's> ways. After that historians and chroniclers borrowed from the imposture of the Egyptians heathen mythology <and conveyed it to the other nations>, and this was how sorcery and witchcraft were invented.[98]

It is important to see that Epiphanius's comment is a transformation of a verse from the Pauline literature, as he himself informs us.[99] In Colossians 3:11, we find, "Here there cannot be Greek and Jew, circumcised and uncircumcised, barbarian, Scythian, slave, free-man, but Christ is all, and in all."[100] This is a lovely index of the semantic shift. For pseudo-Paul, these designations are obviously not the names of "heresies" but of various groupings of collective identities,[101] whereas for Epiphanius they are the names of "heresies," by which he means groups divided and constituted by theological differences fully disembedded from other cultural markers. How, otherwise, could the "heresy" called *Hellēnismos* have originated with the Egyptians?[102] This usage is actually quite common among Greek Christian writers; one might compare the term "Aramean" in Aramaic and Syriac as a name for "pagans" there. Epiphanius, not surprisingly, defines "the topic of the Jews' *eusebeia*" as "the subject of their beliefs."[103] For Epiphanius, as for Gregory, a major category (if not the only one) for dividing human beings into groups is "the subject of their beliefs." The system of identities had been completely transformed during the period extending from the first to the fifth centuries. The systemic change resulting in theological difference as a modality of identity that began, I would suggest, with the heresiological work of Christians such as Justin Martyr works itself out through the fourth century and is closely intertwined with the triumph of orthodoxy. Orthodoxy is thus not only a discourse for the production of difference within but also functions as a category to make and mark the border between Christianity and its proximate other *Ekklesiai*, particularly a "Judaism" and a "Paganism" that it is, in great part, inventing.

There *is* a new moment in fifth-century Christian heresiological discourse. Where in previous times the general move was to name Christian heretics "Jews" (a motif that continues alongside the "new" one), only at this time (notably in Epiphanius and Jerome) is distinguishing Judaizing heretics from orthodox Jews central to the Christian discursive project.[104] As one piece of evidence for this claim, I would adduce an explosion of heresiological interest in the "Jewish-Christian heresies" of the Nazarenes and the Ebionites at this time. At the beginning of the nineteenth century, J. K. L. Gieseler already recognized that "the brightest moment in the history of these two groups doubtless falls about the year 400 A.D., at which time we have the best accounts concerning them."[105] Given that, in fact, it seems unlikely that these sects truly flourished at this particular time,[106] we need to discover other ways of understanding this striking literary flowering. The Ebionites and Nazoreans, in my reading, function much as the mythical "trickster" figures of many cultures in that precisely by transgressing borders that the culture establishes, they reify those boundaries.[107] The discourse of the "Judaizing heretics" thus performs this very function of reinforcing the binaries.

The purpose of Epiphanius's discourse on the Ebionites and Nazarenes is to participate in the imperial project of control of (in this case) Palestine by "identifying and reifying the . . . orthodoxies." Epiphanius explicitly indicates that this is his purpose by writing of Ebion, the heresiarch-founder of the sect: "But since he is practically midway between all the sects, he is nothing. The words of scripture, 'I was almost in all evil, in the midst of the church [קהל] and synagogue [עדה]' [Proverbs 5:14], are fulfilled in him. For he is Samaritan but rejects the name with disgust. And while professing to be a Jew, he is the opposite of Jews—though he does agree with them in part."[108] In a rare moment of midrashic wit (one hesitates to attribute it to Epiphanius himself), the verse of Proverbs is read to mean that I was in all evil *because* I was in the midst between

the church and the synagogue (the Greek is, of course, already a ten-
dentious translation). Epiphanius's declaration that the Ebionites "are
nothing," especially when put next to Jerome's famous declaration that
the Nazarenes think that they are Christians and Jews, when in reality
they are neither, strongly recalls for me the insistence in the modern
period that the people of southern Africa have no religion, not because
they are not Christians, but because they are not pagans.[109] Suddenly
it seems important to these two writers to assert a difference between
Judaizing heretics and Jews. The ascription of existence to the "hybrids"
assumes (and thus assures) the existence of nonhybrid, "pure" *Ekklesiai*.
Heresiology is not only, as it is usually figured, the insistence on some
(or another) right doctrine but on a discourse of the pure as opposed to
the hybrid, a discourse that then requires the hybrid as its opposite term.
The discourse of race as analyzed by Homi Bhabha proves helpful: "The
exertions of the 'official knowledges' of colonialism—pseudo-scientific,
typological, legal-administrative, eugenicist—are imbricated at the point
of their production of meaning and power with the fantasy that drama-
tizes the impossible desire for a pure, undifferentiated origin."[110] We need
only substitute "heresiological" for "eugenicist" in this sentence to arrive
at a major thesis of this chapter.

Jerome, Epiphanius's younger contemporary, is the other most prolific writer about "Jewish-Christians" in antiquity.[111] I want to focus here
on only one aspect of Jerome's discourse about Jews: his discussions of
the "Jewish-Christians." Hillel Newman has argued that Jerome's discourse about the Judaizers and Nazarenes is more or less constructed out
of whole cloth.[112] It thus sharply raises the question of motivation, for, as
historian Marc Bloch notes, "To establish the fact of forgery is not
enough. It is further necessary to discover its motivations. . . . Above all,
a fraud is, in its way, a piece of evidence."[113] I would suggest that Jerome,
in general a much clearer thinker than Epiphanius, moves in the same
direction but with greater lucidity. For him, it is absolutely unambiguous
that rabbinic Judaism is *not* a Christian heresy but a separate *Ekklesia*. The
Mischlinge (by which usage I imply that the discourse of the impure
mixtures of orthodoxies then is not so different from modern racist discourses of miscegenation and its horrors) thus explicitly mark out the
space of illegitimacy, of no orthodoxy and thus no existence (in
nineteenth-century terms, no "religion"):

> In our own day there exists a sect among the Jews throughout all the
> synagogues of the East, which is called the sect of the Minei, and is
> even now condemned by the Pharisees. The adherents to this sect are
> known commonly as Nazarenes; they believe in Christ the Son of God,

born of the Virgin Mary; and they say that He who suffered under Pontius Pilate and rose again, is the same as the one in whom we believe. But while they desire to be both Jews and Christians, they are neither the one nor the other.[114]

This proclamation of Jerome's comes in the context of his discussion with Augustine about Galatians 2, in which Augustine, disallowing the notion that the apostles dissimulated when they kept Jewish practices, suggests that their "Jewish-Christianity" was legitimate. Jerome responds vigorously, understanding the "danger" of such notions to totalizing imperial orthodoxy.[115] What is new here is not, obviously, the condemnation of the "Jewish followers of Jesus" as heretics but that the Christian author condemns them, in addition, for not being Jews, thus at least implicitly marking the existence and legitimacy of a "true" Jewish *Ekklesia* alongside Christianity, as opposed to the falsities of the hybrids. This move parallels, then, Epiphanius's insistence that the Ebionites are "nothing."

I think that it is not going too far to see here a reflection of a social and political process like that David Chidester remarks in an entirely different historical moment: "The discovery of an indigenous religious system on southern African frontiers depended upon colonial conquest and domination. Once contained under colonial control, an indigenous population was found to have its own religious system."[116] Following out the logic of this statement suggests that there may have been a similar nexus between the containment of the Jews under the colonial eye of the Christian Empire that enabled the discovery/invention of Judaism as an *Ekklesia*, eventually named *Synagoga*. Looked at from the other direction, the assertion of the existence of a fully separate-from-Christianity "orthodox Judaism" functioned for Christian orthodoxy as a guarantee of the Christian's own bounded and coherent identity and thus furthered the project of imperial control as marked out by Andrew Jacobs.[117] The discursive processes in the situation of Christian Empire are very different from the earlier projects of mutual self-definition that I have explored elsewhere.[118] Fourth century is not second century. Hegemonic Christian discourse also produced Judaism (and Paganism—e.g., that of Julian) as other *Ekklesiai* or alternative orthodoxies precisely in order to cordon off Christianity, in a purification and crystallization of its essence as a bounded entity. Julian cleverly reverses this procedure and turns it against Christianity.

On at least one reading of Julian's "Against the Galileans," the point of that work is to *reinstate* a binary opposition between Greek and Jew, *Hellēnismos* and *Ioudaismos*, by inscribing Christianity as a hybrid.

Eusebius's claim that the one who leaves Hellenism does not land in Judaism and the reverse now constitutes an argument that Christianity is a monstrous hybrid, a mooncalf: "For if any man should wish to examine into the truth concerning you, he will find that your impiety is compounded of the rashness of the Jews and the indifference and vulgarity of the Gentiles. For from both sides you have drawn what is by no means their best but their inferior teaching, and so have made for yourselves a border of wickedness."[119] Julian further writes, "It is worthwhile . . . to compare what is said about the divine among the Hellenes and Hebrews; and finally to enquire of those who are neither Hellenes nor Jews, but belong to the sect of the Galileans."[120] Julian, as dedicated as any Christian orthodox writer to policing borderlines, bitterly reproaches the "Galileans" for contending that they are Israelites and argues that they are no such thing—neither Jews nor Greeks but impure hybrids.[121] Here Julian sounds very much like Jerome when the latter declares that those who think they are both Jews and Christians are neither or Epiphanius when he refers to the Ebionites as "nothing." This would make Julian's project structurally identical to the projects of the Christian heresiologists who, at about the same time, were rendering Christianity and "Judaism" in their "orthodox" forms the pure terms of a binary opposition with the "Judaizing" Christians, the hybrids who must be excluded from the semiotic system, being "monsters."[122] I suggest, then, a deeper explanation of Julian's insistence that you cannot mix *Hellēnismos* with *Christianismos*. It is not only that *Hellēnismos* and *Christianismos* are separate "orthodoxies" that, by definition, cannot be mixed with each other, but even more that Christianity is always already (if you will) an admixture, a syncretism. Julian wants to reinstate the binary of Jew and Greek. He provides, therefore, another instance of the discursive form that I am arguing for in the Christian texts of his time, a horror of supposed hybrids. To recapitulate, in Julian's very formation of *Hellēnismos*,[123] as a difference not of ethnicity but of systems of belief and worship, he mirrors the efforts of the orthodox churchmen.[124] While he was protecting the borders between *Hellēnismos* and *Ioudaismos* by excluding *Christianismos* as a hybrid, Julian, it seems, was, unbeknownst to himself, smuggling some Christian ideas in his very attempt to outlaw Christianity.[125]

This interpretation adds something to that of Jacobs, who writes that "among the deviant figures of Christian discourse we often find the Jew, the 'proximate other' used to produce the hierarchical space between the Christian and the non-Christian."[126] I am suggesting that the heretic can also be read as a proximate other, producing a hierarchical space between the Christian and the Jew. This point is at least partially anticipated by

Jacobs himself when he writes that "Jews exist as the paradigmatic 'to-be-known' in the overwhelming project of conceptualizing the 'all in all' of orthodoxy. This comes out most clearly in the [Epiphanian] accounts of 'Jewish-Christian' heresies."[127] One way of spinning this would be to see heresiology as central to the production of a projected "Judaism" as the "pure other" of Christian orthodoxy, while the other way of interpreting it would be to see this projection of "Judaism" as essential to the production of orthodoxy over against heresy.[128] My point is that both of these moments in an oscillating analysis are equally important and valid. Seen in this light, orthodoxy itself, orthodoxy as an idea, as a regime (as opposed to any particular orthodox position) is crucial in the formation of Christianity as the universal and imperial *Ekklesia* of the late Roman Empire and, later on, of European Christendom as well.

Orthodox *Ioudaismos*; Catholic *Iudaismus*

While, as we have seen in the preceding chapter, Jewish languages did not have a name for "Judaism" as a religion in contrast to names for other religions, Christian languages certainly did. It is beyond the scope of the present work to pursue a thorough investigation of the usages of Greek *Ioudaismos*, Latin *Iudaismus*, through the Middle Ages (although such a research project is, I reckon, a major desideratum), but a few telling examples will help move us along in the present inquiry.[129] The first is taken from an important Orthodox theologian of the eighth to ninth centuries, Theodor Studite:

[to Theophylact of Nicomedia]

τί δέ σοι ὦπται, ὦ μάκαρ, τὰ παρόντα; ἀλλ᾿ οὐχὶ μικροῦ δεῖν ἰουδαϊσμός, ἤτοι ἑλληνισμός; ἀφῃρέθη ὁ κόσμος τῆς ἐκκλησίας, ἡ ὄψις τῶν ἱερῶν ναῶν, πυρὶ παρεδόθη τὰ ἅγια· ἄλλο τι σχῆμα γνωρίζεται ἐν τῷ χριστιανισμῷ, εἴ γε χριστιανισμόν, ἀλλὰ μὴ ἰουδαϊσμὸν καλεῖν.[130]

Is it [iconoclasm] not nearly *Ioudaismos* or *Hellēnismos*? The adornment (κόσμος) of the Church, the countenance of the holy shrines (ναοί, i.e. churches) have been taken away, the holy things consigned to fire: some other form is there to be discerned in *Christianismos* (if it can be called *Christianismos* and not *Ioudaismos*).

The author speaks of a new order in Christianity with the arrival of iconoclasm, which he calls "quite close to *Ioudaismos* or *Hellēnismos*" (οὐχὶ μικροῦ δεῖν ἰουδαϊσμός, ἤτοι ἑλληνισμός). This kind of *Christianismos* has taken away the adornment of the Church, the beautiful sight/countenance of its shrines, the icons, and now there is some entirely different and new form for *Christianismos* (if it can really be called Christianity and not Judaism: ἐν τῷ χριστιανισμῷ, εἴ γε χριστιανισμόν, ἀλλὰ μὴ ἰουδαϊσμὸν καλεῖν). Now while the use of *Hellēnismos* as the name for the collective of adherents of traditional Greco-Roman cults is well attested at least as far back as Eusebius, this eighth-century text nonetheless well illustrates the use of *Ioudaismos* as the name for a particular cultic formation that, if not "religion" in the modern generic sense, could conceivably be referred to as *a* religion. The strongest clue to this is that *Ioudaismos* is here in the paradigm with *Christianismos*.

One more Greek example should help solidify this point:

Διαιροῦμεν γὰρ θεολογικῶς, ἀλλ᾽ ἀδιαιρέτως, καὶ συνάπτομεν πάλιν, διῃρημένως δέ, οὐ συναλείφοντες, οὐ συγχέοντες τοῦ Υἱοῦ τὰς οὐσίας, οὐκ ἀπεξενωμένα πρόσωπα παρεισάγοντες, ἀλλ᾽ ὡς ἔφαμεν, καὶ ἕνα Θεὸν ὁμολογοῦμεν, καὶ τὰς τρεῖς ὑποστάσεις ἤτουν πρόσωπα οὐκ ἀρνούμεθα· Θεὸς γὰρ ὁ Πατήρ, Θεὸς ὁ Υἱός, Θεὸς τὸ Πνεῦμα τὸ ἅγιον· ἰουδαϊσμὸν καὶ σαβελλισμὸν διαφεύγοντες καὶ ἀρειανισμὸν ἐντεῦθεν ἀναθεματίζοντες, θεότητα φράζοντες, τὴν ὅλην θεότητα δογματίζοντες, ἕνα δὲ πρόσωπον καταγγέλλοντες, ἡγοῦν Πατρός, ἢ Υἱοῦ, ἢ Πνεύματος, κεχωρισμένως τὸ ἑκάστου ἰδίωμα γράφομεν.[131]

For we distinguish theologically, but without dividing, and we join together again, but maintaining distinctions (διῃρημένως), not confounding the essences, not introducing (παρεισάγοντες) alien (ἀπεξενωμένα [lit. 'banished,' connotation of outlandishness]) persons, but as we have said we both confess one God, and do not deny the three hypostases or persons: for God is the Father; God is the Son; God is the Holy Ghost. Avoiding Judaism and Sabellianism, and hence anathematizing Arianism, declaring the whole divinity when we tell of divinity, but proclaiming one person, we write separately of the specific property of each.

Observance of the correct dogma on the Trinity (οὐ συγχέοντες τοῦ Υἱοῦ τὰς οὐσίας, etc.) is an avoidance of Judaism, as well as the Sabellian and Arian heresies (ἰουδαϊσμὸν καὶ σαβελλισμὸν διαφεύγοντες καὶ ἀρειανισμὸν ἐντεῦθεν ἀναθεματίζοντες). The author of this passage articulates powerfully the paradoxes of the Trinity, distinguishing the three persons without dividing them, joining them together while making distinctions between them, confessing one god and asserting three hypostases. This statement is made by way of preface to the subject of the encomium, as part of a section that begins "Ἐντεῦθεν γὰρ προσκυνοῦμεν

Πατέρα καὶ Υἱὸν καὶ ἅγιον Πνεῦμα." At any rate, and should any more proof be necessary for this point, it is crystal clear here that *Ioudaismos* does not function as a verbal noun anymore, not acting as a Jew does but the institution or even abstract essence, Judaism; the final proof being, of course, the concatenation with Sabellianism and Arianism. In any case, we see clearly how *Ioudaismos* is being used to create and police the boundaries of *Christianismos*. It is for that that it was invented and for that that it continues to exist conceptually, serving no need of the Jews but only of the Christians.

Very early in the Latin tradition, *Iudaismus* becomes used as the opposite of *Christianismus*, not manifestly as the name of an *ethnos* but as the name for a theology and set of practices connected with it. Thus (to take one or two of many, many possible examples) we find in the fourth-century Ambrosiaster the following:

> Damasco ergo in Arabiam profectus est ad praedicandum, ubi nullus erat apostolorum, ut ipse hic fundaret ecclesias, ne subripientibus (subrepentibus) pseudoapostolis Iudaismus seminaretur, et inde iterum reversus (regressus) est Damascum, ut visitaret quibus rudis praedicaverat evangelium gratiae dei.[132]

> From Damascus he set out for Arabia to preach where none of the apostles had gone so that he might found an *ecclesia* there—lest *Iudaismus* should be sown surreptitiously/stealthily by Pseudo-apostles, and then he returned again to Damascus, in order to visit those to whom as a novice he had preached the gospel of the grace of God.

Commenting on Galatians 1:17, the author explains Paul's intention in going to Arabia, to found churches there, lest "Judaism be sown" (*Iudaismus seminaretur*) by the creeping in of anti-Pauline, false apostles who demand circumcision and kashruth, *Iudaismus*.

One final Latin example will have to serve for these purposes here. The third- to fourth-century North African Christian grammarian and commentator on Paul's epistles, Marius Victorinus, writes the following:

> Item sic supra dictum: neque Titus qui mecum erat Graecus, conpulsus est circumcidi, non ergo in omnibus nec semper aut multum; postremo propter subinductos fratres, qui erant miscentes Iudaismum Christianismo, et hinc dictum propter Iudaeos

> Likewise, if it has been said above: "nor was Titus the Greek who was with me compelled to be circumcised," then [Paul] has not yielded in everything nor always nor very much; but, finally [he [Titus] was

circumcised], on account of the "brothers" who were being smuggled in, who were mixing Iudaismus with Christianismus, and this was said to be on account of the Jews.[133]

Commenting on Galatians 2:3–4, and the comment is more complicated than we need for this context—roughly: defending Paul's intransigence despite the fact that his disciple Titus was in the end circumcised—the author explains the false brothers "secretly smuggled in" as "mixing Judaism with Christianity" (miscentes Iudaismum Christianismo). Iudaismus and Christianismus are clearly two items of the same type, two species of the same genus, two words of the same semantic paradigm that can be mixed or mixed up.

Given, as I hope to have shown in this book by now, that only Christian writers used Ioudaismos (or any cognate term) in the sense of another member (frequently the other member) of the paradigm that includes Christianismos and especially remembering that in medieval Jewish discourse we never find yahadut as an "other" of Christianity, not even in the Kuzari where it might be most expected, it seems fair enough to conclude that Ioudaismos used as an abstract (not verbal) noun in the sense of the Jewish Ekklesia is indeed a Christian invention.

What Work Does "Judaism" Do?: Judaism as Anti-Judaism

I have proposed that "Judaism" as Ekklesia was essentially extruded by Christian discourse in order to make sense of the paradigmatic status of Christianity. In this final section of the chapter, I would show how consistent this is with the argument (developed independently) that "anti-Judaism," using "Judaism" as a figure for everything abject, has been a virtual constant within Christian cultures (and, to be sure, even before, and not only among Christians: Sunnis referred to Shiites as having "become Jewish"[134]). In a remarkable book, cited several times earlier already, David Nirenberg has shown over and over (to the point of inducing nausea in this reader, not, I hasten to add, owing to Nirenberg's literary skills, which are prodigious but to the matter itself) of the myriad ways that "Judaism"—or in his terms, "anti-Judaism"—has functioned both to enable analysis and also to provide the terms of polemic throughout western thought. We've seen this motion earlier in our brief journey through some patristic texts where "heresies" are named as Judaism and Judaizing. As Nirenberg shows us, "Judaism/Judaizing" is a name for the other, especially in Christian contexts of abjection of the physical as well as, as Nirenberg brilliantly shows, antithetical understandings of language and meaning. So Kant is a Judaizer for Hegelians and Hegel to the neo-Kantians, and for a Schopenhauer *all* the others are engaged in "Judaism," to a mind.[135]

The point that Nirenberg does not, perhaps, emphasize the importance of which sufficiently (although he manifestly understands it and points to it[136]) is that this "Judaism" thing is not something real that is being treated stereotypically and distortedly in all these western discourses but is, indeed, being produced by those very discourses themselves. Thus he writes of Marx, "Marx's fundamental insight here was that the 'Jewish question' is as much about the basic tools and concepts through which individuals in a society relate to the world and to each other, as it is about the presence of 'real' Judaism and living Jews in that society."[137] Just consider how much sharper this insight is if we accept the simple fact that there never was "'real' Judaism" at all for it to be "as it is about." It is not that they are getting "Judaism" wrong but rather that they are making it up as they go along. This phenomenon can be seen, perchance, more clearly in the light of the demonstrations essayed herein of the *lack* of "Judaism" as the name of anything among Jews. "Judaism" is thus generated always as the waste of the production of Christian theology, Catholic or Reformation, as well as other enterprises of Christian thinking, such as, as we have just seen, German Idealist philosophy.

I propose that it was that production of "Judaism" out of the entrails of Christianity—to invoke, once more, Marx's incredibly sharp perception—which is, indeed, the device named "Judaism," of which Nirenberg writes so compellingly, that enabled this imaginary entity, "Judaism," to be the excrement, the abject of Christianity.[138] This has, in fact, as Nirenberg has shown, almost nothing whatever to do with Jews! "Judaism" is then always/already anti-Judaism. This is not to say that these discourses were indifferent regarding the fate of Jewish bodies.

More right than orthodox historians—note, I mean orthodox in their historiography, not in their religion—who imagined (and still do) a Judaism that is somewhere out there and has a history, Marx, it seems, understood instinctively that *Iudaismus* was always being extruded from the entrails of Christendom (even as Luther's *Judenthum* was produced as a back-formation from *Christenthum*), which carries us to our last chapter in this book. How *did* the Jews get religion? Even more: How did they get a religion called "Judaism"?

5

From *Yiddishkayt* to *Judentum*; From *Judentum* to *Yahadut*; or Philology and the Transformation of a Folk

"Judaism," I argue and conclude in this final chapter, is for Jews simply a modern invention.

No "Judaism" in Yiddish

By now, I hope to have more or less securely established that neither Judeo-Greek *Ioudaismos* nor medieval Hebrew *yahadut* are used much like the modern term "Judaism" and its cognates. This is as true of the most widespread of Jewish languages, Yiddish. Max Weinreich, the dean of historians of Yiddish, has written, "However strange it may be, *yidishkeyt* (his idiosyncratic transcription; DB) is a general Yiddish word and *yaades* is only regional—among Polish Jews in the form of /ya:ndes/ in addition the word has no specific Jewishness meaning; it means 'conscience.'"[1] In this fairly bland statement by Weinreich is hidden a world of polemic and controversy that, in itself, will help move us forward in our inquiry here. First, *ya:ndes*: a group of so-called *Maskilim*, beginning with Isaac Ber Levinson (1788–1860) and approbated even by Shai Agnon, derived it as a calque on German *Gewissen*, "conscience" *yad'us* from knowledge, later misunderstood via a folk etymology as related to Jewishness. Although there has been a world of controversy about the origin and usage of this word, it seems that its most secure etymology is, indeed, from a recon-structed Yiddish form /ya:ădus/, which is a reflex of *yahadut*.[2] It is clear that it was understood thus among speakers of Yiddish. As it is, in any case, only known from Poland (and it seems only from the nineteenth century or so[3]), it would be in any case counterevidence to a claim for *yahadut* being used in a general way for an alleged Jewish religion or even for all of Jewish culture.

Two possible antecedents for this usage in rabbinic Hebrew would be the doubtful (but very well-known and much-cited text of Rashi dis-cussed in chapter 3), in which *yahadut* seems to be used to mean mod-esty or something like that, or the oath formula attested in Responsa literature beginning in the sixteenth century, by which someone swears שו״ת משפטי שמואל שמואל שאלה עו: שאני אגיד האמת על נפשי ועל יהדותי, "that I will say the truth, on my soul and on my *yahadut*."[4] It seems to mean, however, an oath by my status as a Jew and, therefore, to contribute less to the cause of *ya:ndes* than might have been hoped for. Following these writers, the only further usages we find of this construction are in fully modern writers of the late nineteenth and twentieth centuries. Jonathan Boyarin, at any rate, seems to have captured its sense best: "The untranslatable term yandes signifies not only a sense of one's ethnic identity but also an active and ethical engagement in the world in conformity with one's awareness of Jewish experience."[5]

Similar issues arise with respect to the word *Yiddishkayt*. As Weinreich has instructed us, "It is misleading to use the term *religion* for traditional *Yiddishkeyt*. When we say *religion* the implication is that there is a sphere in life beyond the boundary of religion. But in *Yiddishkeyt* there is no such delimitation."[6] It is the very semantic essence of "religion," as used in virtually all modern parlance, that it be separate from "politics," for instance. If it is not, we complain of admixture (and a "dangerous" one at that). However, there are cultures (most of the world's cultures, in fact) that make no such separations at all; they do not construct a realm of "religion" that is defined as affective, inner-directed, noncoercive (even when enjoining action in the world) and the like versus a realm of the "political" or the "secular" that represents the obverse of these characteristics. We cannot, moreover, argue that they mix religion and politics since such spheres are not recognized as existent at all. Severin Fowles has brilliantly delineated the perverse process by which scholars first divide cultures up into fragments, separate spheres and then exercise their ingenuity in showing that in that culture these spheres are "mixed up," conflated, confused:

> What most interests me in this literature is the tendency, once again, to parse pre-columbian social life into post-Reformation analytical spheres. "How much of Pueblo Bonito's power was political, economic, and religious?" asks Neitzel (2003:6). . . . In the name of methodological clarity and rigor, the social reality is fragmented, leaving the demonstration of one's interpretive skill to emerge through the reassembling of pieces. I am reminded here of the archaeological joke about a researcher who excavated an ancient room containing a single, beautiful, whole vessel. With a wise nod to his assistant, he took the vessel in his hands and shattered it into a thousand pieces. "Now *that's* a much more significant sample size," he explained with satisfaction.

We cannot escape a certain level of categorization and analytical division; neither can we fully distance ourselves from our own linguistic conventions. But we must be conscious that reassembly is a creative act. A society described as a composite entity in which religion is glued to politics and politics to economics is not the same as a society more simply viewed as a complete vessel. Reassembly, moreover, presents the researcher with an opportunity to shuffle and reglue pieces of the social into new and sometimes Frankensteinian arrangements with emphases and highlights suited more to the researcher's theoretical paradigm than to cultural realities.[7]

Yiddishkayt, indeed, incorporates every aspect of life: worship, study, business dealings, children's games, politics, gendered performance, foodways (not only those defined by kashruth), folkways (even those that violate the halacha), speaking a Jewish language, the customs of Odessa horse thieves, and everything else that defines the Jewish *Lebensform.*

Weinreich, of course, doesn't only declare this conclusion but demonstrates it as well. A fairly brief précis of his writing on *Yiddishkayt* will have to do for this context, even though it hardly does justice to his erudition and the brilliance of his analysis. We begin by citing his approving reference to the work of Matthias Mieses of 1915, who had engaged the question of why separate languages were invented by Jews.[8] After surveying the answers that have been given, Mieses found them all wanting, "until he came to the conclusion that the common creative force in all Jewish languages is the Jewish religion."[9] Weinreich accepted and approved of Mieses's explanation but demurred on one point, crucial for us here:

> We only wish to modify Mieses' term *religion,* for it is bound to evoke contemporary, that is anachronistic, conceptions. Today many Jews and Christians live in essentially the same fashion, and the difference all year is merely that former attend (or can attend) services on Saturday and the latter on Sunday. In relation to the rise of language, one should not speak of the Jewish religion, but of *Jewishness* [*Yiddishkeyt*]. In the traditional Jewishness of diverse culture areas there are many variants and even contradictions; and yet Jewishness has linked all Jews over time and space in a community of historical fate and in a consciousness of this fate.[10]

To gloss this somewhat cryptic utterance, Weinreich objects to the term "religion," for it enters precisely into a system in which Jews are the same as Germans, French, Russians, Americans, except that they have a different religion, go to a different place on a different day to worship but worship just the same. The semantic paradigm into which "Jew" enters is no longer Jew/Frenchman/German/Russian but Jew/Christian/Muslim. This does not, moreover, differentiate between "Orthodox" and other Jews; even the "Orthodox" in our times are most frequently living like everyone else except for their "religion" and "religious practices." (Note that I am not criticizing this situation but noting its difference from the past.)

In contrast to this modern system of "religion" and "religious" difference in which *Judaism* is that circumscribed "religious" component of life, the Saturday versus Sunday bit, Weinreich notes of the past: "There is no element of human conduct that is too trivial for the culture-system of Jewishness; there are details, but no trifles. Therefore traditional Jewishness is not religion and its language is not necessarily the language of religion, unless we say that all of life is religion. . . . It may be said that Jewishness takes the way of religion only with the arrival of the Emancipation."[11] If "all of life is religion," suggests Weinreich, then nothing is. If the word picks out nothing in their form of life, it is semiotically meaningless.[12] Only later can Jews speak of a Jewish religion, or even argue whether "Judaism" is a religion, an ethnicity, a culture—all equally "modern" terms. That shift, that birth of a new Jewish episteme was midwifed by the abandoning, first in Germany, of the distinctive language of *Yiddishkayt*, Yiddish and its replacement by German, with the consequent adoption of the German word *Judentum* into Jewish parlance. The significance of this shift simply cannot be exaggerated. In that process, I suggest, "Judaism" came into being—for Jews.

Judentum: A Tale of Two Cities

"The Jews had been a separate community from time immemorial, and so they were also a separate community in the German lands, not merely a sum of individuals."[13] This important point together with Weinreich's observation that Jews *never* had spoken and written the "standard" language of the communities among whom they dwelled are indicative of the great significance of language for *Lebensform* of Jewry.[14] Since, as was previously shown, Jewish languages did not have a word that means "Judaism," we need to look for that word/concept in the ultimate impact of "Christian" language on the Jews. And that is to be found, I propose, in the beginnings of the usage of standard German by Jewish writers and speakers in the eighteenth century and, in our special case, with the adoption of the word *Judentum*. It was precisely this—"the necessity of granting Jews equal rights [that] was also deduced from a quasi-historical comparison with the problem of the ghetto. Let the sun of tolerance arise anew and the Jews will again become Germans in culture and will

differ from their fellow citizens only in religion"—that destroyed
Yiddishkayt as a form of life.[15]

But first, where did *Judentum* itself come from? Only a brief treatment
of this question can be assayed here. After defining Judentum as "jüdische
Art, namentlich nach der Seite der Religion," the DWB cites Luther's
translation of the New Testament as its earliest example:

> 1) denn jr habt je wol gehöret meinen wandel weiland im jüdenthum,
> wie ich uber die masze die gemeine gottes verfolgete und verstörete sie,
> und nam zu im jüdenthum, uber viel meines gleichen in meinem
> geschlecht, und eivert uber die masze umb das veterliche gesetz. Gal. 1,
> 13. 14; http://www.woerterbuchnetz.de/DWB?lemma=judenthum[16]

The citation is from Luther's translation of Galatians, where the
Greek has *Ioudaismos*. However, as shown by Steve Mason, the Greek
must be taken as a gerund or verbal noun: "acting like a Jew, maintaining
loyalty to Jewish doings," English "Judaize," German *Judenzen* or *Jüdeln*.
German *Judentum* can hardly be derived from these verbs, nor can it be
interpreted in this fashion, since the ending -*thum* clearly marks an
abstract, and not a verbal, noun, similarly to Latin where -*ismus* also does
not function as a verbal noun.[17] In Late Latin, the -ismus suffix became
the ordinary ending for names of religions and ecclesiastical or philosophical systems or schools of thought. According to the OED's entry on
this, in Tertullian (c. third century), the first Latin Christian writer, the
term *Iudaismus* is still used as in Greek, as a verbal noun, even though in
Latin such usage is not supported by the verb system itself. That is, it is
only a loan word. However, later in the Patristic period and in Medieval
Latin, it has morphed into (one of its) modern uses, systems of thought,
beliefs, and practices and become fully productive.[18] No longer to act the
part of a Jew, then, but the name for the whole system. To get a sense of
the difference in semantics, one might compare English "criticism," a
verbal noun from the verb "criticize" with "Catholicism," which is decidedly not a verbal noun from Catholicize but an abstraction, an -ism in our
modern usage. Another appropriate example would be to compare "baptism," the action of baptizing, to its upper-case homologue "Baptism,"
the Church of baptizers, especially in the negative "Anabaptism."
Semantically, *Judenthum* goes with the latter and not the former. Thus
Paul's *Ioudaismos*, "acting like a Jew/Judaizing," turns into "the Jewish
faith" in Luther via Latin *Iudaismus*. I suggest, therefore, that Old High
German word choice here as utilized by Luther (correctly glossed by the
DWB: "jüdische Art, namentlich nach der Seite der religion") manifests
the impact of patristic Latin *Iudaismus* more than it does original Greek

semantics.[19] (Interestingly enough, the first occurrence of "Judaism" in English comes from precisely the same context. The Northern Pauline Epistles [1425] reads, "For yee hafe herde my conuersacyoun sum tyme in Iudaisme," where it is absolutely clear [as duly noted in the OED] that we have an adoption of the Latin term here: English always preferred to borrow and adapt, German to calque.)[20] Just the title of the following work is exemplary of how *Judenthum* was used in the early modern period and also explicitly remarks its origins in Latin *Iudaismus*: *Judaismus oder Judenthumb* [sic], *das ist: außführlicher Bericht von des jüdischen Volckes Unglauben, Blindheit und Verstockung*.[21] In this context, we must not neglect, of course, the infamous Johannes Eisenmenger's *Entdecktes Judenthums* in the next century.[22] The Old High German *Judenthum* (as adopted by Luther) must be taken, then, not at all surprisingly, as a reflex of the Latin Christian *Iudaismus*, despite his having translated from Greek, revealing the Christian (as well as anti-Jewish) routes by which the word entered German (see excursus at end of this chapter) and its consequent Christian entailments upon entering into Jewish *parole* during the long nineteenth century.

Berlin: Mendelssohn, Wolfssohn, and the Adoption of "Judenthum"

Judentum does not exist in Yiddish (until much, much later as a borrowing from German and only means there the Volk itself, Jewry: Chana Kronfeld, personal communication, Fall 2017), and as Weinreich asserts, *Yiddishkayt* does not match *Judentum* in usage at all. *Judentum* had to be carefully taught—to the Jews.

Two of the earliest and most prominent Jewish promoters of *Judenthum* were Moses Mendelssohn (1729–1786), arguably the founder of the Haskalah,[23] in his famous *Jerusalem oder über religiöse Macht und Judentum* (1783),[24] and Aaron Halle-Wolfssohn (1756–1835) who used it in the subtitle for his apology of "Judaism" against the depredations of the Christian antagonist propaganda, *Jeschurun, oder unparteyische Beleuchtung der dem* Judenthume *neuerdings gemachten Vorwürfe* (Hamburg, 1804).[25] Wolfssohn and Mendelssohn, notoriously, were major actors in the project to "convert" German Jews from speaking and writing Yiddish to speaking and writing *sogennante* standard German.[26] The linguistic shifts carried with them fundamental eruptions in the form of life of the Jews as well, for by shifting from a Jewish language to a Christian language, the form of life of the Jews necessarily became Christian au fond in significant and recognizable ways. If Germans they were going to be, speaking German, then *Judentum* would have to be their "religion," ultimately both "Judaism" and "Jewishness" and even as a name for the collective of Jews.

In her book, *How Judaism Became a Religion*, Leora Batnitzky registers the crucial role of Mendelssohn in producing "Judaism" as a "religion" and affords us, as well, quite precise aspects of what that entails.[27] She is, however, less sure-footed in perceiving the role of the language-shift in that very production, writing that she is not concerned with terminology but with concepts: "I am less concerned, in other words, with whether various Jewish thinkers use the term religion to describe Judaism than with whether their conceptions of Judaism are best explained within the framework of a modern concept of religion," and then, "the modern concept of religion also indicates that religion is one particular dimension of life among other particular and separate dimensions, such as politics, morality, science, or economics. Understood as such, religion may or may not have political, moral, scientific, or economic implications but it is nonetheless to be distinguished from other spheres of human life." But as Talal Asad has famously contended, "religion" cannot be defined other than through the very processes that produced it as such a separate sphere,[28] so someone operating with the concept of "religion" as a separate sphere without having learned or adopted the newly repurposed old word strikes me as virtually impossible to imagine. How can we use a "modern concept" to describe another culture that precisely does not operate with the distinctions that concept presupposes? Even the denial that *Judenthum* is a religion constitutes use and recognition of both term and concept. Thus to take an example from Batnitzky's book, one can argue, as she does, that while Buber and Rosenzweig "rebuff the modern term 'religion' as applied to Judaism," they "nonetheless inadvertently affirm the modern idea that Judaism is a religion," without thereby having shown that "religion" exists for them as a concept without a name! I find her argument on the point itself convincing but reject the consequence she draws from it. Even were we to reject the idea that, say, Buber, affirms that Judaism is a religion, the very fact of his engagement in this question, through his denial, as it were, indicates that he is part and parcel of the *dispositif*. And Rosenzweig at least seems to have understood this clearly, as he declared to Scholem, "In a sense we are ourselves guests at our own table, we ourselves, I myself. So long as we speak German (or even if we speak Hebrew, modern Hebrew, the Hebrew of '1921') we cannot avoid this detour that again and again leads us the hard way from what is alien back to our own."[29] We must learn to distinguish clearly between the concept world given, say, for a medieval Jew and the imposition by an early modern Jewish thinker of his conceptual apparatus on that medieval Jewry. So Rabbi Yehuda Halevi, for example, as I've argued at length in the preceding chapter, did not have "Judaism" available, neither in his language nor, as far as can be told, in his conceptual apparatus, but Rabbi Moses Mendelssohn might very well have described "the Judaism" of medieval Sefarad by applying his own conceptual apparatus in which, for instance, "religion" is by definition distinct from politics.

As pointed out by Elizabeth Johnston, Leopold Zunz himself seems to have understood well the impact of adopting Christian language. She remarks how in Zunz's famous maiden voyage, "Etwas über die Rabbinische Literatur," he entitled it "rabbinic literature," but then, later on, even within that document, apparently realizing that this is a highly marked (and pejorative) Christian name for all postbiblical Jewish literature, and even more unambiguously in his later work, named it Hebrew literature or Jewish literature tout court.[30] But of course, as I would claim, *Wissenschaft des Judentums*, nevertheless, is as Christian as anything that the term "rabbinic" has to offer, and it's the *Judentum* that is Christian here, much more than the *Wissenschaft*. In her analysis, Johnston shows, however, how Zunz in his very attempt to de-Christianize (or more precisely, de-protestantize) the depiction of Jewish literature, falls himself into a trap of Christian theological imagination. My contention here is that the use of a "Christian"—not "standard," but Christian—language renders that all but inevitable.

In a helpful article on this same key essay, Leon Wieseltier wrote that "Zunz's pioneering approach to Jewish texts thus bequeathed to subsequent Jewish historiography perhaps its fundamental premise: that the scope of the Jewish historian's activity be no less wide than the scope of Jewish life itself." Wieseltier further remarked:

> It is commonly asserted that Jews in nineteenth-century Germany depicted themselves not as a nation but rather entirely as a religion. Such a self-image was fashioned to serve the purposes of a community thirsting for emancipation and civil equality. Judaism was portrayed as a spiritual creed which need not infringe upon the social and political allegiances of its votaries. . . . Zunz concurred, for these reasons, in denying the Jews the status of a nation. But it would be erroneous to conclude that for Zunz the Jewish difference was, therefore, exclusively religious. He speaks, as we have seen, of a Jewish "church" and a Jewish "state." In fact the entity conceived by the *Etwas* and by Zunz's later work—is neither a church nor a state, but, more precisely, a culture. For Zunz the Jews are less than a state but more than a religion. They

constitute, as one Jewish writer of this century has put it, a civilization. They are, in Zunz's favorite term, a Kulturvolk, a cultural nation, reminiscent in some ways of Humboldt's apolitical estimate of the German people.[31]

It is, however, no contradiction of this point to note that Zunz himself defined *Judentum*, if not always, sometimes at least as precisely a religion: "Judenthum bezeichnet den Glauben und den durch selbigen bedingten Inhalt der Gesetze und Religionsideen der Juden."[32] ("*Judenthum* designates the faith and the contents of the laws and religious ideas of Jews conditioned by that very same [faith].")[33] The contents of the laws and religious ideas are in this definition consequences of the faith called *Judenthum*. *Judenthum* is a faith, a belief system (together, of course, with its dependent consequences in practice) and not, like *Yiddishkayt*, for example, an entire form of life. This enabled Zunz to replace those consequences with others more to his Germanized liking.

As Amos Bitzan has sharply put the point:

> There were two important innovations in Zunz's proposed reform of Jewish religious instruction. First, the content of this instruction was no longer to consist primarily of normative material—specifically, instruction in Jewish law and legal reasoning. Instead, the content was to be Romantic religion that would edify the soul of the student. Second, the person he deemed most qualified to provide this instruction was a man formed by Wissenschaft rather than by Talmudic study. For Zunz, Wissenschaft's power, in this case, derived not from its recovery of historical information that could be relayed to the student—he warned teachers explicitly against feeding children "dry history"—but from its ability to transform the moral and aesthetic feelings of the individual. Zunz's vision of Wissenschaft put it into the service of transforming Judaism into a modern religion, which for German Jews often meant religion according to the criteria of Immanuel Kant and Friedrich Schleiermacher.[34]

My argument here is not that *Judentum* is always in eighteenth- and nineteenth-century Jewish parlance the name of a putative Jewish religion—it certainly is not, not even always or even predominantly for Zunz—but the very fact of this usage and the controversy over whether *Judentum* is a "religion" or a "nation" or a "culture" in itself bespeaks an enormous shift in Jewish discourse. As I have shown elsewhere and earlier in this text, there is no way that the question could be asked or even conceived in Jewish languages, and it was the shift to Christian German that put it on the discursive map of Jewry. There may be no question that with the shift to German attending the desire to be a part of *Deutschtum*, the Jews of Germany—including the Orthodox—were reforming the Jewish form of life and reconstituting it as a confession, *Judentum*, Judaism, *Yahadut*, no longer a member of a paradigm with *Deutschtum* (which itself incorporates "religion" in itself, as pointed out to me by Professor Ismar Schorsch) and, therefore, no longer incongruent with it, but one that included *Christentum*, a religion that was, of course, incompatible with *Judentum*, thus enabling the separation of *Christentum* from *Deutschtum*. This process—well recognized among historians—is known (and contested) as the confessionalization of Judaism, but again one must emphasize that there is no Judenthum, no Judaism at all, until the invention of the problematic of what it is. This movement constitutes nothing but an epistemic shift in the full Foucauldian sense. I would then slightly modify Batnitzky's shrewd title, *How Judaism Became a Religion*, to read *How the Jews Got Religion!*

Vilna and the Birth of Jewish "Judaism"

As pointed out, perhaps somewhat tantalizingly, at the end of chapter 3, a kind of semantic revolution overtakes the word *yahadut* in the second half of the nineteenth century. After the one instance of a phrase *dat yahadut* that we found in the writings of R. Israel Lifshitz Danziger, the next and very explicit usage comes from a Vilna Jewish scholar, educator, and publicist, R. Shmuel Yosef Fünn (1808–1890). This comes from an unpublished manuscript of his discussed in an important article by Eliyahu Stern, who also supplied me with a photograph of the relevant pages of the manuscript.[35] Since the context is vital to my argument here, I'll quote Professor Stern's account of the text. The tract of Fünn was written in response to a slanderous exposé of the Talmud that had been produced by one Alexander McCaul, leader of the British Protestant Church's conversionary mission to Russian Jewry:

> McCaul's work prompted strong responses from all over Jewish Europe. The first and most in depth rejoinders came from the two leading Russian Jewish thinkers, the elder statesman and dean of the Russian Jewish enlightenment Isaac Ber Levinsohn of Kremenets and the young Samuel Josef Fuenn of Vilna. Levinsohn's *Zerubavel* and Fuenn's *Darkhe Hashem* attempted to refute McCaul's arguments specifically and disentangle the granting of civil rights from the project of Christianity. Levinsohn and Fuenn wrote their works for both Jewish and Christian audiences, with the expectation that their words would be translated into Russian or English. They sought to defend Judaism and the

Talmud by marshaling the Catholic and Orthodox idea of tradition to explain the Talmud to those living on Russian and Polish lands.[36]

Here then is the astonishing text that we find in Fünn's work (hardly astonishing to us in *our* usage but to the best of my knowledge, one of the very first instances of such usage). Let us observe, however, carefully, exactly how and with what tone we find the term here: "For you didn't know anything and did not want to know anything, not about the *dat yehudit* and not about the *dat notzrit*, for what is it that you would call by the name *dat* but only the 'theoretical aspect' in the *dat* and that is the matter of the beliefs and opinions?"[37] First of all, we can see clearly here that the term *dat yehudit* appears in contrast with that of the Christians and (in Fünn at any rate) only in such contexts. Fünn, moreover, quite clearly understands that the Protestant McCaul identifies "religion" with theology and faith.

The term, at any rate, morphs from an adjective to a noun only a sentence or two later. Thus, "And if he is speaking of the moral aspect, you have already been shown to understand, also for in morals / ethics the *dat hayahadut* was greater than the *dat hanotzrit*." With respect to practices, *ma'asim*, moreover, Fünn has another novel argument, for the time—namely, that the practices required by Jesus (called the *Notzri*) were simply those of the Torah of Hashem, so there was nothing new there, until Paul and "his associates" came and canceled them, so all that is new is the cancelling of the Torah's required practices. Fünn goes on to argue that Christian practices have developed and changed and are not in accord with the New Testament (as McCaul had claimed) and, therefore, "you don't know what it is that you wish to call by the name of the *dat notzrit* nor what you would name: *yahadut*."

Fünn completes his own argument by summing:

> It results from these matters that if the one who asks us wishes to know a priori the matter of which he is asking us such that we could answer him, he must know a priori that *dat hayahdut* in truth in all three of these aspects [viz the theoretical, the moral, and the practical], is the *dat* of Moses interpreted according to the words of the Sages of Israel (some of whose words are called "The Oral Torah"). The *dat hanotzrit* is *some* of the words of Moses's Torah interpreted according to the words of the Christian Sages from the day that the New Testament was founded. (emphasis added)

Fünn goes on to develop an entire theory of comparative religion, so we might very well say, in which ultimately he argues that both Christianity and Islam, properly understood by their own practitioners—

those born to them—are as true and as salvific for those practitioners as *dat hayahadut* is for born Israelites.

Now there is not the slightest question but that here we have *yahadut* in its full modern sense; it is the name of the "religion" of Israel and comparable with both Christianity and Islam as other members of the genus "religions." I will leave it to the current editor of this astonishing text, Professor Stern, to fully explicate these matters further. To the best of my knowledge, we see nothing like this before Fünn, and if we do here and there, they are the swallows before the summer. We can see, moreover, from here exactly in what context *yahadut* as "Judaism" first appears and in the pen of what kind of a writer, one who is—and this will be immediately crucial—fully versed, fully imbued, and fully identified with traditional Jewish life and learning but who is also, clearly, cognizant of the language, thought, and writing of the larger world. And this is not Berlin, but Vilna.

Ironically, the next crucial step in this story falls to a Berlin and Vilna once again. I jest, only because the author in question was named Berlin, but the story is not a Berlin story but rather a Vilna one. Naftali Zvi Yehuda Berlin (1816–1893), known as the Natziv, was arguably the most important scholar and powerful leader of Lithuanian ultratraditionalist Yeshiva Jewry. However traditionalist he was, he was a reader of the Jewish Press in Hebrew and Yiddish and closely associated with such acculturated Orthodox individuals as Fünn. Just to give a sense, when the Yeshiva in Volozhin where Berlin reigned supreme was in danger of closing, it was Fünn who rescued it on more than one occasion and gave Berlin much advice in practical matters.

It is riveting to see, however, that it is Berlin who makes the next steps in the semantic acceptance and usage of *yahadut* in ultratraditionalist Jewish writing. For example (and I will give only a couple out of many here), Laban in Genesis 31 accuses not only Jacob of having stolen from him but his ancestors and brothers as well, even though it is really only Jacob he suspects. On this Berlin comments in his brilliant Torah commentary, *Ha'ameq Davar*:

העמק דבר בראשית פרק לא
מכל מקום כך דרך אוה"ע כשרואין אחד מישראל שגנב אומר על עבדי ה'
כולם שהמה גנבים, ויש להרע לכולם וחשב דהיהדות גורם היתר לכך, ומש"ה
יש להרע להם ולכלות את היהדות, ומעשה אבות סימן לדורות הבאים

In any case, it is the way of the Gentiles that when they saw one of Israel who has stolen, they say about the worshipers of Hashem all of them that they are thieves. And that one should do evil to all of them, for he [the Gentile] thinks that *yahadut* gives him [the Jew] permission to do that [steal], and because of that one must do evil to them and to destroy the *yahadut*. The acts of the fathers are a watchword for the sons!

What we observe here for the first time in Hebrew writing (if I am not mistaken) is *yahadut* being used as the subject of a sentence, almost an agent. It is something that can give permission, allow, the subject of its sovereignty, as it were, to steal. Moreover, we observe here that *yahadut* in its second occurrence here shows a kind of equivocation that will be entirely typical of its modern usages—namely, it wavers between that subject, that sovereign agent that permits or forbids, and as the name for the Jewish People.

An unambiguous usage of *yahadut* for the People, as in *Judentum*, can be found in this work at Deuteronomy 26:5, where we read the following:

> לגוי. כבר ביארנו דמשמעות גוי הוא אומה שיש לה ארץ ומלוכה בפ״ע, וא״כ
> היה ראוי לכתוב לעם, מזה יצא הדרש שהיו מצוינים שם, וה״ז כדכתיב ואשרו
> אתכם כל הגוים כי תהיו אתם ארץ חפץ וגו' (מלאכי ג'), פי׳ היהדות היא
> כאומה בארץ בפ״ע

> As a nation; I have already explained that the meaning of *goy* is a nation with a land and sovereignty in its own right, and therefore it would have been appropriate here to write ʿ*am* [which generally is taken to make a People without its own land and sovereignty; DB]. From this point issues the midrash that they were distinguishable there, and this is what is written: "And all of the nations [*goyim*] will bless you, for you will be the Land of Desire." Its interpretation: *Yahadut* will be a nation in the land/the world in its own right!

Even though mixed with other peoples and not having land and sovereignty of its own, *yahadut*, the People of Israel, will be seen by the others as a nation in its own right because they remain distinguishable and faithful to their ways. *Yahadut* here must refer to the collective and not its practices, beliefs, and so on. In other contexts, however, Berlin uses *yahadut* almost exclusively as the name for the abstraction, the "religion," and not the people, so a certain Gentile wants to uproot *yahadut* from the hearts of Jewish children (Genesis 31:29), which is, of course, another usage in which *Judentum* can appear. In other words, Berlin's usage of *yahadut* is a perfect calque on German *Judentum*, matching the usage of no earlier Hebrew word or phrase. It would be, I think, a serious mistake not to see *Judentum* lurking here in the semantic background.

"Judaism" as a Subject

Even though the Natziv is a representative of the vision of the eternal
Israel as "distinguishable" there, nonetheless, by adopting the shifted
sense of *yahadut* as calque on *Judentum*, he covertly, perhaps willy-nilly,
imports the means for the destruction of that very distinction. I have
observed that at least once in the writing of Rabbi Berlin, *yahadut* functions as the subject of a sentence, as a virtual agent. In chapter 3, I have
established that this is *never* the case in earlier Jewish writing. The word
yahadut and its exceedingly rare Judeo-Greek predecessor are never the
grammatical subjects of a sentence, whereas in the twentieth century
and onward, *yahadut* and its English congener, "Judaism" (not quite
equivalent), both frequently are. Also and most importantly, *Judentum* can
also function in this way: *Judentum lehrte*, and so on. This distinction
when looked at makes a startling difference.

We find this usage frequently in another important late-nineteenth-
century document, a translation from the German commentary on the
Torah written by the leader of German-Jewish orthodoxy, Rabbi
Shimshon Raphael Hirsch (1808–1888) early in the second half of the
nineteenth century. This author was, of course, one of the most prolific
of German Jewish writers to use the term *Judentum/Judenthum* as previously shown. Not surprisingly, in the Hebrew translation made of his
great commentary later in the nineteenth century (first publication
1896?), we find *yahadut* doing many things.

The translation was made by Moshe Zalman Aronsohn (1848–1906),
one of the founders of Russian Jewish orthodoxy and translator of much
of Hirsch to Hebrew. A couple of examples (out of many) will serve to
illustrate the point:

רש״ר הירש בראשית פרק א

האליליות פיצלה את העולם כולו לקבוצות ולחוגים רבים; בראש כל חוג עמד
שליט, שריכז בידיו סמכויות מיוחדות. היתה זו תוצאה עקבית של הטעות
היסודית שהוזכרה לעיל. אם חומר העולם היה קדום, היה האל המעצב כפות
ומוגבל לחומר; כך ירד האל והפך לכח—טבע, שאיננו חפשי ביצירתו. אל זה
לא יכול לחולל ניגודים של ממש ותופעות שונות זו מזו ביסודן. אולם, העולם
מלא ניגודים, ומצויות בו תופעות שונות זו מזו; הוא נוסד אפוא ע״י אלהים
רבים—כמספר הקבוצות של תופעות מנוגדות. ואילו היהדות כופרת באלהים
הרבים ובשלטון שהופקד בידיהם; את כוחם היא מעבירה לידי האל היחיד,
ורק לו היא קוראת אלהים.

Paganism divided the whole world into multiple groups and circles;
at the head of each circle, there stood a sovereign, who concentrated
into his hands special powers. This was a consistent result of the

fundamental error that was mentioned above [that the world was produced out of pre-existing matter]. If the matter of the world were primordial, the god, the designer, would have been constrained by the
material. That is how the god deteriorated and became a power,
Nature, which is not free in its creativity. A god like this is incapable of
doing contradictory things and [producing] phenomena that are different from each other in their very foundation. The world, however, is
full of contradictions and phenomena that are very different from each
other. It was created, therefore, by many gods according to the number
of contradictory phenomena. *Yahadut*, however, denies the existence of
many gods and the sovereignty that was deposited with them. Rather it
transfers all their powers to one god, and only he does it call God.

Yahadut here denies, transfers, calls something God.

If we have already seen the beginnings of such usage in Berlin of
Vilna (undoubtedly as previously shown under the impact of *Judentum*),
in literature such as the translated Hirsch of Berlin, we find a whole array
of activities that this new agent, *yahadut*, can engage in. Thus we find "it"
doing various things to its practitioners:

רש״ר הירש דברים פרק יד
אין התורה מכירה קירבת ה' ומעלה אנושית המושגות רק ברוח—תוך כדי
הפקרת הצד הגופני החושני ומסירתו לחילול מוסרי. היהדות תופסת את האדם
כולו ומכניסה אותו לתחום אצילותה, והיא מורה שקדושת החיים החושניים
היא התנאי הראשון של התרוממות האדם אל ה', ודבר זה כבר בא לידי ביטוי
במצות מילה.

The Torah does not recognize closeness to God and high human attain-
ment only in spirit with abandon of the sensuous body and giving it
over to moral profanity. *Yahadut grabs* ahold of the whole human and
introduces him to his most noble state, and it *teaches* that the holiness of
the sensual life is a necessary condition for exaltation of the human to
Y. And this matter has already been exemplified by the command of
circumcision.

We find here *yahadut* as the subject of three active verbs. These and
many others are the things that *yahadut* does. He speaks of the content
of *yahadut*, of the literature of *yahadut*, of a characteristic feature of
yahadut, the special quality of *yahadut*. There is no question here but
that *yahadut* is functioning in its fully modern usages and contexts; all
these usages could be matched in later twentieth-century Hebrew, as well
as in parallels, such as English "Judaism." The Hirsch translation is,
in effect, the proof of the pudding. The word *yahadut* is transformed in
Hebrew under the powerful impact of German *Judentum*. In effect, this is

not only the transformation of a word and its usage but part and parcel of the reinvention of People Israel into the religion "Judaism," part and parcel of what is known to historians as the confessionalization of Israel.

An Enemy of Yahadut

We have a vitally important contemporary witness to these very events in Jewish sociocultural history from a witness who observed them and resisted them. The context is a three-part article in the Hebrew Journal, *Halevanon*, published during the second half of the nineteenth century, originally in Jerusalem, then in Paris, and finally in Mainz and London.[38] The article in question, written by one H. Y. Flensberg, is entitled "The Talmud and *Yahadut*." It was published in 1873 during the Mainz period of *Halevanon*, which throughout its existence was the organ of the highly conservative old Orthodox community of Jerusalem and its supporters in Europe. The article is itself yet another defense of the Talmud similar in goal, if not in style or even content, to that of Fünn referred to earlier. The passage I shall discuss here is taken from the third installment of the article, volume 9, no. 22, published on January 29, 1873. The article itself is rather disjointed, consisting largely of a polemic against Jewish antagonists of the Talmud. At a certain point, however, the author, after first finally announcing his theme (well into the third installment), apparently as the relationship of the Talmud to *yahadut*, with the latter entirely dependent on the former, makes statements like "wherever the Torah plummets, *yahadut* falls ten times over . . . , for without the Torah, there is no commandment, and no godly *dat*, and without all of these, what is the *yahadut* of which we would hope for its continuation?" But then, seemingly in a kind of panic at his own use of the word *yahadut*, the author shifts directions quite suddenly:

> But, indeed, hear my honored reader! Indeed the name/noun "*yahadut*, *Judenthum* [in Hebrew transliteration]" which is pronounced openly[39] by many and honorable writers, when they are speaking about the spiritual situation of Israel, is an affliction to me. I am amazed to know who birthed this vain hallucination and from whose belly did it go out? And I thought to know this, behold I investigated it, and thus it is [i.e., a calque from the German]: I know, dear reader, that you will, it is possible, ask me what evil have I found in this honorable noun, which is formed as perfect Hebrew [lit. the holy language], which finds its way among all of the great writers and all folks of all walks of life and all the Hebrew journals use it as a word, and you will find no evil in it from its beginning? But stop over the words for a moment. I will make you know and testify before you. The spirit of criticism does not speak in

me, for writerly envy has never been mine. No it is because this word is a new creation in our holy tongue, it has just arrived; none of the prophets of heaven for whom *yahadut* was the breath of their nostrils and all day long they spoke of it imagined it.[40] God forfend from me, If only our holy tongue would grow and become a mighty vine, in which every European thought will be comfortable in its mouth.[41] They will speak and it will be refreshing to them, for it will be useful for all of their needs. But on this a tempest has seized me, for in this concept *Judenthum* which is bottled up in the noun *yahadut*, which the writers or the new scholars have introduced into the vineyard of Israel, they have made a line of *tohu* and an anchor of *bohu* on the house of Israel and on their faith, to turn them from the way of rationality and knowing what God demands of them and they [those writers] will rest in a congregation of ghosts and reformers.

ואולם שמע נא קורא נכבד! כי שם "היהדות, יודענטהום" היוצא מפורש
מפי סופרים רבים ונכבדים, בעת שידובר ביניהם על דבר מצב הרוחני של
ישראל, עמל הוא בעיני; פליאה דעת ממני מי הרה את מקסם הכזב ההוא
ומבטן מי יצא? ואחשבה לדעת זאת, הנה חקרתיה כן היא: ידעתי קורא יקר,
כי מלאת מלין לשאלני מה עול מצאתי בשם הנכבד הזה העשוי על טהרת
שפת קודש, אשר לו מהלכים בין כל הסופרים הגדולים, ולכל מכ"ע העברים
יהיה להם למלה, ורעה לא תימצא בו מעודו? אך עצור נא במלין כמעט רגע,
אזכירך ואערכה לעיניך.—הן רוח הבקרת לא ידבר בי, כי קנאת סופרים לא
אכלתני, לא יען כי השם ההוא הוא בריאה חדשה בשפת קדשנו, מקרוב בא,
לא שערוהו כל חוזי עליון אשר היהדות היתה רוח אפם, ותמיד כל היום עליה
נשאו מדברותיהם—חלילה לי מזה, מי יתן ותגדל שפת קודשנו והיתה לגפן
אדרת אשר גם כל הגות רוח לאומי אייראפא תמצאנה מנוחה על פיה, בה
ימללו וישיחו כל העולה על רוחם, ידברו ותרוח להם, כי תהיה דרושה לכל
חפציהם. אולם אך על זאת יאחזני שער, כי בהמושג הזה "יודענטהום" העצור
בשם "היהדות" אשר הביאו הסופרים או החכמים החדשים בכרם בית ישראל,
הטו קו תהו ומשקלת בהו על בית ישראל ועל אמונתם, להתעותם מדרך השכל
וידע מה ה' אלקיהם דורש מהם, ובקהל רפאים או רעפארמער יניחו.[42]

Flensberg gives us everything on a platter: *yahadut*, in this sense, is an entirely new usage. It is a calque on German *Judentum*. The reason for this calque is to enable authors in Hebrew to express themselves in consonance with European (read: Christian) thinking, and he doesn't like it. On my reading, Flensberg—having himself utilized the word *yahadut*—does a double take and flinches at the word because it really does disturb him. He then explains why it disturbs him in spite of it being a correctly formed Hebrew word, further remarking that he does not, in general (perhaps ironically), oppose linguistic innovation in Hebrew that enables it to become a full modern language fit for "European" thoughts. There are, however, two reasons that he cannot tolerate this word, the first being that he clearly identifies it as a loan-translation from German *Judentum* and the second that it has semantic consequences that he finds intolerable, to wit that it produces a category, *Judentum*, that includes all Jews as the name for Jewish "religion as well," for *Judentum*, indeed, means both the entirety of Jewry and the Jewish "religion." As he argues, *yahadut*, the accursed calque on *Judentum*, does as well. He accordingly curses its users that they will remain "ghosts"—those who have left off entirely observing the Torah and lost all contact with Jewishness—and "reformers," members of the Reform Movement.[43]

Our author goes further in a sequel, since he argues that the word *yahadut* applies to the entire genus of those descended from Judea, as he says, to Karaites, and Sadducees, and Samaritans; all are incorporated in *Judentum/Yahadut*, but what sets "us" apart is our commitment to the Torah and the Talmud. The author goes on and on condemning this new usage. In other words, *yahadut* is not only a new word but one that signifies a new invention, some kind of a name for a "Judaism," a *Judentum* that incorporates all sorts of heresies and deviations:

> And now what is this voice of *yahadut* that we hear from the writers and the new sages? Not the voice of Torah, and not the voice of the Commandment, but it is the voice of *yahadut*, *Judentum* that we hear! This is the genus which includes in it the Karaite who partially assents [to the Torah] and also the *apikoros* who denies everything. Only in the congregation the writers raise their voices like the clarion of the Shofar and to its banner gather all those who call out its name and those who are awakened to use; is this not imbecility and a great evil to use the genus and to leave aside the species which divides between the righteous and the evil-doers, between those who worship G-d and those who do not worship Him, and is the righteous equal to the evil-doer? Behold there is [more] than enough of mocking and anger! Will thus be the work of the writers of the House of Israel? Their work is foreign!

> ועתה, מה קול היהדות אשר אנחנו שומעים מן הסופרים והחכמים החדשים?
> לא קול תורה ולא קול מצוה, זולתי קול יהדות, יודענטהום, אנחנו שומעים,
> הוא הסוג אשר יכללו בו את הקראי המודה במקצת, גם את האפיקורס הכופר
> הכל, רק בעדה ירימו הסופרים כשופר קולם, ולדגלה יתאספו כל הקוראים
> בשמה, והמתעוררים להחזיק בה, האין זאת אולת ורעה רבה לאחוז את הסוג,
> ומן המין המבדיל בין צדיק לרשע בין עובד אלקים לאשר לא עבדו יניחו את
> ידם, והיה כצדיק כרשע? הלא כדי בזיון וקצף! הכזו תהיה עבודת הסופרים
> בבית ישראל? נכריה עבודתם!

ח״י פלנסברג, תלמוד ויהדות (ג), הלבנון, שנה ט, כג טבת תרל״ג, 29.1.1873,
עמ׳ 177-178.[44]

Now whether or not we agree with his polemic against all the new and liberal winds blowing among Jews, we must certainly accept his explicit testimony, consistent as it is with the philological material exposed until here, to convince us beyond a shadow of a doubt not only that *yahadut* was a newly formed concept for Jewish writers, a calque, or loan translation from German *Judentum* but that it inevitably brought with it the cultural connotations of the latter, as well, but it was *perceived* as such too, for good or (in this case) for ill. I would suggest that his argument is founded on the double sense of *Judentum* as Jewry and "Judaism," precisely matched in the double sense of modern Hebrew *yahadut*, proving incidentally the point that modern Hebrew *yahadut* is a calque on German *Judentum*! As Jewry it includes everyone, but then it seems as if all Jewry and their views are included in "Judaism." Flensberg is in favor of modernizing the language to make it speak European philosophy, but the word *yahadut* causes him to be in distress, seized by an emotional storm owing to its connotations. Among his targets, it would seem, is that radically Orthodox modernizer, the Natziv. I, of course, do not subscribe to the suggestion that words are reified and their meanings unchangeable (certainly, the Natziv did not intend to include Karaites, atheists, or even Reformers in his *yahadut*!), and neither did Flensberg imagine such of his own great teacher but rather he asserts that words with strong associations and ideologies behind them willy-nilly produce change in the social formations that adopt them.[45] As the Rabbis have said: "Death and life are in the hands of language"! Here, then, is the "smoking gun" for the argument of this chapter and the cumulative argument of this book.

The key word "Judaism," it seems, was, indeed, for Jews a modern notion.

EXCURSUS: DANIELA SCHMIDT* ON JUDENTHUM

The word *"Judentum"* was mostly translated in German dictionaries from the seventeenth century until the early nineteenth century with the Latin word *"Judaismus."* *"Judaismus"* is very pervasive as a Latin key word in German-Latin dictionaries—for example, in the Vocabularius ex quo of 1469[†] or in the Dictionarium Latinogermanicum of 1541.[‡] Kaspar Stieler referred to this word in the first germanophone dictionary in 1691.[§]

In Middle High German prevailed the word jüdischeit.[¶] According to the current research, there is no account for the word judentuom in Middle High German. Thus Old High German dictionaries contain the word judentuom.[**] This is based on five manuscripts of a file glossary (readers' guide for the Latin text in order of word appearance) of the Expositio libri comitis (Collectiones in epistulas et evangelia), which was written in 812. The scripture of Smaragdus of Saint-Mihiel contains commentary of the pericopes of the epistles and gospels of the liturgical year. The compilation was very popular among the preachers and offered excerpts of patristic compositions as well as contemporary commentaries.[††] The respective gloss is to be found in the context of Galatians 1:13.

---

[*] These remarks (and a lot more detail as well) were offered me by Daniela Schmidt, who is a graduate student in the Institut für Religionswissenschaft und Jüdische Studien at Potsdam University, following my initial oral presentation of the first part of this chapter at my von Humboldt Festakt lecture in April 2017. I am very grateful to her for this expert commentary. The notes in this excursus are supplied by her as well.

[†] Vocabularius Ex quo. Nikolaus Bechtermünz, "Judaismus est mos vel ritus iudeorum vel gentes iudeorum" (Eltville, 1469), http://tudigit.ulb.tu-darmstadt.de/show/inc-ii-34/0157.

[‡] Petrus Cholinus, Johannes Frisius, and Daniel Sternberg, "Judaismus, Iüdisch gsatz vnd brauch," Dictionarium Latinogermanicum (Tigurum, 1541), 495, http://reader.digitale-sammlungen.de/de/fs1/object/display/bsb10147558_00507.html.

[§] Kaspar Stieler, Der Teutschen Sprache Stammbaum und Fortwachs oder Teutscher Sprachschatz (Nürnberg, 1691), col. 903.

[¶] Georg Friedrich Benecke, Wilhelm Müller, and Friedrich Zarncke, Mittelhochdeutsches Wörterbuch 1 (Leipzig, 1854), 775, http://www.woerterbuchnetz.de/BMZ?lemma=juedischeit (meaning descriptions: 1. judaismus, jüdische Religion, 2. Judenschaft, die Juden. Lexer, Matthias [1872–1878] Mittelhochdeutsches Handwörterbuch); Mittelhochdeutsches Wörterbuch 1 (Leipzig, 1872), col. 1486, http://www.woerterbuchnetz.de/Lexer?lemma=juedischeit (meaning descriptions: Judaismus, jüd. Religion; Judenschaft, jüd. Volk).

[**] Cf. as latest work: Althochdeutsches Wörterbuch. Auf Grund der von Elias von Steinmeyer hinterlassenen Sammlungen, im Auftr. der Sächsischen Akademie der Wissenschaften zu Leipzig. Begr. von Elisabeth Karg-Gasterstädt und Theodor Frings, ed. von Rudolf Grosse 4 (Berlin, 2002), col. 1833, http://awb.saw-leipzig.de/cgi/WBNetz/wbgui_py?sigle=AWB&lemma=judentuom.

[††] Cf. Hans Hubert Anton, Smaragd von Saint-Mihiel, in Biographisch-Bibliographisches Kirchenlexikon (BBKL) 10 (Herzberg, 1995), col. 644–648. Cf. Rolf Bergmann, ed., Althochdeutsche und altsächsische Literatur (Berlin, 2013), 437.

In total, there are ten manuscripts* of the glossing of this work, of which only five contain the word judentuom and are all Bavarian provenience.[†] Two of the five manuscripts are in important composite gloss traditions together with glossing about Saint Gregory the Great.[‡] The manuscripts originate in a time around 1000 until the twelfth century.[§]

The DWB overlooked in this case the etymology, though at the time of composition of the series of articles "Jude-" (1877) there existed already two works on glossaries, which noted the Old High German usage.[¶]

Furthermore, the word can be found in an Early Modern High German legal source (1530)—at the same time as Luther—that was written in Bern and formulates the consequences of the reform of faith for civil rights issues.[**] The connection of "römisches Judentum" [Roman Judaism] is interesting in Middle Low German (1593) where it is transferred and used as a polemic against the papacy.[††]

In the following centuries there are remarkable entries in Frisch (1741)[‡‡] with the specification "Religion" as well as the commentary in Adelung's works (1775/1793), "ein Wort, welches anfängt zu veralten":[§§] a word which begins to become obsolescent. Campe's dictionary need also be mentioned

---

*   Cf. Bergmann, 438.

†   Bergmann, 438.

‡   Bergmann, 438. One of these important composite manuscripts is available as digital copy online: clm 19440 http://daten.digitale-sammlungen.de/bsb00036881/image_177, evidence on the top of the page, first line. Handschrift b in der Sammlung von Elias Steinmeyer and Eduard Sievers, Die althochdeutschen Glossen, 5 vol. (Berlin, 1879–1922), vol. 1, 805, manuscripts, 803. Regarding germanophone glosses, see Peter Schmitt, Glossen, Glossare. II: Deutsche Literatur, in LexMA 4 (1989), col. 1510f.

§   Bergmann, Althochdeutsche und altsächsische Literatur, 438.

¶   Johann Schilter, Thesaurus Antiquitatum teutonicarum, ecclesiasticarum, civilium, litterariarum: Tomis tribus (1728), vol. 3, 498; and Eberhard Gottlieb Graff, Althochdeutscher Sprachschatz oder Wörterbuch der althochdeutschen Sprache 1 (Berlin, 1834), col. 596.

** Frühneuhochdeutsches Wörterbuch. Hrsg. von Ulrich Goebel; Anja Lobenstein-Reichmann; Oskar Reichmann. Begr. von Robert R. Anderson; Ulrich Goebel; Oskar Reichmann. Vol. 8: I—kuzkappe, Berlin 2013, https://fwb-online.de/lemma/judentum.s.2n?q=judentum&page=1: "Rennefahrt, Staat/Kirche Bern 417, 1 (halem., 1530): Da die kilchwychinen [sc. Kirchweihe—D.S.] vom bapstûmb, ja? vom ceremonischen judenthûmb [. . .] harflissent."

†† Mittelniederdeutsches Handwörterbuch, begründet von Agathe Lasch und Conrad Borchling, hrsg. nach Gerhard Cordes und Annemarie Hübner von Dieter Möhn und Ingrid Schröder, I ff. (Hamburg 1928–) Neumünster 1956 ff., vol. 2 (2004), 485.

‡‡ Johann Leonhard Frisch, Teutsch-Lateinisches Wörter-Buch 1 (Berlin, 1741), p. 92.

§§ Johann Christoph Adelung, Versuch eines vollständigen grammatisch-kritischen Wörterbuchs der hochdeutschen Mundart, mit beständiger Vergleichung der übrigen Mundarten, besonders aber der Oberdeutschen 2 (Leipzig, 1775), 1446; and Johann Christoph Adelung, Grammatisch-kritisches Wörterbuch der hochdeutschen Mundart 2, 2nd ed. (Leipzig, 1796), 1445, http://www.woerterbuchnetz.de/Adelung?lemma=judenthum.

(1807–1811), in which the description of "die Gebräuche" (practices) is intro-*
duced, which is then continued, presumably by taking in translations of
Judaismus.

A dictionary that particularly focuses on the contemporary language of
that time is the work of the Jewish dictionary author Daniel Sanders. He did
not include the key word Judentum *in this work. Only in his supplement*
dictionary (1885)[†] he included a lemma for Judentum *with evidence that*
criticized from a Jewish perspective the use of Judentum to denote
Jewish people.

Willmans[‡] notes regarding the word formation of Judenthum *that the*
-thum formations in Old High German were masculine. They are usually
combined with substantives mostly with a personal meaning. The formations
with -tuom are denoted by "Würde und Stand, Sitte und Gewohnheit"[§] (dig-
nity and stand, convention and manner). Willmans notes further that it is very
close to the formation of -heit and -schaft. Such can similarly be found in
Henzen, who concludes regarding the meaning of this derivation, "Sie
schwankt vom Abstrakten zu Konkreten verschiedener Färbung, wahllos dabei
in das Revier der Suffixe -heit und -schaft übergreifend (besonders bei
Eigenschafts- und Kollektivbezeichnungen)"[¶] (It fluctuates between abstract
and concrete of the different coloring, randomly interfering with the grounds
of the suffixation -heit and -schaft [especially in the feature and collective
descriptions]). The change of gender, which is generally shown in Wilmanns's
-tuom formation, is proven in the dictionaries: Old High German and Middle
Low German list "Judentum" as a masculine word while in Early Modern
High German it became a neuter.

---

[*]   Joachim Heinrich Campe, Wörterbuch der deutschen Sprache 2 (Braunschweig, 1808),
      852.
[†]   Daniel Sanders, Ergänzungs-Wörterbuch der deutschen Sprache: Eine Vervollständi-
      gung und Erweiterung aller bisher erschienenen deutschsprachlichen Wörterbücher
      (einschließlich des Grimm'schen), Mit Belegen von Luther bis auf die neueste Gegen-
      wart (Berlin, 1885), 288.
[‡]   Wilhelm Wilmanns, Deutsche Grammatik. Gotisch, Alt-, Mittel- und Neuhochdeutsch,
      Zweite Abteilung: Wortbildung (vol. 2, II, 1) 2nd ed. (Berlin, 1930), 392f.
[§]   Wilmanns, Deutsche Grammatik, 392f.
[¶]   Walter Henzen, Deutsche Wortbildung, Halle (Saale, 1947), 193.

Epilogue

Talal Asad has indicted the stakes involved here: "the attribution of implicit meanings to an alien practice regardless of whether they are acknowledged by its agents is a characteristic form of theological exercise, with an ancient history."[1] I have argued here that this is the case with attributing the concept of a "religion," "Judaism," to premodern Jews who acknowledged no such meaning to their practice. Even until our present moment, moreover, it could be defensibly argued that modern "Judaism" both is and is not a "religion." On the one hand, for many purposes, it—like Hinduism—operates as a religion within multireligious societies. Contemporary Jews claim for their religion a semantic, cultural status parallel to that of Christianity in the West. We study Judaism in programs of religious studies, claim religious freedom, have sections on Judaism at the American Academy of Religion—even one on comparative Judaism and Hinduism—and in general function as members of a "faith"—or system of ultimate meaning, or whatever—among other faiths. On the other hand, there are many ways that we continue to be uncomfortable and express our discomfort with this very definition. For both Zionists and many non-Zionist Jews (including me), versions of description or practice with respect to Judaism that treat it as a faith that can be separated from ethnicity, nationality, language, and shared history have felt false. Precisely that very position of Judaism at the American Academy of Religion has been experienced by us, sometimes, as in itself a form of ambivalently capitulating behavior (which is not, I hasten to add, altogether unpleasurable). Something about the difference between Judaism and Christianity is captured precisely by insisting on the ways that Judaism is not now, and never was, a religion—for Jews.[2] When Jews teach Judaism in a department of religious studies, they are as likely to be teaching Yiddish literature or the history of the Nazi genocide as anything that might be said (in Christian terms) to be part of a Jewish religion!

Jonathan Boyarin writes, "The question of the imbalance between a totalizing categorical usage of the term 'diaspora' and the discourses within various diasporic formations that may not recognize that category leads us to the necessary recognition that whatever the criterion for judging our own discourse may be, it cannot rest on a simplistic notion of pluralist (different but in the same ways) tolerance."[3] Empowered by the Christian interpellation of Judaism as a religion, the Jews, nevertheless, significantly resisted the (ambiguous) tolerance enacted by the Theodosian Empire's emplacement of a "frontier all the more mysterious . . . because it is abstract, legal, ideal."[4] Refusing to be different in quite the same ways—not a religion, not quite—Judaism (including the bizarrely named Jewish orthodoxy of modernity) remained something else, neither quite here nor quite there. Among the various emblems of this different difference remains the fact that there are Christians who are Jews, or perhaps better put, Jews who are Christians, even up to this very day.

What is, then, the value of theory for this kind of research? It is an *askesis* designed to help us avoid the dogmatism that adheres to us when we do not realize that it is dogmatism, an *askesis* that helps us learn not to look at other languages with lenses entirely constructed of our own. *Askesis* implies a rigorous practice by which we train ourselves over and over and over many years. In other words, I study theory such as Wittgenstein's and Lienhardt's to help me disentangle myself from anachronistic conceptual frameworks (also known as theory); fire fighting fire, as it were. As Lienhardt—and before him Benjamin and Pannwitz and, after him, Asad—has realized, some or another version of a deformation of our language is imperative for us to translate another form of life.

Since the statement "Judaism exists" makes no ontological sense and only has meaning in a language in which the word "Judaism" (or an equivalent) exists, it would follow that any talk of "Judaism" in antiquity, or in the Middle Ages for that matter, is *eo ipso* an ideological intervention, an assertion of the timelessness of the Christian concept "Judaism," a Form in the Platonic sense that can exist without anyone knowing that it does. Since "to imagine a language means to imagine a form of life" [PI §19], a language that has no word "Judaism" has no Judaism as part of the form of life. For us to imagine that form of life would require the fashioning of a language without "Judaism." We can learn from colonized peoples, who have always done this, how to make a language speak the language of the other. Just as they have had to imagine a form of life with "religion" in it, and we must needs imagine forms of life with no religion, so if Jews had no word that corresponds to "Judaism," we must be able to describe Jewish "doings" that don't incorporate a concept for the Jewish religion. It is marking the very differences between "us" and "them" that constitutes cultural translation, even (especially) when we have met them and they seem to be us.

There is a kind of comfort and certainly self-authentication in finding ourselves in the past, but finding an other there can be an even richer and more wonderful experience. Sheldon Pollock has recently written, "At the same time, and more positively now, philology on Plane 1 (historicism) helps us to better comprehend the nature, or natures, of human existence and the radical differences it has shown over time, that is, the vast variety of ways of being human."[5] I would cite this sentence as a kind of credo. For Camus, the strongest motivation for letting another individual be herself, an other and not a reflection of self, is to avoid being alone in the world. Similarly, letting the others, even our own ancestors, be as truly themselves as we can allow them, as complexly different from us as we can imagine them, expands our sense of the myriad forms of life that humans have produced and has the potential to render the imagined potentialities of our own collective human lives immeasurably richer as well.[6] In investigating different languages, we investigate different forms of life and imagine different possibilities.[7] As Wittgenstein himself wrote, and on a very similar philosophical occasion, "Our world looks quite different if we surround it with different possibilities."[8]

Greenfield, December 31, 2017

Acknowledgments

I had first thought to dedicate this book to Max, Max, and Alex in recognition of the tremendous support I have received from the Max Planck Institute for the History of Knowledge (Berlin) and its director, Professor Lorraine Daston, who supported my residency there in the summer of 2016, from the Max Weber Kolleg in Erfurt and its directors, Professors Jörg Rüpke and Martin Mulsow, who hosted me in the fall of 2016, and especially to the Alexander von Humboldt Foundation, which awarded me a von Humboldt Senior Research Prize for the spring and summer of 2017. This munificent and magnificent support for the "human sciences" in Germany is a ray of light in a dark world. Professor Dr. Rainer Kempling and Professor Dr. Markham Geller performed above and beyond the call of any possible duty in producing the incredibly demanding application for that prize and have made my stay here richer and more productive in many ways. In the end, I made a better, warmer, and more appropriate dedication to the most meaningful support and friend behind this book, but there are still many to thank.

To scholar friends at the Freie Universität who hosted me during the tenure of the von Humboldt Fellowship, I am also exceedingly grateful, including again Professors Kempling and Geller, Professor Florentina Badalanova Geller, Professor Tal Ilan, Dr. Islam Dayeh, Dr. Nora Schmidt, and Dr. Hannah Tzuberi. To the great support staff at the FU Seminar für Katholische Theologie (may it survive and thrive), Sara Han, Matthias Adrian, and my student helper Boris Kaplunovitch, who performed yeoman service and more.

I wish to thank the organizers of the Bampton Lectures in America, which enabled me to present my discussion of ancient *Ioudaismos* for the first time, and thank as well the amazing audiences at Columbia University who heard and commented on those lectures. I am grateful to audiences at Brown University, the Graduate Theological Union, Institute for Cultural Inquiry (Berlin), Spree-Athen (Berlin), the Max Weber Kolleg in Erfurt, as well as the Universities of Berlin (FU and von Humboldt), Bonn, Düsseldorf, Erfurt, Frankfurt, Halle, Münster, Nantes, and the Luther Propaganda Seminar in Jena, where chapters or parts of chapters of this book were "tried out." The audiences in all of those venues were helpfully critical.

This book was written with a little help from my friends (actually quite a bit).

I stepped out of my comfort zone to produce this synthetic study. Professor Eliyahu Stern helped me crucially with modernity, the existence of which I had barely suspected beforehand; Professor Amos Bitzan was similarly helpful with matters of his specialty. Drs. Islam Dayeh, Nora Schmidt, and Lena Salaymeh offered crucial aid with the Arabic of the Kuzari; Professor Yosef Schwartz read the Kuzari chapter and made invaluable comments (and gave me confidence with his endorsement of the argument; all faults remain mine). Professor Shamma Boyarin helped as well with some of the medieval and early modern texts, Professor Elliot Wolfson with the extremely difficult Abraham Abulafia, and Professor Dr. Florentina Geller with the Old Church Slavonic text in chapter 3. Early readers of parts or all of the manuscript included Professor Carlin A. Barton and Professor Jonathan Boyarin, who both kept me off blind alleys and showed me light at the end of tunnels. My colleague and friend Professor James Porter read the manuscript toward the end of its gestation and also helped me avoid pitfalls and not miss the point. Prof. Chana Kronfeld was, as usual, enormously helpful with details of Yiddish and early modern Hebrew philology and more. Only I, of course, am responsible for the synthesis and its failures.

The editors of this series were helpful above and beyond the call of editorial duty, and I am very grateful to them, as well. Andy Bush's tough love and ability to see where an argument contradicts itself were invaluable, and Deborah Dash Moore tried her best with my style and to make me clearer (all failings that remain are my own damn fault).

Thanks as well to Lisa Milloy, masseuse nonpareil, who helped keep body and soul together when the soul and its bent-over exertions threatened to overwhelm the body.

Notes

PREFACE — WHAT ARE WE TALKING ABOUT WHEN WE TALK ABOUT
"JUDAISM"?

1. John J. Collins, "Cult and Culture: The Limits of Hellenization in Judea," in *Hellenism in the Land of Israel*, ed. John J. Collins and Gregory Sterling, Christianity and Judaism in Antiquity (Notre Dame, IN: University of Notre Dame, 2000), 39.

2. The discussion in Brent Nongbri, "Paul without Religion: The Creation of a Category and the Search for an Apostle beyond the New Perspective" (PhD diss., Yale University, 2008) would make a fine starting point.

CHAPTER I — THE DEBATE OF THE TERMS

1. Daniel Dubuisson, *The Western Construction of Religion: Myths, Knowledge, and Ideology*, trans. William Sayers (Baltimore: Johns Hopkins University Press, 2003), 38.

2. Arnaldo Momigliano, "The Rules of the Game in the Study of Ancient History," trans. Kenneth W. Yu, *History & Theory* 55, no. 1 (2016): 39–45, reprint, 1974,

3. Seth Schwartz, "How Many Judaisms Were There? A Critique of Neusner and Smith on Definition and Mason and Boyarin on Categorization," *Journal of Ancient Judaism* 2, no. 2 (2011): 238. See too Quentin Skinner, "Meaning and Understanding in the History of Ideas," *History and Theory* 8 (1969): 24.

4. See the illuminating discussions in Naomi Seidman, *Faithful Renderings: Jewish-Christian Difference and the Politics of Translation*, Afterlives of the Bible (Chicago: University of Chicago Press, 2006), esp. 93–94. This discussion was crucial for me in developing my thoughts here.

5. See too in support of this point, "We may tend to assume that in discussing *mageia* or *sacerdos* or *thusia* or *sacrificium* as 'magic' or 'priest' and 'sacrifice' we are reflecting the 'emic' sensibilities of the Greeks or Romans whose voices we are interpreting, but this is quite erroneous" (David Frankfurter, "Comparison and the Study of Religions in Late Antiquity," in *Comparer en Histoire Des Religions Antiques: Controverses et Propositions*, ed. Claude Calame and Bruce Lincoln, Religions 1 [Liège: Presses universitaires de Liège, 2012], 88). I agree totally (and am pleased to note Frankfurter's ironizing of "emic" here). I am perhaps less convinced than Frankfurter that it is *only* through comparative work that the gross distortions can be rectified but allow for the possibility that I am wrong. On the cost to comparison of greater accuracy and nuance in description, see the following:

By this account of the matter, the first consequence of the adoption of polythetic classification in social anthropology is that comparative studies, whether
morphological or functional or statistical, are rendered more daunting and
perhaps even unfeasible. Yet polythetic classes are likely to accommodate better
than monothetic the variegation of social phenomena: they have, as Sokal and
Sneath put it, a high content of information, and they carry less risk of an arbi-
trary exclusion of significant features. In other words, it could be said, the
polythetic principle is truer to the ethnographic materials. If this is so, then
the increased difficulty of comparison is a price that simply has to be paid—if
there is some way of meeting it. (R. Needham, "Polythetic Classification: Convergence and Consequences," *Man* n.s. 10 [1975]: 359)

There is a final point to be made here and elsewhere. The field typically contrasts
"emic" as the view of the insider and "etic" as the view of the outsider scientist; this is
simply inadequate. "Emic" analysis, if it means anything, means discovering and
describing what distinctions make a difference within the culture that one is analyzing,
even when the insiders only tacitly know this or even deny it—for instance, being told
by informants that first-cousin marriages are forbidden and then finding several
examples. "Etic" can mean only one of two things: either describing many distinctions
that make no difference in the culture in question (as phonetic analysis in linguistics
does) or, and this is more useful, naming the analyst's "subsequent attempt to take the
descriptive information they have already gathered and to organize, systematize,
compare—in a word, to redescribe—that information in terms of a system of their
own making." Russell T. McCutcheon, ed., *The Insider / Outsider Problem in the Study of
Religion: A Reader*, Controversies in the Study of Religion (London: Cassell, 1999), 17
(from the editor's introduction). I am much more interested in discovering the systems
of their making than in making systems of my own.

6. Talal Asad, "The Concept of Cultural Translation in British Social Anthropology,"
in *Writing Culture: The Poetics and Politics of Ethnography*, ed. James Clifford and
George E. Marcus (Berkeley: University of California Press, 1986), 151.

7. Cited in Walter Benjamin, "The Task of the Translator," in *Walter Benjamin: Selected
Writings*. Vol. 1, *1913–1926*, ed. Marcus Bullock and Michael W. Jennings. [1913–1926.]
[Selections. English] (Cambridge, MA: Belknap Press of Harvard University Press,
1996), 261–262. See Arnold Krupat, *Ethnocriticism: Ethnography, History, Literature* (Berkeley: University of California Press, 1992), 196–198, on different modes of appropriation
of Benjamin / Pannwitz. Cf. Jonathan Z. Smith, *Relating Religion: Essays in the Study of
Religion* (Chicago: University of Chicago Press, 2004), 269–270, for a very different—nearly
opposite—use of the figure of "stretching" an old language.

8. Lilith Acadia, "Discourses of 'Religion'" (unpublished manuscript, University of
California, Berkeley, 2016), referring to Talal Asad, *Genealogies of Religion: Discipline and*

Reasons of Power in Christianity and Islam (Baltimore: Johns Hopkins University Press, 1993), 24.

9. Asad, "Cultural Translation."

10. Godfrey Lienhardt, "Modes of Thought," in *The Institutions of Primitive Society, a Series of Broadcast Talks*, ed. and comp. E. E. Evans-Pritchard and et al. (Glencoe, IL: Free Press, 1954), 96–97.

11. James I. Porter, personal communication. Cultures, are, of course (all cultures) incoherent as often as they are coherent. Cf. "I want to insist that to argue for a form of coherence by which a discourse is held together is not ipso facto to justify or defend that discourse; it is merely to take an essential step in the problem of explaining its *compulsiveness*" (Asad, "Cultural Translation," 145–146). Agreeing with Asad, I would nonetheless want to argue for something less than coherence, as things can make sense within the doings of a collective even if they contradict other things that make sense there too. For this issue, see Skinner, "Meaning and Understanding," 16–18. Asad, it seems, emphasizes "coherence" in a context in which it was regularly insisted that "primitive thought" was *incoherent* as a form of reproach (Skinner, 18.)

12. Smith, "Trading Places," in *Relating Religion*, 221–222. For further elaboration of his approach, see too Smith, *Relating Religion*, 30–32. The best and most attractive of Smith's presentations of his theoretical approach is "A Twice-Told Tale: The History of the History of Religion's History," in *Relating Religion*, 362–374, but even that one does not convince me for reasons that I can only give here the "chapter headings" for: (1) There are not "two orders" in Smith's own account but three, one of which he simply ignores. Let us call the first order the "raw data" that an anthropologist—any kind of anthropologist, including a philologian—finds with respect to a given form of life. The second order is, then, to be understood as the sense that people in the given collective give to their doings, including their verbal doings. The third order would be, then (equivalent to Smith's second order), some other kind of sense that analysts from the outside mobilizing their own cultural norms and "stipulative procedures" provide. It is no accident that Smith glosses over what I (having learned this from my colleague Anders Klostergaard Peterson) call here the "second order"—namely, the categories and understandings that the doers give to their doings, the ways that they understand the world. This does not simply collapse into the "raw data" of, say, an acoustic (= phonetic) description but requires careful and lengthy study of the language and other data available for that form of life to uncover those understandings, especially the ones that are inchoate. An "outsider" category such as "religion" can only interfere with that discovery. Note that this does not preclude either diachronic analysis (this once meant x but later it means y) or the critical uncovering of unarticulated meanings and categories. (2) Phonetic (in its anthropological form, amputated to give the unfortunate "etic") is in no way a superior mode of analysis as the linguistic analogy demonstrates, for phonemic (emic) analysis provides for the units of meaningful distinction within the language while phonetic (etic) only gives us physical

information without any rendering of meaning or structure possible. It follows from these two premises that the object of analysis is as complete and subtle an account of the data observed and a rigorous attempt to understand the categories and representations within which "they" understood what is, after all, *their* world. If the object is not to understand what "they" consider "magic" and how they interpret it, then what could it possibly be? I emphasize, once more, that not all meanings are articulated.

13. See too, "In all such cases, the coherence or lack of it which is thus discovered very readily ceases to be an historical account of any thoughts which were ever actually thought. The history thus written becomes a history not of ideas at all, but of abstractions: a history of thoughts which no one ever actually succeeded in thinking, at a level of coherence which no one ever actually attained" (Skinner, "Meaning and Understanding," 18.)

14. See the following:

> Thus, the anthropological concept of culture, for example, as Wagner argued, is the equivocation that emerges as an attempt to solve intercultural equivocality, and it is equivocal in so far as it follows, among other things, from the "paradox created by imagining a culture for people who do not imagine it for themselves" (1981:27) [a fortiori, a religion, adds Boyarin]. Accordingly, even when misunderstandings are transformed into understandings—like when the anthropologist transforms his initial bewilderment at the natives' ways into "their culture," or when the natives understand that what the Whites called, say, "gifts" were in reality "commodities"—even here such understandings persist in being not the same. The Other of the Others is always other. If the equivocation is not an error, an illusion or a lie, but the very form of the relational positivity of difference, its opposite is not the truth, but the univocal, as the claim to the existence of a unique and transcendent meaning. The error or illusion par excellence consists, precisely, in imagining that the univocal exists beneath the equivocal, and that the anthropologist is its ventriloquist. (Eduardo Viveiros de Castro, "Perspectival Anthropology and the Method of Controlled Equivocation," *Tipití: Journal of the Society for the Anthropology of Lowland South America* 2, no. 1 [2004]: 12)

15. Cf. Smith again: "One cannot escape the suspicion that it is precisely this latter possibility (speaking the other language) that defines the goal of many students of religion" (Smith, *Relating Religion*, 31). Guilty as charged! Smith seems there to equate the desire to speak the other language and make our language speak it as well with "those scholars who would emphasize totality and congruency when describing religion." This is a non sequitur; one can surely be as committed as Smith to the partiality of understanding, to its fragmentary and provisional status, to the need for constant rectification (corrigibility), without subscribing to his program of the comparison of "second order" redescriptions.

16. Viveiros de Castro, "Perspectival Anthropology," 5.

17. Asad, "Cultural Translation," 147.

18. As Asad puts it, "Here I draw attention briefly to Lienhardt's use of the word 'translation' to refer not to linguistic matter per se, but to 'modes of thought' that are embodied in such matter" (Asad, "Cultural Translation," 142). Viveiros de Castro again: "Therefore, the aim of perspectivist translation—translation being one of shamanism's principal tasks, as we know (Carneiro da Cunha 1998)—is not that of finding a 'synonym' (a co-referential representation) in our human conceptual language for the representations that other species of subject use to speak about one and the same thing. Rather, the aim is to avoid losing sight of the difference concealed within equivocal 'synonyms' between our language and that of other species, since we and they are never talking about the same things" (Viveiros de Castro, "Perspectival Anthropology," 7).

19. Asad, "Cultural Translation," 151. Wittgenstein apparently himself authorized "way of living" as a translation for *Lebensform*. See discussion in Anna Boncompagni, "Elucidating Forms of Life: The Evolution of a Philosophical Tool," in "Wittgenstein and Forms of Life," special issue, *Nordic Wittgenstein Review* (2015): 158.

20. See on this Asad, "Cultural Translation," 157. For a brilliant account of what happens when this principle is not observed, too lengthy even to summarize here, see Viveiros de Castro, "Perspectival Anthropology," 17.

21. P. M. S. Hacker, "Forms of Life," in "Wittgenstein and Forms of Life," special issue, *Nordic Wittgenstein Review* (2015): 17.

22. Theodor W. Adorno, "The Essay as Form," in *Notes to Literature. Vol. 1*, ed. Rolf Tiedemann, trans. Shierry Weber Nicholsen, European Perspectives (New York: Columbia University Press, 1991), 13.

23. Cf. Smith to the following by Adorno: "If science and scholarship, falsifying as is their custom, reduce what is difficult and complex in a reality that is antagonistic and split into monads to simplified models and then differentiate the models in terms of their ostensible material, the essay, in contrast, shakes off the illusion of a simple and fundamentally logical world, an illusion well suited to the defense of the status quo" (Adorno, 15).

24. I would go so far as to suggest that one of the reasons that it became comfortable at a certain time to speak of "Judaisms" in antiquity is that we perceive Judaisms in our world.

25. Adorno, "The Essay as Form," 11.

26. Benson Saler, "Religio and the Definition of Religion," *Cultural Anthropology* 2, no. 3 (1987): 398.

27. Inter alia, Annette Yoshiko Reed has pointed to the contours of ancient knowledge production that are encompassed by neither modern "science" nor "religion." Annette Yoshiko Reed, "'Ancient Jewish Sciences' and the Historiography of Judaism," in

Ancient Jewish Sciences and the History of Knowledge in Second Temple Literature, ed. Jonathan Ben-Dov and Seth Sanders (New York: New York University Press, 2013), 201.

28. It is hardly my intention here to propose that there is one true reading of the past text. I am rather insisting that the attempt at as nuanced and complex a reading of the "other" language as possible is an increase in knowledge. See Sheldon Pollock, "Philology in Three Dimensions," *Postmedieval: A Journal of Medieval Cultural Studies* 5 (2014): 406. Note that this version of translation has little in common with what Smith faults as mere restatement in the lack of discrepancy between datum and model as in Christian descriptions of the New Testament wherein "the model remains essentially as a paraphrase" (Smith, *Relating Religion*, 206.) Let me put this another way. If, as Smith remarks and I tend to agree, the arguments produced in NT studies, for example, are frequently more like the data analyzed in other branches of the human sciences than like the arguments advanced as the results of such analysis, this does not free us of the requirement to carefully analyze those data in actors' (NT scholars who are committed Christians) terms.

29. Cf. Asad, "Cultural Translation," 162.

30. This does not, however, necessitate the positing of unconscious meaning. As Asad has remarked, once more, "Here I want to note that reference to the linguistic patterns produced by speakers does not make a good analogy because linguistic patterns are not meanings to be translated, they are rules to be systematically described and analysed. A native speaker is aware of how such patterns should be produced even when he cannot verbalize that knowledge explicitly in the form of rules. The apparent lack of ability to verbalize such social knowledge does not necessarily constitute evidence of unconscious meanings" (Asad, 161). See on this exact point as well Skinner, "Meaning and Understanding," 28–29.

31. Cf. once more:

There is "all the difference in the world" (Wagner 1981:51) between a world where the primordial is experienced as naked transcendence, pure antianthropic alterity (the non-constructed, the non-instituted, that which is exterior to custom and discourse) and a world of immanent humanity, where the primordial takes on human form (which does not make it necessarily tranquilizing; for there where everything is human, the human is something else entirely). *Describing this world as though it were an illusory version of our own, unifying the two via a reduction of one to the conventions of the other, is to imagine an overly simple form of relation between them.* This explanatory ease ends up producing all sorts of uneasy complications, since this desire for ontological monism usually pays with an inflationary emission of epistemological dualisms—emic and etic, metaphoric and literal, conscious and unconscious, representation and reality, illusion and truth, et cetera. (Viveiros de Castro, "Perspectival Anthropology," 14; emphasis added)

NOTES TO PAGES 8–10   165

32. Ian Hacking, "'Style' for Historians and Philosophers," *Studies in History and Philosophy of Science Part A* 23, no. 1 (1992): 5.

33. Elenore Smith Bowen, pseudonym, *Return to Laughter* (New York: Harper, 1954).

34. P. M. S. Hacker and G. P. Baker, *Wittgenstein: Understanding and Meaning. Part I, Essays*, Analytical Commentary on the Philosophical Investigations 1 (Oxford: Blackwell, 2005), 61.

35. I find Anna Wierzbicka, *Understanding Cultures through Their Key Words: English, Russian, Polish, German, and Japanese*, Oxford Studies in Anthropological Linguistics (New York: Oxford University Press, 1997), 22–23, very useful on this necessity and on the necessity for extensive analytical work to decide what is the same and what different.

36. I am happy to grant that Smith does support this point. See especially Smith, *Relating Religion*, 383.

37. "When Nietzsche defined philology as 'slow reading' (Nietzsche, [1881] 1980a, 5), he meant, or should have meant, reading in a state of heightened self-awareness about what exactly we are doing when we are reading. Such self-awareness arises in direct proportion to the time-space distance that separates us from the origins of the text. The closer the text is, the less conscious we are of the processes by which we make sense of it: 'The more language is a living operation the less we are aware of it' (Gadamer, 1976, 65)." Pollock, "Philology in Three Dimensions," 400. I believe that this idea can be mapped onto Fischer and Marcus's idea of a function for ethnography as well: George E. Marcus and Michael M. J. Fischer, *Anthropology as Cultural Critique: An Experimental Moment in the Human Sciences* (Chicago: University of Chicago Press, 1986). See too, "No less problematic is the attempt to erase the reader's own historicity. It is less ironical than inevitable that Spinoza's own reading should reveal such presentism: as many commentators on the Tractatus have remarked, 'the true meaning' of the Bible turns out to be the meaning that conforms to Spinoza's philosophy. Finally, the proposition that there exists a singular, unchanging meaning that is entirely historicist and determined in accordance with the procedures of the natural sciences evinces a radically unhistorical understanding of meaning." Pollock, "Philology in Three Dimensions," 404.

38. Annette Yoshiko Reed, "Categorization, Collection, and the Construction of Continuity: 1 Enoch and 3 Enoch in and Beyond 'Apocalypticism' and 'Mysticism,'" *Method & Theory in the Study of Religion* 29, no. 3 (2017): 268–311.

39. Carlin A. Barton and Daniel Boyarin, *Imagine No Religion: How Modern Categories Hide Ancient Realities* (Bronx: Fordham University Press, 2016).

40. Jonathan H. Turner, et al., *The Emergence and Evolution of Religion by Means of Natural Selection*, Evolutionary Analysis in the Social Sciences (London: Routledge, 2017), 3.

41. Timothy Fitzgerald, *The Ideology of Religious Studies* (New York: Oxford University Press, 2000), and Timothy Fitzgerald, *Discourse on Civility and Barbarity: A Critical*

History of Religion and Related Categories (New York: Oxford University Press, 2007). I find Benson Saler, *Conceptualizing Religion: Immanent Anthropologists, Transcendent Natives, and Unbounded Categories*, Studies in the History of Religions, vol. 56 (Leiden: E. J. Brill, 1993), particularly useful for the way that explains the everyday usage of the term "religion" in contemporary English (somewhat misread by the otherwise excellent Fitzgerald).

42. Brent Nongbri, "Paul without Religion: The Creation of a Category and the Search for an Apostle beyond the New Perspective" (PhD diss., Yale University, 2008), 10. I subscribe as well to Nongbri's comment a page later:

> This working notion of "religion" bears a strong resemblance to the type of definition that Benson Saler developed in his important study, *Conceptualizing Religion: Immanent Anthropologists, Transcendent Natives, and Unbounded Categories* (Leiden: Brill, 1993). Saler also noted that what is needed is not a "better" or "more inclusive" definition of religion. He writes, "Religion is a word that has traditional meanings for us and for the audience for which we write, and by so widening or otherwise altering what it includes, it may well cease to have much utility as a research and literary tool" (157). Saler advocates instead a polythetic definition, relying on Wittgenstein's notion of family resemblances. He also invokes prototype theory in order to prevent the polythetic classification from being too free-floating. The prototypes he chooses are Christianity, Judaism, and Islam. *I differ from Saler in that I regard the concepts of Judaism and Islam as having been (to a large degree) constructed in the mold of Christianity by heresiologists and Christian thinkers.* (Nongbri, "Paul without Religion," 11, emphasis added)

43. Reed, "Categorization."

44. See Anders Klostergaard Petersen, review of *Imagine No Religion: How Modern Abstractions Hide Ancient Realities*, by Carlin A. Barton, Daniel Boyarin, *Bryn Mawr Classical Review* 6 (2017): 325. My junior colleague in Erfurt, Emiliano Urciuoli, where much of this book was first conceived, raised the following difficulty, and addressing it will help clarify the ambitions of this book:

> I do think that the statement about the absence of a semantically and/or functionally separated religious sphere in the past—which is true—is not the best argument for ruling out the legitimacy of the concept of "religion" for ancient folks. The problem here is less the truthfulness of the two statements than the fact that there may be no necessary connection between them.
>
> However broadly conceived as "form of life," language does not completely cover and use up what goes on at the level of social ontologies. Language and societies—to mimic Foucault when he argued against the Annales—are not transitive to each other. You perfectly recognize that when saying, few lines after, that

"any given collective—i.e.: including ancient collectives—makes distinctions that are not articulated (that are tacit, that 'go without saying')." Wonderfully said! Yet it seems to me that you do not draw all the consequences. Insofar you admit the sotto voce existence of doxai as unspoken articulations of distinctions for ancient people, the scientific task shouldn't be—I totally agree with you—to "reduce the unknown to the known," which is a colonialist move, but rather to "bring out the unspoken," or "to make it visible," which is a critical move. You rightly ban the former, but you gloss over—or exclude?—the latter.

Now, among the unspoken distinctions to bring up, I would not include the semantically and/or functionally divided spheres, but the neither necessarily Christian nor modern fields. As fields I mean, with Bourdieu, the partially autonomous social arenas differentiated from each other by the different goods at stake, the different capitals circulating within them. The fact that there is no religion, as a collectively shared abstraction setting apart a distinct set of empirical data, does not necessarily mean that there is no religious field, that is, a non-formally institutionalized sub-universe of meaningful practices, social productions and experiences, material and symbolic investments, and social recognition processes that is separated from—for instance—the public-political field less by the means of semantics and law than by its tacit logic of functioning, interests, goods, and kinds of capitals at stake. I personally reflected upon and wrote about the rise and the gradual structuration of a "Mediterranean religious field" around I-II CE. [p.c. December, 2016]

I certainly grant now the theoretical possibility (indeed perhaps necessity) that such tacit fields are present within forms of life and not directly accessibly to language but would nevertheless like to be instructed in *how* one establishes such fields for a culture unknown other than through its language. Moreover, I hope to show later how we can actively see in some cases, at any rate (the case of Josephus as an example), that this distinction of fields is actively *not* made. In any case, naming such fields a priori with such names as "religious field" seems once again to reproduce them as reductions. Wittgenstein's notion of language as *Lebensform* seems to me a more productive basis for our philological investigations (but I'm more than willing to be shown wrong).

45. Adorno, "The Essay as Form," 6.

46. George Foot Moore, *The Rise of Normative Judaism* (Cambridge: Reprinted from *Harvard Theological Review* 17, no. 4 [October 1924] and 18, no. 1 [January 1925]. Includes bibliographical references. I. To the reorganization at Jamnia–II. To the close of the Mishnah, 1925), 307.

47. Moore, 308.

48. Moore, 327.

49. George Foot Moore, "Intermediaries in Jewish Theology: Memra, Shekinah, Metatron," *Harvard Theological Review* 15, no. 1 (January 1922): 42.

50. Moore, 55.

51. Daniel Boyarin, "Daniel 7, Intertextuality, and the History of Israel's Cult," *Harvard Theological Review* 105, no. 2 (2012): 135–162.

52. Erwin R. Goodenough, *By Light, Light: The Mystic Gospel of Hellenistic Judaism* (New Haven: Yale University Press, 1935).

53. Jacob Neusner, recently deceased, was a revolutionary figure in the study of ancient Jewry, one of the first to seek to put that study right in the middle of the humanities in the American academy. He succeeded perhaps at that project more fully than in his own scholarly constructions, which have tended more and more to seem wildly overdrawn and schematized, as in the instance being presented here. I have found Michael Satlow, "Defining Judaism: Accounting for 'Religions' in the Study of Religion," *Journal of the American Academy of Religion* 74, no. 4 (2006): 843–847, very helpful in laying out Neusner's views here.

54. Jacob Neusner, *The Way of Torah: An Introduction to Judaism*, The Religious Life of Man Series (Encino, CA: Dickenson, 1974), 8.

55. Neusner, *The Way of Torah*, 7.

56. Satlow, "Defining Judaism," 845.

57. Satlow, 845.

58. Jonathan Z. Smith, *Imagining Religion: From Babylon to Jonestown* (Chicago: University of Chicago Press, 1982), 18.

59. Satlow, "Defining Judaism," 846.

60. Satlow, 847.

61. Satlow, 846–847.

62. Insofar as this would result in a kind of dialect map of features and characteristics joining and separating one group to and from the others, we might very well have a polythetic account of what joins and separates all groups that call themselves "Israel," but we have not advanced much beyond the dialect map model for describing the different proposed (or identified) "Israels." Schwartz, "How Many Judaisms," 219. This model had explicitly recognized that groups that we call "Judaisms" frequently had overlapping characteristics shared with groups that we call "Christianities" but which divided them from other groups called "Judaisms" and "Christianities," respectively. Daniel Boyarin, *Dying for God: Martyrdom and the Making of Christianity and Judaism*, The Lancaster/Yarnton Lectures in Judaism and Other Religions for 1998 (Stanford: Stanford University Press, 1999). Seth Schwartz is exactly right in claiming that such polythetic methods end up including much of what we (or even they) called Christianity within the same complex as rabbinic, Qumran, and other groups and texts. For me—and, I imagine, for Satlow—this is not a negative consequence. Schwartz's general critique of polytheticism (including mine but especially J. Z. Smith's) is well worth reading carefully ("How Many Judaisms," 219–221), although, naturally, I am much less

concerned than Schwartz to find a way to place a boundary between "Judaism" and "Christianity" prior to the fourth century.

63. Cf. Daniel Boyarin, "Beyond Judaisms: Meṭaṭron and the Divine Polymorphy of Ancient Judaism," *Journal for the Study of Judaism in the Persian, Hellenistic, and Roman Periods* 41 (July 2010): 323–365, among others for the "inter alia."

64. Shaye J. D. Cohen, *The Beginnings of Jewishness: Boundaries, Varieties, Uncertainties*, Hellenistic Culture and Society 31 (Berkeley: University of California Press, 1998).

65. Paula Fredriksen, "Mandatory Retirement: Ideas in the Study of Christian Origins Whose Time Has Come to Go," *Studies in Religion* 35, no. 2 (2006): 231–246.

66. Elizabeth A. Castelli, *Martyrdom and Memory: Early Christian Culture-Making* (New York: Columbia University Press, 2004), 50.

67. Schwartz, "How Many Judaisms," 233.

68. Οἰδὼν δὲ Αχιὼρ πάντα, ὅσα ἐποίησεν ὁ Θεὸς τοῦ Ἰσραήλ, ἐπίστευσε τῷ Θεῷ σφόδρα καὶ περιετέμετο τὴν σάρκα τῆς ἀκροβυστίας αὐτοῦ καὶ προσετέθη πρὸς τὸν οἶκον Ἰσραὴλ ἕως τῆς ἡμέρας ταύτης.

69. Matthew Thiessen, *Contesting Conversion: Genealogy, Circumcision, and Identity in Ancient Judaism and Christianity* (Oxford: Oxford University Press, 2011).

70. Schwartz, "How Many Judaisms," 238.

71. Saler, "Religio," 395.

72. Cited as a personal communication in Brent Nongbri, *Before Religion: A History of a Modern Concept* (New Haven: Yale University Press, 2013), 156.

73. Barton and Boyarin, *Imagine No Religion*.

74. This section of the current chapter is a much abridged version of part of that study (Barton and Boyarin, 123–151.)

75. Barton and Boyarin, *Imagine No Religion*, 15–52.

76. My systematic disagreement with him on this point does not in any way qualify the myriad ways that my work and I have learned from him over the years.

77. "Some people, when they see a word, think the first thing to do is to define it. Dictionaries are produced and, with a show of authority no less confident because it is usually so limited in place and time, what is called a proper meaning is attached. I once began collecting, from correspondence in newspapers, and from other public arguments, variations on the phrases 'I see from my Webster' and 'I find from my Oxford Dictionary.' Usually what was at issue was a difficult term in an argument. But the effective tone of these phrases, . . . was to appropriate a meaning which fitted the argument and to exclude those meanings which were inconvenient to it but which some benighted person had been so foolish as to use." Raymond Williams, *Keywords: A Vocabulary of Culture and Society* (Oxford: Oxford University Press, 2015), xxviii–xxix.

See too the following:

Philosophy has arrived at a thoroughgoing critique of definitions from the most divergent perspectives—in Kant, in Hegel, in Nietzsche. But science has never adopted this critique. Whereas the movement that begins with Kant, a movement against the scholastic residues in modern thought, replaces verbal definitions with an understanding of concepts in terms of the process through which they are produced, the individual sciences [including in this case the science of religion, the Wissenschaft des Judentums, DB], in order to prevent the security of their operations from being disturbed, still insist on the pre-critical obligation to define. (Adorno, "The Essay as Form," 12)

78. Daniel R. Schwartz, *Judeans and Jews: Four Faces of Dichotomy in Ancient Jewish History*, Kenneth Michael Tanenbaum Series in Jewish Studies (2014), 93.

79. The following few paragraphs are taken from Barton and Boyarin, *Imagine No Religion*, 124–127.

80. Carlin A. Barton, *Roman Honor: The Fire in the Bones* (Berkeley: University of California Press, 2001), 7.

81. The exception for Philo as for certain early Christian writers is the apologetic context in which the Empire is being importuned to allow the Jews/Christians their cult or worship alongside the others in the Empire.

82. Philo texts according to *Thesauraus Linguae Graecae*; translation my own.

83. Philo, as is well known, does not reject the "outer" performances of Jewish practice and writes sharply against those who do.

84. For Philo, it would seem, as I learn by unpacking the sentence as I have, that the notoriously-difficult-to-define *hosiotēs* refers as well to inner dispositions.

85. Lois Shawver, "Commentary on Wittgenstein's Philosophical Investigations," http://users.rcn.com/rathbone/lwtocc.htm.

86. See especially the now classic articulation of this point for history of ideas: Skinner, "Meaning and Understanding," 37.

87. An unpublished lecture of Hans Sluga's, once heard, set me thinking this way. This is where a certain understanding of Wittgenstein meets Bakhtin's "alien word" and Kristeva's "intertextuality" as well.

88. David Bloor, *Wittgenstein: A Social Theory of Knowledge*, Contemporary Social Theory (London: Macmillan, 1983), 27.

89. Stanley Cavell, *The Claim of Reason: Wittgenstein, Skepticism, Morality, and Tragedy* (Oxford: Clarendon Press, 1979), 178.

90. See Smith, *Relating Religion*, 133–134. Making a not dissimilar argument, cf. Smith, 144, n. 51. Just to clarify at this point: this is not a claim that phenomena do not exist that are not named in the language but only that the abstractions that organize phenomena into categories cannot be asserted other than through their usage in language.

91. For a version of this idea, see Wierzbicka, *Understanding Cultures*. See to start with the extraordinarily sharp statement of John Locke's, quoted there on 4. Already then, and by him, it was clearly understood that abstractions are frequently (even usually) untranslatable. It is not inapposite to observe here, although the force of this observation will appear later, that the account that J. Z. Smith (Smith, *Relating Religion*, 127–131) gives of the philological dismantling of the concept of *mana* between Durkheim and Levi-Straus matches the sorts of arguments that are being mounted against *religion* in Barton and Boyarin, *Imagine No Religion*.

92. See C. P. Jones, "῎Εθνος and γένος in Herodotus," *Classical Quarterly*, n.s., 46 (1996): 316, who, in an exemplary study, makes this point compellingly.

93. See too, "I've suggested elsewhere (Asad 1983a) that the attribution of implicit meanings to an alien practice regardless of whether they are acknowledged by its agents is a characteristic form of theological exercise, with an ancient history." Asad, "Cultural Translation," 161. Compare too Skinner's similar use of "mythology" (Skinner, "Meaning and Understanding," 7–10) or "metaphysical belief" (19–20).

94. Ludwig Wittgenstein, *Philosophische Untersuchungen* = *Philosophical Investigations*, trans. G. E. M. Anscombe, P. M. S. Hacker, and Joachim Schulte (Chichester, West Sussex, UK: Wiley-Blackwell, 2009), 11.

95. J. F. M. Hunter, "'Forms of Life' in Wittgenstein's 'Philosophical Investigations,'" *American Philosophical Quarterly* 5, no. 4 (1968): 233–243.

96. Hacker, "Forms of Life," 1–20.

97. Hacker, 2.

98. I would generally associate my view with the interpretation described in Boncompagni: "If forms of life are to be found on an empirical level, and if we identify them with the social and cultural features of a human society, then we can affirm that each human aggregate constitutes a form of life, if it is characterized by the existence of shared practices and a shared background of knowledge, language, know-how, history, culture. Each form of life is then a possible subject for anthropological research. Empirical pluralism can be associated, for instance, with Max Black, Naomi Scheman, Norman Malcolm." Boncompagni, "Elucidating Forms of Life," 165. For a good account of the problems attending "culture," see Saler, *Conceptualizing Religion*, 232–233.

99. For "form of life" as "converging on the idea of culture," see G. P. Baker, *Wittgenstein: Understanding and Meaning: Volume 1 of an Analytical Commentary on the Philosophical Investigations, Part II: Exegesis 1–184* (Hoboken: Wiley, 2008), 74. In the Brown Book, Wittgenstein observes that to imagine a language is to imagine a culture. Ludwig Wittgenstein, *Preliminary Studies for the "Philosophical Investigations," Generally Known as the Blue and Brown Books* (Oxford: Blackwell, 1969), 134. Since that book was written in English, it is clear that for him, *Lebensform* is a virtual equivalent of English "culture," but, paradoxically for English, "form of life," seems less theoretically pitfall-ridden than "culture."

100. Hacker, "Forms of Life," 18.

101. I must confess that "merely a surface ornament" confounds me quite totally.

102. Hacker so well sums up his compelling point:

> Wittgenstein's aim was to undermine such conceptions of philosophy, philoso-
> phy of logic and language [as those of Frege, Russel, and his own *Tractatus*] and
> to replace them with an anthropological and ethnological conception. Accord-
> ing to the latter (which incidentally harmonizes "in the large" with von Hum-
> boldt's observations on thought and language), language is not the totality of
> sentences that can be generated from a set of primitive indefinables, definitions,
> formation- and transformation-rules. It is rather an uncircumscribable motley
> of human activities, of the playing of language-games, in the medley of human
> life. (Hacker, "Forms of Life," 4)

103. Hacker, "Forms of Life," 11.

104. See "In recent years, scholars working on Paul have come to focus with some
urgency upon the relationship of Paul with 'Judaism,' and the unhistoricized, essential-
ized notion of 'religion' as a system of practices and beliefs leading to some sort of 'salvation' has operated unnoticed in these debates." Nongbri, "Paul without Religion," 4.

105. Laurence Foschia, "Le Nom du culte, et ses derives a l'Epoque Imperiale," in
*L'HELLENISME D'EPOQUE ROMAINE: NOUVEAUX DOCUMENTS, NOUVELLES
APPROCHES (Ler s. a. C.—111e s. p. C.) Actes du colloque international a la memoire de Louis
Robert Paris, 7–8 Juillet 2000* (Paris: De Boccard, 2004).

106. Incidentally, one clear argument against *eusebeia* being glossed as "religion" is
that it is required and practiced with respect to parents, teachers, kings, and queens,
showing that its usage simply does not match our "religion."

107. Schwartz, *Judeans and Jews*, 97–98.

108. Schwartz, 98. It needs to be said that Schwartz has simply set up a straw man
here. To the best of my knowledge, no one has ever insisted that *thrēskeia* means only
worship. What Steve Mason, Schwartz's adversary on this issue, *has* written is the following: "Josephus also favours a noun that integrates 'divine worship, ritual, cult, and
piety' (*thrēskeia*) and its cognate verb 'to worship.' Though rarely used by non-Judaean
writers the word group had some currency among other Judaean authors before Josephus picked it up. He found it singularly convenient for his claims about the Judaean
disposition toward piety and worship." Steve Mason, *The Jewish-Roman War of 66 to 74:
A Historical Inquiry* (Cambridge: Cambridge University Press, 2016).

109. This "fullness of time" still needs to be fully explored. For the nonce, see Nongbri, *Before Religion*, referring as well to earlier research.

110. The very fact that in some corpora *thrēskeia* is an antonym of *eusebeia* and in
others a virtual homonym shows strongly that it would be a mistake to consider it a

"neutral" term that only picks up semantic content from the context. It is *used* differently by different authors and, therefore, means differently. See Wierzbicka, *Understanding Cultures*, 65–68, for a similar but not identical reasoning.

111. Smith, *Relating Religion*, 17. See also Fitzgerald, *Discourse on Civility*, 21.

112. For extensive documentation of the pitfalls of ascribing "religion" to ancient Greek and Roman (including Hellenistic Jewish) societies, see Barton and Boyarin, *Imagine No Religion*.

113. See for the nonce, Weston La Barre, *The Ghost Dance: Origins of Religion* (London: Allen and Unwin, 1972). Carlin Barton is now pursuing research demonstrating precisely the same emotional realm experienced and described in accounts of the "war band" and of cultic formations.

114. Sylvie Honigman, *Tales of High Priests and Taxes: The Books of the Maccabees and the Judean Rebellion against Antiochos IV*, The S. Mark Taper Foundation Imprint in Jewish Studies (Oakland: University of California Press, 2014), 4.

115. Honigman, 17.

116. Remarkably, Saler admits this point explicitly, arguing that "most families of religion are connected in complex ways to the development of religion as a Western category, and ideas about them continue to influence how Westerners and persons educated in the West use the term religion." Saler, *Conceptualizing Religion*, 227.

117. In future work, I hope to actually describe this process in detail for particular cases.

118. Quentin Skinner, "The Idea of a Cultural Lexicon," *Essays in Criticism* 29 (1979): 207.

CHAPTER 2 — JEWRY WITHOUT JUDAISM

1. Philip R. Davies, *On the Origins of Judaism*, BibleWorld (London: Equinox, 2011), 1.

2. Davies, 4.

3. Davies, 9.

4. Davies, 11.

5. Davies, 12.

6. Matthew Thiessen, *Contesting Conversion: Genealogy, Circumcision, and Identity in Ancient Judaism and Christianity* (Oxford: Oxford University Press, 2011).

7. *Panegyricus* 50, cited in Jonathan M. Hall, *Hellenicity: Between Ethnicity and Culture* (Chicago: University of Chicago Press, 2002), 209.

8. See too Daniel R. Schwartz, "'Judean' or 'Jew'? How Should We Translate *IOUDAIOS* in Josephus?," in *Jewish Identity in the Greco-Roman World = Jüdische Identität in der Griechisch-Römischen Welt*, ed. Jörg Frey, Daniel R. Schwartz, and Stephanie Gripentrog, Ancient Judaism and Early Christianity 71 (Leiden: E. J. Brill, 2007), 3–27.

9. See also 49.22, where he again refers to the Jews as a *genos*.

10. In the same century, we also find ὁ ἡγούμενος τοῦ ἔθνους, "the governor of the province," POxy.1020.5 (iii A. D.), or in Dio Chrysostom, "ὁ τυραννήσας τοῦ ἔθνους," D.Chr.43.11.

11. Daniel R. Schwartz, *Jewish Background of Christianity*, Wissenschaftliche Untersuchungen Zum Neuen Testament (Tübingen: J. C. B. Mohr, 1992), 13.

12. Leora Batnitzky, *How Judaism Became a Religion: An Introduction to Modern Jewish Thought* (Princeton: Princeton University Press, 2011).

13. Yehoshua Amir, "The Term Ιουδαϊσμός: On the Self Understanding of Hellenistic Judaism," in *Proceedings of the Fifth World Congress of Jewish Studies, the Hebrew University, Mount Scopus-Givat Ram, Jerusalem, Jerusalem [Sic], 3–11 August, 1969*, ed. Pinchas Peli (Jerusalem: World Union of Jewish Studies, 1972–1973), 264.

14. Amir, "The Term Ιουδαϊσμός," 265.

15. See, for example, 2 Maccabees 4:13: ἦν δ᾽ οὕτως ἀκμή τις Ἑλληνισμοῦ καὶ πρόσβασις ἀλλοφυλισμοῦ διὰ τὴν τοῦ ἀσεβοῦς καὶ οὐκ ἀρχιερέως Ἰάσωνος ὑπερβάλλουσαν ἀναγνείαν, which Schwartz translates as "and there was such an apogee of Hellenism and inroad of foreignism due to the extreme impurity of that impious and unhighpriestly Jason." In a context in which behaving ("improperly") like a Greek would be designed *Hellēnismos* and even *alluphulismos* acting like a foreigner can be found, it is hardly surprising to find the antonym of these as *Ioudaismos*.

16. Amir, "The Term Ιουδαϊσμός," 266.

17. Steve Mason, "Jews, Judaeans, Judaizing, Judaism: Problems of Categorization in Ancient History." *Journal for the Study of Judaism* 38, no. 4–5 (2007), 465.

18. Mason, 467.

19. Inter alia in Daniel Boyarin, "Semantic Differences: Linguistics and 'the Parting of the Ways,'" in *The Ways That Never Parted: Jews and Christians in Late Antiquity and the Early Middle Ages*, ed. Adam H. Becker and Annette Yoshiko Reed, Texte und Studien Zum Antiken Judentum 95 (Tübingen: Mohr Siebeck, 2003), 65–85. The point about *Ioudaismos* had, moreover, already been anticipated as far back as Jonathan A. Goldstein, trans. and ed., *II Maccabees: A New Translation with Introduction and Commentary*, The Anchor Bible 41a (New York: Doubleday, 1983). There may be no doubt that Mason worked out the argument and strengthened it decisively in his thorough paper.

20. Mason, "Jews, Judaeans, Judaizing, Judaism." Let it, nonetheless, be said clearly that (as Seth Schwartz has already noted) I have accepted some of Mason's conclusions and not others (I see, however, no flaw in that; we are, after all, dealing here in scholarly "facts" and their interpretation, not authority).

21. Cf. Martha Himmelfarb, "Judaism and Hellenism in 2 Maccabees," *Poetics Today* 19 (1998): 196. I think that Himmelfarb gets this one (uncharacteristically) exactly upside

down. Starting from *Ioudaismos* as the given and translating it as "Judaism," she assumes that *Hellēnismos* here must mean "Hellenism," not "Hellenizing."

22. It does need to be conceded that as attested in the literature, *Hellēnismos* generally is used positively and quite restricted to writing style. Nonetheless, given the productivity of this paradigm, and especially its utility for "othering," *hellēnizō* would seem to be a perfectly ordinary formation to indicate Judeans acting like Greeks and being loyal to the Hellenic cause.

23. K. J. Dover, *Aristophanic Comedy* (Berkeley: University of California Press, 1972), 214.

24. Ραζὶς δέ τις τῶν ἀπὸ Ἰεροσολύμων πρεσβυτέρων ἐμηνύθη τῷ Νικάνορι, ἀνὴρ φιλοπολίτης καὶ σφόδρα καλῶς ἀκούων καὶ κατὰ τὴν εὔνοιαν πατὴρ τῶν Ἰουδαίων προσαγορευόμενος. 38 ἦν γὰρ ἐν τοῖς ἔμπροσθεν χρόνοις τῆς ἀμειξίας κρίσιν εἰσενηνεγμένος Ἰουδαϊσμοῦ, καὶ σῶμα καὶ ψυχὴν ὑπὲρ τοῦ Ἰουδαϊσμοῦ παραβεβλημένος μετὰ πάσης ἐκτενίας. Translation by Daniel R. Schwartz, *2 Maccabees*, Commentaries on Early Jewish Literature (CEJL) (Berlin: Walter de Gruyter, 2008), 465.

25. Ἰουδας δὲ ὁ καὶ Μακκαβαῖος καὶ οἱ σὺν αὐτῷ παρεισπορευόμενοι λεληθότως εἰς τὰς κώμας προσεκαλοῦντο τοὺς συγγενεῖς καὶ τοὺς μεμενηκότας ἐν τῷ Ἰουδαϊσμῷ προσλαμβανόμενοι συνήγαγον εἰς ἑξακισχιλίους.

26. Seth Schwartz, "How Many Judaisms Were There? A Critique of Neusner and Smith on Definition and Mason and Boyarin on Categorization," *Journal of Ancient Judaism* 2, no. 2 (2011), 225.

27. Schwartz, 226.

28. οἱ μὲν οὖν οὕτως ὠμῶς ἀπεσφάγησαν ἅπαντες πλὴν Μετιλίου, τοῦτον γὰρ ἱκετεύσαντα καὶ μέχρι περιτομῆς ἰουδαΐσειν ὑποσχόμενον διέσωσαν μόνον, τὸ δὲ πάθος Ῥωμαίοις μὲν ἦν κοῦφον, ἐκ γὰρ ἀπλέτου δυνάμεως ἀπαναλώθησαν ὀλίγοι, Ἰουδαίων δὲ προοίμιον ἁλώσεως ἔδοξεν.

29. καὶ τὰς μὲν ἡμέρας ἐν αἵματι διῆγον, τὰς δὲ νύκτας δέει χαλεπωτέρας· καὶ γὰρ ἀπεσκευάσθαι τοὺς Ἰουδαίους δοκοῦντες ἕκαστοι τοὺς ἰουδαΐζοντας εἶχον ἐν ὑποψίᾳ, καὶ τὸ παρ' ἑκάστοις ἀμφίβολον οὔτε ἀνελεῖν τις προχείρως ὑπέμενεν καὶ μεμιγμένον ὡς βεβαίως ἀλλόφυλον ἐφοβεῖτο.

30. Goldstein, *II Maccabees*, 230, n. 13.

31. καὶ τὰς ἐξ οὐρανοῦ γενομένας ἐπιφανείας τοῖς ὑπὲρ τοῦ Ἰουδαϊσμοῦ φιλοτίμως ἀνδραγαθήσασιν ὥστε τὴν ὅλην χώραν ὀλίγους ὄντας λεηλατεῖν καὶ τὰ βάρβαρα πλήθη διώκειν. Translation slightly modified from Daniel R. Schwartz, *2 Maccabees*, 170. See next note.

32. Goldstein writes, "Vied with one another," utilizing the more usual meaning of φιλοτίμως, while D. Schwartz translated, "Fought with manly vigor for *Ioudaismos*." My "strived for" is meant to capture this ambiguity.

33. Goldstein keenly observes, "Our verse contains the earliest known occurrence of the Greek word *Ioudaismos* ('Judaism'). The writer probably chose deliberately to use a

word of this form in the same context as 'barbarian,' for he thus induced his literate Greek audience to remember the struggle of the loyal Hellenes against the 'barbarian' Persians and against the 'Medism' of Greek collaborators with the Persian empire." Goldstein, *II Maccabees*, 192, n. 21.

34. I have converted Schwartz's "conversion" to "change," as Schwartz's translation rather sells the pass by using such a marked term as "conversion." The Greek is μεταθέσει, which might be translated as "displacement" also.

35. 22 Ἡ δὲ τοῦ βασιλέως ἐπιστολὴ περιεῖχεν οὕτως· «Βασιλεὺς ᾿Αντίοχος τῷ ἀδελφῷ Λυσίᾳ χαίρειν. 23 τοῦ πατρὸς ἡμῶν εἰς θεοὺς μεταστάντος, βουλόμενοι τοὺς ἐκ τῆς βασιλείας ἀταράχους ὄντας γενέσθαι πρὸς τὴν τῶν ἰδίων ἐπιμέλειαν, 24 ἀκηκοότες τοὺς ᾿Ιουδαίους μὴ συνευδοκοῦντας τῇ τοῦ πατρὸς ἐπὶ τὰ Ἑλληνικὰ μεταθέσει, ἀλλὰ τὴν ἑαυτῶν ἀγωγὴν αἱρετίζοντας καὶ διὰ τοῦτο ἀξιοῦντας συγχωρηθῆναι αὐτοῖς τὰ νόμιμα αὐτῶν·25 αἱρούμενοι οὖν καὶ τοῦτο τὸ ἔθνος ἐκτὸς ταραχῆς εἶναι, κρίνομεν τό τε ἱερὸν αὐτοῖς ἀποκατασταθῆναι καὶ πολιτεύεσθαι κατὰ τὰ ἐπὶ τῶν προγόνων αὐτῶν ἔθη. 26 εὖ οὖν ποιήσεις διαπεμψάμενος πρὸς αὐτοὺς καὶ δοὺς δεξιάς, ὅπως εἰδότες τὴν ἡμετέραν προαίρεσιν εὔθυμοί τε ὦσι καὶ ἡδέως διαγίνωνται πρὸς τὴν τῶν ἰδίων ἀντίληψιν». See also Cana Werman, "On Religious Persecution: A Study in Ancient and Modern Historiography," *Zion* 81, no. 3–4 (2016): 18–19, in Hebrew, with English summary. Werman, for some reason, cites the less clear second letter there vv. 27–37 rather than this one but nonetheless reads that letter very similarly to my own interpretation of the significance of this one. See also next note.

36. Himmelfarb, "Judaism and Hellenism." Cf. Werman, "On Religious Persecution," 18–19. While I agree with Werman that this text all but refutes Honigman's thesis (see text immediately following), it does little to support Werman's notion of a separate "religious" sphere either.

37. Sylvie Honigman, *Tales of High Priests and Taxes: The Books of the Maccabees and the Judean Rebellion against Antiochos IV*, The S. Mark Taper Foundation Imprint in Jewish Studies (Oakland: University of California Press, 2014).

38. Werman, "On Religious Persecution."

39. Honigman, *Tales of High Priests*, 145. Incidentally, I quite agree with her explanation of why *Ioudaismos* and *Hellēnismos* do not appear together in the same context in 2 Maccabees—namely, that they don't belong together within the narration, although I don't need to accept her construction of the text or her appeal to royal inscriptions to conclude thus. See also Erich Gruen, "Hellenism and Persecution: Antiochus IV and the Jews," in *Hellenistic History and Culture*, ed. Peter Green (Berkeley: University of California Press, 1993), 238–264. The contrast is within the semantic system of the text as a whole, not an immediate context. (Consequently, refuting her reconstruction of the royal narrative does not, pace Werman, force us to accept older interpretations.) Finally, Honigman refers to *Ioudaismos* as an abstraction (e.g., Honigman, *Tales of High*

Priests, 199) without once, to the best of my memory, attempting to demonstrate this anachronistic grammatical construal, while I argue, with Mason, that it is a verbal noun, a gerund, no more an abstraction than "walking" or "eating." Now, again, Honigman clearly gets the error of translating *Ioudaismos* and *Hellēnismos* as "Judaism" and "Hellenism" and then referring to their modern meanings, but she hasn't gone far enough.

40. So, for instance, Honigman writes, "Put simply, 'religion' ('Judaism') and 'culture' ('Hellenism') fail to match any recognizable semantic fields in the social and cultural environment of the author." So far, so excellent, but then, "and therefore it is impossible that the author was restricting his own understanding of *Hellēnimos* to 'cultural' aspects" (Honigman, *Tales of High Priests*, 202). The problem here, of course, is the notion that something refers to "culture," an anachronism as well to be sure, and implies that it is out of the sphere of a putative "religion" rather than seeing that a culture, according to most modern construals, incorporated so-called religion (as well as the military, economic relations, etc.). Honigman's oddly restricted and restrictive sense of what "culture" means has led her quite widely astray (Honigman, 212), and moreover, given power to her opponents.

41. Honigman, 105.

42. Honigman, 143.

43. 21καὶ τὰς ἐξ οὐρανοῦ γενομένας ἐπιφανείας τοῖς ὑπὲρ τοῦ Ἰουδαϊσμοῦ φιλοτίμως ἀνδραγαθήσασιν ὥστε τὴν ὅλην χώραν ὀλίγους ὄντας λεηλατεῖν καὶ τὰ βάρβαρα πλήθη διώκειν 22 καὶ τὸ περιβόητον καθ' ὅλην τὴν οἰκουμένην ἱερὸν ἀνακομίσασθαι καὶ τὴν πόλιν ἐλευθερῶσαι καὶ τοὺς μέλλοντας καταλύεσθαι νόμους ἐπανορθῶσαι τοῦ κυρίου μετὰ πάσης ἐπιεικείας ἵλεω γενομένου αὐτοῖς.

44. I, therefore, agree with Werman's rejection of Honigman's explanation of *Ioudaismos* but not for the same reasons (Werman, "On Religious Persecution," 16–18). Our differences emerge especially on 17, where Werman assumes that refutation of Honigman's interpretation necessitates a return to the notion that there is a religion ("a personal religion," no less) called "Judaism" in antiquity. In fine, my own reading of *Ioudaismos/Hellēnismos* is closer to Werman than to Honigman but does not support in any way the idea central to Werman's argument of a distinct "religious" persecution, still less of the existence of *yahadut* (a verbal anachronism by about a millennium and a conceptual one of about two millennia, as we will see in the next chapters of this book). Werman simply assumes that if Honigman can be dismissed, then we are perforce left with the older historical doctrine of a "religion" called *yahadut*, quite thoroughly disregarding all other scholarship and all other published ideas and interpretations.

45. Honigman, *Tales of High Priests*, 145.

46. 11καὶ τὰ κείμενα τοῖς Ἰουδαίοις φιλάνθρωπα βασιλικὰ διὰ Ἰωάννου τοῦ πατρὸς Εὐπολέμου τοῦ ποιησαμένου τὴν πρεσβείαν ὑπὲρ φιλίας καὶ συμμαχίας

πρὸς τοὺς Ῥωμαίους παρώσας καὶ τὰς μὲν νομίμους καταλύων πολιτείας παρανόμους ἐθισμοὺς ἐκαίνιζεν 12ἀσμένως γὰρ ὑπ' αὐτὴν τὴν ἀκρόπολιν γυμνάσιον καθίδρυσεν καὶ τοὺς κρατίστους τῶν ἐφήβων ὑποτάσσων ὑπὸ πέτασον ἤγαγεν 13ἦν δ' οὕτως ἀκμή τις Ἑλληνισμοῦ καὶ πρόσβασις ἀλλοφυλισμοῦ διὰ τὴν τοῦ ἀσεβοῦς καὶ οὐκ ἀρχιερέως Ἰάσωνος ὑπερβάλλουσαν ἀναγνείαν 14ὥστε μηκέτι περὶ τὰς τοῦ θυσιαστηρίου λειτουργίας προθύμους εἶναι τοὺς ἱερεῖς ἀλλὰ τοῦ μὲν νεὼ καταφρονοῦντες καὶ τῶν θυσιῶν ἀμελοῦντες ἔσπευδον μετέχειν τῆς ἐν παλαίστρῃ παρανόμου χορηγίας μετὰ τὴν τοῦ δίσκου πρόσκλησιν 15καὶ τὰς μὲν πατρῴους τιμὰς ἐν οὐδενὶ τιθέμενοι τὰς δὲ Ἑλληνικὰς δόξας καλλίστας ἡγούμενοι.

47. Mason, "Jews, Judaeans, Judaizing, Judaism." 463.

48. Mason, 469.

49. ἀλλ' ὅτε εἶδον ὅτι οὐκ ὀρθοποδοῦσιν πρὸς τὴν ἀλήθειαν τοῦ εὐαγγελίου, εἶπον τῷ Κηφᾷ ἔμπροσθεν πάντων Εἰ σὺ Ἰουδαῖος ὑπάρχων ἐθνικῶς καὶ οὐκ Ἰουδαϊκῶς ζῇς, πῶς τὰ ἔθνη ἀναγκάζεις ἰουδαΐζειν.

50. Mason, "Jews, Judaeans, Judaizing, Judaism," 464.

51. See discussion of dating in Martin Hengel, "Die Synangoninschrift von Stobi," ZNW 57, no. 3 (1966): 147–148, 150–159.

52. Hengel's entire discussion there on 179–181 is also illuminating and important.

53. And, indeed, this is undoubtedly the reason he ignores them.

54. Mason, "Jews, Judaeans, Judaizing, Judaism," 468.

55. Anna Wierzbicka, *Understanding Cultures through Their Key Words: English, Russian, Polish, German, and Japanese*, Oxford Studies in Anthropological Linguistics (New York: Oxford University Press, 1997), 15–17.

56. Duncan MacRae, "Diligentissumus Investigator Antiquitatis? 'Antiquarianism' and Historical Evidence between Republican Rome and the Early Modern Republic of Letters," in *Omnium Annalium Monumenta: Historical Writing and Historical Evidence in Republican Rome*, ed. Christopher Smith and Kaj Sandberg (Leiden: E. J. Brill, 2017).

57. Naomi Seidman, *Faithful Renderings: Jewish-Christian Difference and the Politics of Translation*, Afterlives of the Bible (Chicago: University of Chicago Press, 2006), 23.

58. See Carlin A. Barton and Daniel Boyarin, *Imagine No Religion: How Modern Categories Hide Ancient Realities* (Bronx: Fordham University Press, 2016), for this key argument.

59. Louis Ginzberg, *The Legends of the Jews*, trans. Henrietta Szold (Philadelphia: Jewish Publication Society of America, 1909–1938), intro. I was reminded of this passage by Moshe Dembitzer.

60. Josephus, *Flavius Josephus, Translation and Commentary.* Vol. 10, *Against Apion*, ed. Steve Mason, trans. and commentary by John Barclay. Josephus, Flavius. Works. English. 2000, vol. 10 (Leiden: E. J. Brill, 2007). It is worth noting in this context that the title is *not* from Josephus's pen but is a latter-day imposition on the work.

61. Josephus and Barclay, *Against Apion*, 262, n. 638.

62. "Josephus synthesizes early political and legal theory with Jewish socio-religious values to coin the concept of theocracy as an alternative to the classical models of government. Critiquing the instability and tyrannical tendencies of imperial rule, Josephus insists that a lasting polity must instead be built upon the foundations of law. By limiting the role of men and relying instead upon sacral laws, theocracy promises to be such a system. Notwithstanding the violence done to this term over time, or its later transformation, theocracy for Josephus represents a constitutional scheme carefully designed to achieve libertas and lawfulness." David C. Flatto, "Theocracy and the Rule of Law: A Novel Josephan Doctrine and Its Modern Misconceptions," *Dine Yisrael* 28 (2011): 7. For the formulation that *theokratia*, as used by Josephus, is the opposite of its modern usage, see Flatto, "Rule of Law," 5. This point if sustained—and I believe it is—quite undoes the conclusion reached by Honigman (Honigman, *Tales of High Priests*, 115–117), to wit that Josephus's term refers to a previously existing concept of rule by priests.

63. Eusebius reads "laws," not "words," here, but in any case, as mentioned so is it glossed in the next sentence by Josephus, so even without emending the text, that is the sense. As Copeland remarks, "The Nomos concept was quite prominent and bore universal connotations both in the Bible and in Greek thought, and because Law and Word were intimately related in both contexts." E. Luther Copeland, "Nomos as a Medium of Revelation—Paralleling Logos—in Ante-Nicene Christianity," *Studia Theologica* 27 (1973): 51–52.

64. For this dualism within rabbinic culture, see the following: "Rabbi Tarfon and the Elders were reclining in the upper room of the House of Natza in Lydda and the following question was asked of them: Which is greater: Is study greater or the deed? Rabbi Tarfon responded and said, the deed is greater. Rabbi Akiva responded and said, study is greater. All then responded and said, study is greater, as it conduces to the deed" [TB Qiddushin:40b].

65. Josephus and Barclay, *Against Apion*, 267, n. 677, citing *Ant. rom.* 2.28.

66. See for this usage Flavius Josephus, *Judean War 2*, trans. and commentary by Steve Mason and Honora Chapman. Josephus, Flavius. Works. English. 2000, vol. 1B (Leiden: E. J. Brill, 2008), 116 [*War* 145]: "There is great reverence among them for—next to God—the name of the law-giver."

67. Ἡμῖν δὲ τοῖς πεισθεῖσιν ἐξ ἀρχῆς τεθῆναι τὸν νόμον κατὰ θεοῦ βούλησιν οὐδ᾽ εὐσεβὲς ἦν τοῦτον μὴ φυλάττειν.

68. Severin M. Fowles, *An Archaeology of Doings: Secularism and the Study of Pueblo Religion* (Santa Fe: School for Advanced Research Press, 2013), 78.

69. Robert M. Cover, "Supreme Court, 1982 Term—Foreword: Nomos and Narrative" (1983).

70. Amir, "The Term Ἰουδαϊσμός," 266. See discussion in Mason, "Jews, Judaeans, Judaizing, Judaism," 465. Cf. Daniel R. Schwartz, "More on Schalit's Changing Josephus: The Lost First Stage," *Jewish History* 9, no. 2 (Fall 1995): 9–20.

CHAPTER 3 — GETTING MEDIEVAL *YAHADUT*

1. There has been extensive research and scholarly comment and analysis of this book and its translations for a century now. My task here is to study the language and translation language of a small, limited semantic field. It would not surprise me at all were more sophisticated philology to bring further nuance and even corrections of my views here. Very useful and important is the short essay by Daniel J. Lasker, "Translations of Rabbi Yehuda Halevis Kuzari," http://seforim.blogspot.com/2017/06/translations -of-rabbi-judah-halevis.html.

2. For ibn Tibbon's Hebrew, I have used Yehudah HaLevi, *The Kuzari: In Defense of the Despised Faith*, newly translated and annotated by N. Daniel Korobkin (Jerusalem: Feldheim, 2009); Judah ha-Levi, trans. Hartwig Hirschfeld, *Judah Hallevi's Kitab al Khazari*, The Semitic Series (London: G. Routledge, 1905). For the Arabic, I have consulted Yehudah Halevi, *Sefer Hakuzari: Maqor Wetargum*, ed. and trans. Yosef ben David Qafih (Kiryat Ono: Mekhon Mishnat ha-Rambam, 1996). I have also had the great privilege of being able to consult the (as yet unpublished) translation of the Arabic by Professor Barry S. Kogan, for which privilege I thank him. My translations given here of the Arabic text follow Kogan's renderings except for when I feel that he has used terminology that is anachronistic, such as "religion," which is, of course, the whole novellum of my research here.

3. See C. P. Jones, "Ἔθνος and γένος in Herodotus," *Classical Quarterly*, n.s., 46 (1996): 316, who, in an exemplary study, makes this point compellingly.

4. Cf. Reinhold Glei and Stefan Reichmuth, "Religion between Last Judgement, Law and Faith: Koranic Dīn and Its Rendering in Latin Translations of the Koran," *Religion* 42, no. 2 (April 2012): 247–271, an important article in its own right, but I think not sufficiently attentive to the nuances of the usage of *religio* in ancient Latin. See now Carlin A. Barton and Daniel Boyarin, *Imagine No Religion: How Modern Categories Hide Ancient Realities* (Bronx: Fordham University Press, 2016). I am certainly not clear on what they base their statement that "contrary to widespread assumptions, the emergence of a generalized uncountable notion ('Kollektivsingular') 'Religion' could be traced here for Latin already to the 1st century BCE" (Glei and Reichmuth, "Religion between Last Judgement," 268). Moreover, it must be said that simply giving passages of Arabic and translating *dīn* as "religion" hardly constitutes an argument that indeed that is its usage. See, for example, Glei and Reichmuth, 256. Aside from these quibbles, it does seem instructive that, according to Glei and Reichmuth, a decisive turn in the usage/translation of *dīn* does seem to occur in early modernity (Glei and Reichmuth, 265–266).

5. For this term, see Severin M. Fowles, *An Archaeology of Doings: Secularism and the Study of Pueblo Religion* (Santa Fe: School for Advanced Research Press, 2013).

6. See the distinction in Kalām (Islamic rational theology) between "intellectual obligations" and "traditional obligations," as explored by Ehud Krinis, "The Arabic Background of the *Kuzari*," *Journal of Jewish Thought and Philosophy* 21 (2013): 20–22.

7. Here again we see ibn Tibbon's reluctance to use *dat* with reference to Jewry.

8. I have back-formed this non-existent biblical form from *date* to distinguish it from medieval Hebrew *datot*.

9. See too Esther 9:10, where a *"dat* is given in Shushan, the capitol, and the ten sons of Haman were hanged."

10. See "For the respective ethnic or religious groups (both of which are very difficult to distinguish in the Koran in any case) terms such as umma or milla ('people, community') are used," Glei and Reichmuth, "Religion between Last Judgement," 254.

11. It has been suggested to me that the reason for this is entirely extraneous to my query, since these are used as "code" terms, so as not to arouse the ire of Christians and Muslims who would not find themselves in Edom and Ishma'el. I find this explanation not at all attractive, at the least because it would require an uncommon level of incomprehension on the part of those Gentiles (Christian or Muslim) in not recognizing these millennium-old terms. A further alternative suggestion is that it was precisely the deep-time (even biblical, of course) associations of those very ethnonyms that made them so attractive to Hebrew writers. In a sense, however, this can be seen as a notational variant of the thesis advanced here, that in those climes and times, "religious" categories had not replaced the traditional "ethnic" ones!

12. Lena Salaymeh, personal communication, September 2016.

13. Timothy Fitzgerald, *The Ideology of Religious Studies* (New York: Oxford University Press, 2000).

14. I am very, very grateful for the help of Professor Florentina Badalanova Geller, who in the middle of reading proofs for an eight-hundred-page book in Russian took time off to retranslate this passage for my use, informing me that the published translation was inaccurate.

15. This story, incidentally, is very similar to a rabbinic fable of God offering the Torah to various peoples and being turned down because of various prohibitions.

16. Dmitrieva, L. A. [sostavlenie i obshchaia redaktsiia] and D. S. Likhacheva, *Pamiatniki Literatury Drevnei Rusi: Konets XV-Pervaia Polovina XVI Veka*, Pamiatniki Literatury Drevnei Rusi (Moskva: "Khudozh. lit-ra," 1984), 98–101. I cite here a new translation of the Old Church Slavonic text made for me by Professor Florentina Badalanova Geller, for which I am very grateful as well as for her other invaluable help.

17. We find the same usage in the thirteenth century in the Torah commentary of Rabbi Hayyim Paltiel. Interestingly, and perhaps tellingly, we find a variation of this usage in Rashi's commentary on the Tractate Yevamot 24b, but in the MSS of Rashi, it does not appear. Presumably later than Rashi himself (1040–1105), the context is nonetheless interesting and perhaps very important. The context there is, once again, a discussion of *gerut*. The case is of a man who is suspected of having had relations with a non-Jewish woman who later underwent *gerut*. The Mishna says he may not marry

her, as it would confirm the suspicion (of their affair and her insincerity in *gerut*), but if he did marry her, he is not forced to divorce her. On this the Talmud remarks that it is clear, nonetheless, that she is indeed a *gioret* (the feminine form of *ger*)—that is, that even though the original suspected lover is forbidden to marry her, she is nonetheless in the status of *ger* (i.e., she is a Jew). On this the printed Rashi remarks, ואף על גב דלא נתגיירה לשם יהדות אלא בשביל שישאנה זה, "Even though she did not enter the state of *gerut* for the sake of *yahadut* but only in order that this man would marry her." Superficially, this is the same usage that we see in the Sekhel Tov passage cited here—namely, "in order to become a Jew, to enter into Jewry" (i.e., a juridical condition). On further analysis, however, we can see that this is not the case here, for in the passage discussed in the main text, the complement of "for the sake of *yahadut*" is immersion, and immersion can be for many other reasons than entering into Jewry, but *gerut* is always for the purpose of entering into Jewry whatever ulterior motive for *that* might obtain (in this case, desire for this particular Jewish man). Becoming a *gioret* for the sake of *yahadut*, therefore, must mean out of conviction and devotion to the Jewish God, and we would see here a transition to a usage something like modern *yahadut* as the name of a "religion," even a "faith." Unfortunately, since we don't know when (terminus ante quem = late fifteenth century when Talmud first printed) or by whom this gloss was added to Rashi's text, we cannot make too much of it. Rashi himself in the MSS reads simply, "She did not become a *gioret* except for desire to marry this man"—no *yahadut* in sight. In any case, by the time of the editio princeps of the Talmud, as well as such writers as R. Y. Karo, such usage must have been possible, suggesting the beginnings of an early modern partial preparatory turn toward modern usage. Cf. Moshe Idel, "Abraham Abulafia and the Pope: An Account of an Abortive Mission," *AJS Review* 7 (1982): n. 75, in Hebrew.

18. I do not use here the term "conversion" as it is a particularly loaded theological term in western languages already comprising emotional or even mystical changes of heart, while *gerut*, of course carrying its own loaded meanings, connotes a moving from identification with and membership in one collective to another without necessarily or originally indicating an altered emotional state. This particular usage continues into the modern period, for instance in the work Ḥasde David by Rabbi David Pardo (1718–1790) on the Tosefta, A"Z chapter 3, halacha 4. That sort of idea will await the modern period within Jewry as well, as we shall see anon.

19. My gratitude to my friend Professor Menahem Kahana נר"י, who steered me in the right direction on this.

20. Further support for this conclusion can be found from the fact that the same Rabbenu Tam is cited using this very locution, שם של יהדות, his name of *yahadut*—that is, the name he bore as a Jew at Tosafot Gittin 34b, lemma והוא דאתתחזק. Finally, this is the version cited by Rabbi Ḥayyim Paltiel (1240–1300) to Genesis 35:10. A fascinating question, beyond the scope of the present writing, is why in one manuscript tradition of the text, it was emended to predate it to the Roman imperial period.

בית יוסף יורה דעה סימן קנז .21

ערקתא דמסאנא. שרוך הנעל שאם דרך הגוים לקשור כך ודרך ישראל לקשור בענין אחר
כגון שיש צד יהדות בדבר ודרך ישראל להיות צנועים אפילו שינוי זה שאין כאן מצוה אלא
מנהג בעלמא יקדש השם בפני חביריו ישראל. וז"ל הרי"פ (שם יז:) אפילו ערקתא דמסאנא
פירוש הגוים שבאותו זמן היו רצועות של מנעליהם אדומות וישראל היו עושים שחורות כדי
שלא ילבשו מלבוש נכרי וכתב מהרי"ק בשורש פ"ח דבדוקא נקט הרי"ף שהגוים היו עושים
אדומות והיהודים שחורות דבכהאי גוונא הוא דיש להקפיד שאין דרך הצנועים להיות אדום
ללבושם וצבע השחור הוא דרך צניעות והכנעה והיינו כדפירש רש"י דדוקא שיש בו צד
יהדות וצניעות

תשובות, שערי צדק | מחבר: שרירא גאון בר׳ חנניה .22

Montefiore Library London 98. I am very grateful to Dr. Gabriel Birnbaum of the
Hebrew Lexicon Project of the Hebrew Language Academy, who supplied me with this
text.

23. For other examples, see Eliezer Ben-Yehuda, *Milon Ha-Lashon Ha-ʿIvrit Ha-
Yeshanah Veha-Ḥadashah* (Yerushalayim, 1910–1959), vol. 16, 250, and others could be
added as well.

24. E. E. Urbach, "*Yahadut* in the Language of the Sages," *Leshnonenu* 25 (1961): 145, in
Hebrew.

25. See Idel, "Abraham Abulafia."

26. Hebrew text cited in Idel, 7.

27. Idel, 12–14.

28. Cf. Elliot R. Wolfson, "Textual Flesh, Incarnation, and the Imaginal Body: Abraham Abulafia's Polemic with Christianity," in *Studies in Medieval Jewish Intellectual and
Social History: Festschrift in Honor of Robert Chazan*, ed. David Engel, Lawrence Schiffman, and Elliot Wolfson, Supplements to the Journal of Jewish Thought and Philosophy 15 (Brill: E. J. Leiden, 2012), 200, n. 41.

29. Wolfson, "Textual Flesh," 208.

30. Abraham Abulafia, *Imrei Shefer*, edited by Amnon Gross (Jerusalem, 1999), 104, in
Hebrew.

31. Abraham Abulafia, *Otsar Eden Ganuz*, edited by Amnon Gross (Jerusalem, 2000),
190, in Hebrew.

32. Aqedat Yitzhak, ad Genesis, Gate 18.

33. Toldot Yitzhaq, chapter 31.

34. See chapter 5 for further discussion of this usage.

35. Toldot Yitzhaq, Numbers 17.

36. Abarbanel, Deuteronomy 30.

37. In chapter 2 of the same commentary, Alsheikh returns to using *yahadut* in its
most common medieval usage—namely, the state of being a Jew (i.e., immersion for

the sake of *yahadut* as opposed, in this case, to immersion for the sake of becoming a Hebrew slave and thus clearly a status and nothing else).

38. A further fascinating occurrence in R. Lifschitz can be found in the introduction, where Lifschitz writes the following:

להוציא לאור ספר זה והנה התיגעתי עד אשר . . . מצאתי את שאהבה נפשי, שמצאתי
דאתא לידי מדפיס א אשר התרצה להקים דפוס יהדות פה וחפץ ה׳ בידו הצליח למצוא
אותיות יפות

To publish this book and I labored until I succeeded to find what which my soul loves, for I found a printer who desired to establish here a [printing] press of *yahadut* and God desired that he would succeed and he found beautiful letters [beautiful fonts].

This is almost certainly the first totally unambiguous usage of *yahadut* in this abstract sense to be found in the literature.

CHAPTER 4 — "JUDAISM" OUT OF THE ENTRAILS OF CHRISTIANITY

1. Leora Batnitzky, *How Judaism Became a Religion: An Introduction to Modern Jewish Thought* (Princeton: Princeton University Press, 2011).

2. Nirenberg, *Anti-Judaism*.

3. Nirenberg, 3, emphasis added.

4. Had Nirenberg carried his own insight to its end, I wonder if he had been so critical of Marx's allegedly not carrying *his* to the end. On the other hand, a certain ambivalence in Marx cannot be denied as well.

5. And Cynthia M. Baker, *Jew*, Key Words in Jewish Studies (New Brunswick: Rutgers University Press, 2017) must be mentioned here for good as well.

6. Brent Nongbri, "Paul without Religion: The Creation of a Category and the Search for an Apostle beyond the New Perspective" (PhD diss., Yale University, 2008).

7. As justly pointed out by Nongbri:

Boyarin refers to Gregory of Nazianzus' refutation of Julian in an unfortunate translation which regularly renders the Greek θρησκεια with the English 'religion' and the articular infinitive το ἑλλενιζειν with the loaded term 'Hellenism,' which leads Boyarin into a number of difficulties. (Nongbri, "Paul without Religion," 52)

Indeed. I hope that my subsequent extensive philological work on these words (in Barton and Boyarin, whether good or bad, is not for me to judge) would, at any rate, expiate the sin.

8. Nongbri, 50–62. Nongbri goes sometimes too far, in my opinion, in dismissing some of my interpretations there and somewhat mischaracterizes others but no matter, in essence he is right. In what follows, I simply delete the previous interpretations

that I consider now partly or largely invalid and rephrase what remains in new terms that I think, today, make more sense.

9. Nongbri, 62.

10. Rowan Williams, "Does It Make Sense to Speak of Pre-Nicene Orthodoxy?," in *The Making of Orthodoxy: Essays in Honour of Henry Chadwick*, ed. Rowan Williams (Cambridge: Cambridge University Press, 1989), 3.

11. See the brilliant and pellucid Paula Fredriksen, *Augustine and the Jews: A Christian Defense of Jews and Judaism* (New Haven: Yale University Press, 2010), xiv–xv:

> In the Christian literature that begins to appear early in the second century, however, these arguments against other Jews transform into condemnations of Judaism itself. From this point on, many gentile authors, whether disputing with Jewish contemporaries or contesting with each other over questions of authority and identity, increasingly expressed the principles of their various Christian beliefs and practices by appealing to a vast web of interconnected anti-Jewish themes. . . . By Augustine's period, after three hundred years of vigorous development, this interpretive anti-Judaism had become a defining feature of orthodox identity and of orthodox theology.

12. On the promulgation of the Codex, see now John Matthews, *Laying Down the Law: A Study of the Theodosian Code* (New Haven: Yale University Press, 2000); earlier the essays in Jill Harries and I. N. Wood, *The Theodosian Code*, ed. Jill Harries (Ithaca, NY: Cornell University Press, 1993); Tony Honoré, *Law in the Crisis of Empire, 379–455 AD: The Theodosian Dynasty and Its Quaestors; with a Palingenesia of Laws of the Dynasty* (Oxford: Clarendon Press, 1998).

13. For an analogous and similarly ramified shift in the meanings of terms within an imperial situation, see Robert Young, *Colonial Desire: Hybridity in Theory, Culture, and Race* (London: Routledge, 1995), 50, on the vicissitudes of "civilization" and "culture."

14. Maurice Sachot, "«*Religio/Superstitio*». Historique d'une subversion et d'un retournement," *Revue d'histoire des religions* 208, no. 4 (1991): 355–394.

15. Sachot, "«*Religio/Superstitio*»," 375. As Michele R. Salzman, "'Superstitio' in the Codex Theodosianus and the Persecution of Pagans," *Vigiliae Christianae* 41 (1987): 174, makes clear, this meaning is already a development from even earlier meanings. See now Carlin A. Barton and Daniel Boyarin, *Imagine No Religion: How Modern Categories Hide Ancient Realities* (Bronx: Fordham University Press, 2016), 46–49 and passim.

16. Peter Brown, *Authority and the Sacred: Aspects of the Christianization of the Roman World* (Cambridge: Cambridge University Press, 1995), 35.

17. Cf. the following quotation cited in the previous chapter from the *Kuzari*:

> Some of them said, "No one has ever come to us to tell us that after his death he has been to Paradise or Hell," but most of them preferred an orderly and harmonious society and accepted the service.

This is a good description of Ciceronian "religio" but hardly of Christianity! (Thanks to Andrew Bush.) For Cicero himself, see Barton and Boyarin, *Imagine No Religion*, 39–52.

18. *Religio ver dei cultus est, superstitio falsi*, 4.28.11.

19. Mary Beard, John A. North, and S. R. F. Price, *Religions of Rome* (Cambridge: Cambridge University Press, 1998), 216. See earlier Maurice Sachot: "Dans la bouche de chrétien *religio* renvoie désormais non plus seulement à pratiques et à des institutions individuelles, familiales ou civiles, mais aussi et avant tout à un rapport absolu à la vérité." Maurice Sachot, "Comment le Christianisme est-il devenu *religio*," *Revue des sciences religiuses* 59 (1985): 97. This should almost surely be connected up with other semantic shifts in Latin as well, notably the shift in the meaning of *verus* itself. Carlin A. Barton, "The 'Moment of Truth' in Ancient Rome: Honor and Embodiment in a Contest Culture," *Stanford Humanities Review* (1998): 16–30.

20. Barton and Boyarin, *Imagine No Religion*, 43–46.

21. And see the quotation from Seth Schwartz in the next paragraph.

22. Lee I. Levine, "The Jewish Patriarch (Nasi) in Third Century Palestine," in *Aufstieg und Niedergang der Römischen Welt II, Principat 19,2* (Berlin: Walter de Gruyter, 1979), 685, and see Günter Stemberger, *Jews and Christians in the Holy Land: Palestine in the Fourth Century* (Edinburgh: T & T Clark, 1999).

23. Peter Schäfer, ed., *The Talmud Yerushalmi and Graeco-Roman Culture III*, Texte und Studien Zum Antiken Judentum 93 (Tübingen: Mohr Siebeck, 2002), 59.

24. Amnon Linder, *The Jews in Roman Imperial Legislation*, ed. and trans. Amnon Linder (Detroit: Wayne State University Press, 1987), 68.

25. Stemberger, *Jews and Christians*, 29.

26. Clyde Pharr, *The Theodosian Code and Novels, and the Sirmondian Constitutions a Translation with Commentary, Glossary, and Bibliography*, in collaboration with Theresa Sherrer Davidson and Mary Brown Pharr, intro. by C. Dickerman Williams (Princeton: Princeton University Press, 1952), 469.

27. For this issue, see Elliott S. Horowitz, "The Rite to Be Reckless; on the Perpetration and Interpretation of Purim Violence," *Poetics Today* 15, no. 1 (1994): 9–54.

28. See the discussion in Stemberger, *Jews and Christians*, 155.

29. Pharr, *Theodosian Code*, 468. "It does remain likely that there were rabbis among the *primates* mentioned in the law codes." Seth Schwartz, *Imperialism and Jewish Society from 200 B.C.E. to 640 C.E.* (Princeton: Princeton University Press, 2001), 118. See also J. H. W. G. Liebeschuetz, *Antioch: City and Imperial Administration in the Later Roman Empire* (Oxford: Clarendon Press, 1972), 12, 16; Vasiliki Limberis, "'Religion' as the Cipher for Identity: The Cases of Emperor Julian, Libanius, and Gregory Nazianzus," *Harvard Theological Review* 93, no. 4 (2000): 382.

30. Stemberger, *Jews and Christians*, 308.

31. Linder, *Roman Imperial Legislation*, 69.

32. Schwartz, *Imperialism and Jewish Society*, 116. For the Patriarch as a perceived threat to Christianity, see Wilhelm Karl Reischl and Joseph Rupp, *Cyrilli Hierosolymarum Archiepiscopi Opera Quae Supersunt Omnia*, ed. Wilhelm Karl Reischl (Hildesheim: Olms, 1967), 2:24, and discussion by Andrew S. Jacobs, "The Imperial Construction of the Jew in the Early Christian Holy Land" (PhD diss., Duke University, 2001), 51. Compare the roughly analogous insistence in the code that the high priest of Egypt must *not* be a Christian, XII.1.112, and see the discussion in David Frankfurter, *Religion in Roman Egypt: Assimilation and Resistance* (Princeton: Princeton University Press, 1998), 24. According to Stemberger, even this, however, is an understatement with respect to the Patriarch. He shows that in the fourth century, the Patriarch was higher in authority than the governor (Stemberger, *Jews and Christians*, 242–243). Levine writes that in the fourth century, the Patriarch was more powerful than the Herodian kings (Levine, "The Jewish Patriarch," 651).

33. "Iudaei sint obstricti caerimoniis suis: nos interea in conservandis eorum privilegiis veteres imitemur, quorum sanctionibus definitum est, ut privilegia his, qui illustrium patriarcharum dicioni subiecti sunt, archisynagogis patriarchisque ac presbyteris ceterisque, qui in eius religionis sacramento versantur nutu nostri numinis perseverent ea, quae venerandae christianae legis primis clericis sanctimonia deferuntur." Pharr, *Theodosian Code*, 468. See also Schwartz, *Imperialism and Jewish Society*, 103–104, although "the patriarch, or *nasi*, by the middle of the fourth [century] had become a very estimable figure indeed, the rabbis did not have any officially recognized legal authority until the end of the fourth century and even then it was severely restricted and in any case not limited to rabbis." Moreover, and very importantly, "As for the patriarchs, they acquired much of their influence precisely by relaxing their ties to the rabbis and allying themselves instead with Palestinian city councillors, wealthy diaspora Jews, and prominent gentiles." See also Stemberger, *Jews and Christians*, 34.

34. Pharr, *Theodosian Code*, 469.

35. Schwartz, *Imperialism and Jewish Society*, 187.

36. Homi K. Bhabha, *The Location of Culture* (London: Routledge, 1994), 85.

37. This would suggest a possible qualification to claims such as those made by Shaye Cohen, "Pagan and Christian Evidence on the Ancient Synagogue," in *The Synagogue in Late Antiquity*, ed. Lee I. Levine (Philadelphia: American Schools of Oriental Research, 1987), 170–175.

38. Although this term does not, to the best of my knowledge, exist, Beard, North, and Price, *Religions of Rome*, 237, strongly imply that its virtual synonym, *religio illicita*, does, but only in Christian texts—a fact that, if it could be verified, would strengthen my case.

39. Stemberger, *Jews and Christians*, 35, suggests that, when the CTh XII.1.158 writes, "Irrespective of what religion (*superstitio*) they profess," this too includes Orthodox Christianity as one of the religions.

40. Linder, *Roman Imperial Legislation*, 428.

41. "Idem aa. philippo praefecto praetorio per illyricum. nullus tamquam iudaeus, cum sit innocens, obteratur nec expositum eum ad contumeliam religio qualiscumque perficiat."

42. See "It is our desire that all the various nation which are subject to our clemency and moderation, should continue to the profession of that religion [*religio*] which was delivered to the Romans by the divine Apostle Peter, as it has been preserved by faithful tradition and which is now professed by the Pontiff Damasus and by Peter, Bishop of Alexandria, a man of apostolic holiness. According to the apostolic teaching and the doctrine of the Gospel, let us believe in the one deity of the father, Son and Holy Spirit, in equal majesty and in a holy Trinity. We authorize the followers of this law to assume the title Catholic Christians; but as for the others, since in our judgment they are foolish madmen, we decree that the shall be branded with the ignominious name of heretics, and shall not presume to give their conventicles the name of churches. They will suffer in the first place the chastisement of divine condemnation and the second the punishment of out authority, in accordance with the will of heaven shall decide to inflict. (XVI 1.2)." It is clear from this citation that the other "religions" are "heretical" (non-Nicene) Christian groups.

43. "Sed hoc christianis, qui vel vere sunt vel esse dicuntur, specialiter demandamus, ut iudaeis ac paganis in quiete degentibus nihilque temptantibus turbulentum legibusque contrarium non audeant manus inferre religionis auctoritate abusi." Pharr, *Theodosian Code*, 476.

44. Caroline Humfress, "Religion," in *The Evolution of the Late Antique World*, by Peter Garnsey and Caroline Humfress (Oxford: Orchard Academic Press, 2001), 135–170.

45. Hal A. Drake, "Lambs into Lions: Explaining Early Christian Intolerance," *Past and Present*, no. 153 (1996): 27–29.

46. Note that since belief is the crucial modus for determining Christian legitimacy, the Quartodeciman heresy is described as a belief and not a practice. Orthodox Judaism would tend to do the opposite, describing wrong beliefs as bad practice.

47. Pharr, *Theodosian Code*, 469.

48. Virginia Burrus, "'In the Theater of This Life': The Performance of Orthodoxy in Late Antiquity," in *The Limits of Ancient Christianity: Essays on Late Antique Thought and Culture in Honor of R. A. Markus*, ed. William E. Klingshirn and Mark Vessey, Recentiores: Late Latin Texts & Contexts (Ann Arbor: University of Michigan Press, 1999), 81.

49. Just a note of orientation: This suggestion is very different, nearly opposite, from my claims toward the end of Daniel Boyarin, *Border Lines: The Partition of Judaeo-Christianity*, Divinations: Rereading Late Ancient Religions (Philadelphia: University of Pennsylvania Press, 2004), and see Virginia Burrus, Richard Kalmin, Haim Lapin, and Joel Marcus, "Boyarin's Work: A Critical Assessment," *Henoch* 28 (2006): 7–30.

50. This is true, I warrant, as well of the term *aposynagogos* in the Fourth Gospel as well, which only means kicked out of the synagogue, not excommunicated or rendered a non-Israelite! Misunderstanding of this has led to unwarranted suggestions that something called "Christianity" was a separate "religion" at the time of the Fourth Evangelist.

51. The case is dependent on taking certain terminology found in Tertullian's writings about Marcion as being drawn from that author as claimed explicitly by Judith Lieu, *Image & Reality: The Jews in the World of the Christians in the Second Century* (Edinburgh: T & T Clark, 1996), 344, and see more extensive discussion in Markus Vinzent, *Tertullian's Preface to Marcion's Gospel*, Studie Patristica Supplementa (Leuven: Peters, 2016), 342–347.

52. William R. Schoedel, *Ignatius of Antioch: A Commentary on the Letters of Ignatius of Antioch*, ed. Helmut Koester, trans. and ed. William R. Schoedel, Hermeneia—a Critical and Historical Commentary on the Bible (Philadelphia: Fortress Press, 1985), 126. See Lieu, *Image*, 28ff. and passim, for an exploration of the anxieties that this fuzzy border gave rise to. This position is partially pace Keith Hopkins, "Christian Number and Its Implications," *Journal of Early Christian Studies* 6, no. 2 (1998): 187, who seems to regard such fuzziness (or "porosity," in his language) as particularly characteristic of Christianity. Hopkins's paper is very important and will have to be reckoned with seriously in any future accounts of Judeo-Christian origins and genealogies. See also on this passage Shaye J. D. Cohen, "Judaism without Circumcision and 'Judaism' without 'Circumcision' in Ignatius," *Harvard Theological Review* 95, no. 4 (2002): 398–399.

53. Schoedel, *Ignatius of Antioch*, 40.

54. Schoedel, 41.

55. Henning Paulsen and Walter Bauer, *Die Briefe Des Ignatius von Antiochia und der Brief Des Polykarp von Smyrna*, Handbuch Zum Neuen Testament (Tübingen: Mohr Siebeck, 1985), 25.

56. Other interpretations, seeing this as a reference to the name Ephesus, seem to me quite far-fetched.

57. Schoedel, *Ignatius of Antioch*, 126. I shall have more to say about this passage anon.

58. See also Ignatius to the Romans 3:2.

59. For φύσει in this sense, cf. Trallians 1:1, and discussion in Schoedel, *Ignatius of Antioch*, 138.

60. Schoedel, 40.

61. Pace Schoedel, 43.

62. Schoedel, 95, 140.

63. Judith Lieu, "'I Am a Christian': Martyrdom and the Beginning of 'Christian' Identity," in *Neither Jew Nor Greek? Constructing Christian Identity* (Edinburgh: T & T Clark, 2003); Barton, "The 'Moment of Truth.'"

64. Similarly, it seems to me that 7:1 of that letter in which Ignatius writes, "For some are accustomed with evil deceit to carry about the name, at the same time doing things unworthy of God" (Schoedel, *Ignatius of Antioch*, 59), it is *not* the name "Christ" that these folks are carrying about (pace Schoedel: "that is, they move from place to place looking for converts to their version of Christianity") but the name *Christian*. Cf. Justin's remark: "For I made it clear to you that those who are Christians in name, but in reality are godless and impious heretics, teach in all respects what is blasphemous and godless and foolish" (Dialogue 80.3–4), A. Lukyn Williams, ed. and trans., *Justin Martyr: The Dialogue with Trypho*, Translations of Christian Literature (London: SPCK, 1930), 169–171; Justin, *Dialogus Cum Tryphone*, ed. Miroslav Marcovich, Patristische Texte und Studien Bd. 47 (Berlin: Walter de Gruyter, 1997), 208–209.

65. As Lieu remarks, "The claiming of this identity involves the denial of other alternatives . . . I Am." Hence the importance of the name, martyrdom, and *Ioudaismos* in Ignatius. If one can be a Jew and a Christian, then Ignatius's martyrdom would, indeed, be in vain.

66. Schoedel, *Ignatius of Antioch*, 12, who sees "heresy" and "heterodox" as quasi-technical terms in Ignatius. But cf. Schoedel, 147: "But we should note first that in referring to the 'strange plant' as 'heresy' Ignatius is mainly concerned about the false teachers themselves rather than their teaching. 'Heresy,' then, is still basically a matter of people who disrupt unity and create 'faction.'"

67. Schoedel, 28. See also C. K. Barrett, "Jews and Judaizers in the Epistles of Ignatius," in *Jews, Greeks and Christians: Religious Cultures in Late Antiquity. Essays in Honor of William David Davies*, ed. Robin Scroggs, SJLA 21 (Leiden: E. J. Brill, 1976), 220–244.

68. Schoedel, *Ignatius of Antioch*, 104.

69. Schoedel, 108.

70. Pace Schoedel, 118, who considers Ignatius's usage the same as that of 2 Maccabees, Paul, and the Pastoral Epistles. It is clear to readers of this book and especially of chapter 2 that I do not accept Schoedel's interpretation of those texts either.

71. Schoedel, 200 (emphasis added).

72. Schoedel, 202–203.

73. Schoedel, 203. See too Shaye J. D. Cohen, "Judaism without Circumcision," 403–404.

74. I slightly disagree with Nirenberg in his formulation to the effect that "in the tradition of Saint Paul Judaizing had always been a Christian vice, not a Jewish one," a statement hard to sustain given that for Paul there were not yet any Christians. On the other hand, I totally affirm the next sentence that "it [Judaizing, Judaism] had also always been understood as a linguistic error, a basic miscomprehension of how words work to relate humans to each other, their God, and their world" (Nirenberg, *Anti-Judaism*, 229). This is certain, it would seem, from Ignatius on.

75. Contra Schoedel, *Ignatius of Antioch*, 118, I do not see here a near-technical term for heresy, preferring the view of Martin Elze, "Irrtum und Häresie," *Kairos* 71 (1974): 393–394.

76. Schoedel, *Ignatius of Antioch*, 201. There is a great deal of controversy regarding the question of Ignatius's knowledge and use of written gospel texts. I am convinced from my reading of his works that for him "gospel" is the good news of Christ's death and resurrection, just as he says here, suggesting strongly that he does not have written gospels. For this judgment, Koester remains definitive. Helmut Koester, *Synoptische Überlieferung bei Den Apostolischen Vätern* (Berlin: Akademie-Verlag, 1957). More recently, Koester has continued to maintain this view. Helmut Koester, "Ancient Christian Gospels: Their History and Development" (Harrisburg: Trinity Press International, 1990), 7.

77. Schoedel, *Ignatius of Antioch*, 123, n. 3.

78. "But Ignatius makes a characteristic move when he links the resurrection with the mystery of Christ's death and emphasizes the latter as that through which faith comes. For it is Christ's death that stands out as a 'mystery' in Ignatius' mind (*Eph.* 19.1). One purpose of Ignatius here is to present the passion and resurrection (not Scripture as misinterpreted by the Jews and Judaizers) as that which determines the shape of Christian existence (and makes sense of Scripture)" (Schoedel, *Ignatius of Antioch*, 123–124).

79. Cohen, "Judaism without Circumcision," 397.

80. Schoedel, *Ignatius of Antioch*, 207. See discussion immediately following.

81. For further discussion of this difficult passage, see Schoedel, 207–209, and especially William R. Schoedel, "Ignatius and the Archives," *Harvard Theological Review* 71 (1978). For another recent discussion of these passages, see Birger Pearson, "The Emergence of the Christian Religion," in *The Emergence of the Christian Religion: Essays on Early Christianity* (Harrisburg: Trinity Press International, 1997), 11–14. For the interpretation that I have suggested here, see also Einar Molland, "The Heretics Combatted by Ignatius of Antioch," *Journal of Ecclesiastical History* 5 (1954): 1–6. See also the important argument of C. K. Barrett. Arguing that Ignatius indicates that he has heard this preaching, he writes, "Presumably in some kind of church meeting like that in which Ignatius prophesied [7.1]—an important point, for it must mean that the persons in question were Christian, even if (in Ignatius' eyes) unsatisfactory Christians. Ignatius is unlikely to have made his way into the synagogue." C. K. Barrett, "Jews and Judaizers in the Epistles of Ignatius," in *Jews, Greeks and Christians: Religious Cultures in Late Antiquity. Essays in Honor of William David Davies.* ed. Robin Scroggs, SJLA 21 (Leiden: E. J. Brill, 1976), 233. Finally, cf. Paulsen and Bauer, *Die Briefe*, 85–86.

82. For this correct translation, see Charles E. Hill, "Ignatius, 'the Gospel', and the Gospels," in *Trajectories through the New Testament and the Apostolic Fathers*, ed. Andrew F. Gregory and Christopher M. Tuckett (Oxford: Oxford University Press, 2005), 272. I confess to remaining unpersuaded by Hill's overall argument, but this is not the venue for detailed examination.

83. παρακαλω δε υμας μηδεν κατ εριθειαν πρασσειν, αλλα κατα χριστομαθιαν. επει ηκουσα τινων λεγοντων οτι· Εαν μη εν τοις αρχειοις ευρω, εν τω ευαγγελιω ου πιστευω· και λεγοντος μου αυτοις οτι· Γεγραπται, απεκριθησαν μοι οτι· Προκειται. εμοι δε αρχεια εστιν Ιησους Χριστος, τα αθικτα αρχεια ο σταυρος αυτου και ο θανατος και η αναστασις αυτου και η πιστις η δι αυτου· εν οις θελω εν τη προσευχη υμων δικαιωθηναι.

Schoedel, *Ignatius of Antioch*, 207.

84. I partly disagree with Schoedel's remark there that "we may observe in this connection that Ignatius speaks of Judaism where Paul would more naturally have spoken of the law. Thus Ignatius' contrast is between grace and Judaism and not, as in Paul, between grace and law." For Schoedel's "grace" here, I would put "gospel," so the contrast is between gospel and *Ioudaismos*, or, better put, between gospel and Scripture with the reliance on the latter defined as *Ioudaismos*. To be sure, this makes Ignatius a distant ancestor to Marcion only in this, his rejection of Scripture. I think that Ignatius simply does not operate with an opposition between grace and law at all, as we can see from Mag. 2: "because he is subject to the bishop as to the grace of God and to the presbytery as to the law of Jesus Christ." Indeed, Schoedel's remark is somewhat puzzling, since he himself argues that "Ignatius uses 'grace' and 'law' as parallel expressions," Schoedel, *Ignatius of Antioch*, 239. Ignatius's Judaizers are apparently *uncircumcised*, making them very, very different from Paul's opponents indeed (cf. Phil. 6:1; see discussion in Josep Rius-Camps, *The Four Authentic Letters of Ignatius, the Martyr: A Critical Study Based on the Anomalies Contained in the Textus Receptus*, Xpictianicmoc [Roma: Pontificium Institutum Orientalium Studiorum, 1979], 41, who nonetheless insists that the "Judaizers" and the "Gnostic-docetics" must be two "irreducibly" different groups. This flows from Rius-Camps's misapprehension that Ignatius's "Judaizers" are the representatives of "Judaizing tendencies similar to those that sprang up in the Pauline communities," notwithstanding the fact that virtually the entire content of the Pauline opposition was their insistence on Jewish law especially circumcision, while Ignatius's Judaizing opponents' "error" is christological and not connected with any insistence on Jewish practice, notwithstanding their maintenance of the Sabbath). Lightfoot's arguments all stand up to Rius-Camps's attempt at withering critique of them in Rius-Camps, *Four Authentic Letters of Ignatius*, 40–51. Rius-Camps seems to believe that by defining "Judaizing" as a form of Christianity that "inculcates Jewish observances and practices" (42), he has then proven that if Ignatius refers to those who expound *Ioudaismos*, they must too be inculcating such observances and practices, in spite of the fact that Ignatius himself refers to them as "uncircumcised"!

85. Nirenberg, *Anti-Judaism*, 238.

86. See just for one example the remarks of Nirenberg, 193: "The Middle Ages created for the Jews a political and legal status analogous to their hermeneutic one."

87. Daniel Boyarin, "The Gospel of the Memra: Jewish Binitarianism and the Crucifixion of the Logos," *Harvard Theological Review* 94, no. 3 (2001): 243–284.

88. Schoedel, *Ignatius of Antioch*, 234. To be sure, Schoedel in accord with his view would see this as only applicable in the case of the "Gnostic docetics," while I would extend the point, either by seeing all the opponents as essentially one, particularly so if they are being polarized by Ignatius himself, or as applicable to both of the cases if the "two heresy" view holds.

89. For the text and analysis, see Nirenberg, *Anti-Judaism*, 212–213.

90. Nirenberg, 222.

91. J. Rebecca Lyman, *Christology and Cosmology: Models of Divine Activity in Origen, Eusebius, and Athanasius*, Oxford Theological Monographs (Oxford: Oxford University Press, 1993).

92. Eusebius, *Preparation for the Gospel*, trans. Edwin Hamilton Gifford (Grand Rapids: Baker Book House, 1981).

93. Eusebius, *The Proof of the Gospel*, ed. and trans. W. J. Ferrar, Translations of Christian Literature (London: SPCK, 1920), I. 7. See too Jacobs, "Imperial Construction," 33.

94. I have deleted the word "religions" here, which does not exist in the Greek.

95. 1.2.9 σκόπει τοιγαροῦν εἰ μὴ τοῦτ᾽ αὐτὸ ἦν τὸ μεταξὺ ἰουδαϊσμοῦ καὶ ἑλληνισμοῦ τρίτον ἡμῖν ἀποδεδειγμένον τάγμα, παλαίτατον μὲν καὶ πάντων τυγχάνον πρεσβύτατον, νεωστὶ δὲ διὰ τοῦ ἡμετέρου σωτῆρος πᾶσι τοῖς ἔθνεσι κατηγγελμένον.... (10) ὥστε τὸν ἐξ ἑλληνισμοῦ ἐπὶ τὸν χριστιανισμὸν μετατιθέμενον οὐκ ἐπὶ ἰουδαϊσμὸν ἐκπίπτειν, οὐδ᾽ αὖ πάλιν τὸν ἐκ τῆς ἰουδαϊκῆς ἐθελοθρησκείας ἀναχωροῦντα εὐθὺς Ἕλληνα γίνεσθαι,

96. Nongbri, "Paul without Religion," 59.

97. Epiphanius of Salamis, *The Panarion of Epiphanius of Salamis, Book I, Sections 1–46*, trans. Frank Williams (Leiden: E. J. Brill, 1987), 16–50. Cf., however, Eusebius's *Demonstratio evangelica* 1.2.1 (Eusebius, *Proof*, 9). See important comments of Nongbri, "Paul without Religion," 61, n. 119.

98. Epiphanius, *Panarion of Epiphanius of Salamis*, 19. I have not quoted the Greek here, since the only Greek text I can find is corrupt and doesn't match Williams's *Vorlage*.

99. Epiphanius, *Panarion of Epiphanius of Salamis*, 9.

100. Cf. Jacobs, "Imperial Construction," 55–56.

101. For a highly salient and crystal-clear delineation of the terms "ethnic" and "cultural," see Jonathan M. Hall, *Hellenicity: Between Ethnicity and Culture* (Chicago: University of Chicago Press, 2002), esp. 9–19.

102. As has been noted by previous scholars, for Epiphanius, "heresy" is a much more capacious and even baggy-monster category than for most writers (Aline Pourkier, *L'Hérésiologie chez Épiphane de Salamine*, Christianisme Antique 4 [Paris: Editions Beauchesne, 1992], 85–87; Frances Young, "Did Epiphanius Know What He Meant by

'Heresy'?," *Studia Patristica* 17, no. 1 [1982]: 199-205). See the discussion in Jacobs, "Imperial Construction," 56. Epiphanius certain did know that "Hellenism" has to do originally with Greeks.

103. Epiphanius, *Panarion of Epiphanius of Salamis*, 24.

104. Justin's discussion of Jewish heresies is a different move from this, as analyzed earlier.

105. Johann Karl Ludwig Gieseler, "Über die Nazaräer und Ebioniten," *Archive für alte und neue Kirchengeschichte* 4, no. 2 (1819): 279, as cited in Glenn Alan Koch, "A Critical Investigation of Epiphanius' Knowledge of the Ebionites: A Translation and Critical Discussion of *Panarion 30*" (PhD diss., University of Pennsylvania, 1976), 10.

106. Stemberger, *Jews and Christians*, 80, writes, "It seems that there were no significant Jewish-Christian communities left in Palestine itself, and the primary problem for the wider church was the attraction of Judaism for the members of Gentile Christianity."

107. Nathaniel Deutsch, *Guardians of the Gate: Angelic Vice Regency in Late Antiquity*, Brill's Series in Jewish Studies 22 (Leiden: E. J. Brill, 1999), 19.

108. Epiphanius, *Panarion of Epiphanius of Salamis*, 120.

109. David Chidester, *Savage Systems: Colonialism and Comparative Religion in Southern Africa* (Charlottesville: University Press of Virginia, 1996), 11-16.

110. Bhabha, *Location*, 71.

111. For a useful (if methodologically uncritical) summary of the material, see Ray A. Pritz, *Nazarene Jewish Christianity: From the End of the New Testament Period until Its Disappearance in the Fourth-Century* (Jerusalem: Magnes Press, 1992), 48-70.

112. Hillel Newman, "Jerome's Judaizers," *Journal of Early Christian Studies* 9, no. 4 (December 2001): 421-452.

113. Marc Bloch, *The Historian's Craft: Reflections on the Nature and Uses of History and the Techniques and Methods of Those Who Write It*, trans. Peter Putnam (New York: Vintage Books, 1953), 93.

114. usque hodie per totas orientis synagogas inter Iudaeos heresis est, quae dicitur Minaeorum, et a pharisaeis huc usque damnatur, quos uulgo Nazaraeos nuncupant, qui credunt in Christum, filium dei natum de Maria uirgine, et eum dicunt esse, qui sub Pontio Pilato et passus est et resurrexit, in quem et nos credimus, sed, dum uolunt et Iudaei esse et Christiani, nec Iudaei sunt nec Christiani. Jerome, *Correspondence*, ed. Isidorus Hilberg, Corpus Scriptorum Ecclesiasticorum Latinorum (Vienna: Verlag der Osterreichischen Akademie der Wissenschaften, 1996), vol. 55, 381-382.

115. See the discussion in Jacobs, "Imperial Construction," 114.

116. Chidester, *Savage Systems*, 19.

117. For fuller documentation and demonstration of this point, see my earlier discussion in Daniel Boyarin, "The Christian Invention of Judaism: The Theodosian Empire

and the Rabbinic Refusal of Religion," *Representations* 85 (2004): 21–57. Caveat lector; the changes in my view of "religion" that I have indicated here in the palinode and throughout apply.

118. Daniel Boyarin, "Justin Martyr Invents Judaism," *Church History* 70, no. 3 (September 2001): 427–461.

119. Julian and Wilmer Cave France Wright, "Against the Galileans," in *The Works of the Emperor Julian*, trans. Wilmer Cave France Wright, Loeb Classical Library (London: Heinemann, 1913), 389.

120. Julian and Wright, 319–321.

121. Julian and Wright, 393–395.

122. For a somewhat different, but I think largely compatible, interpretation of Julian's program, see Nongbri, "Paul without Religion," 63–66.

123. Hall, *Hellenicity*, xix.

124. Limberis, "Cipher."

125. Wright points out that Julian has Christ-like figures in his own theology (Julian and Wright, "Against the Galileans," 315).

126. Jacobs, "Imperial Construction," 30.

127. Jacobs, 57.

128. Although I have omitted here any lengthy discussion of Justin Martyr, work being pursued on this figure in other quarters will bear out this analysis with respect to him as well.

129. I wish to thank my former research assistant, now Dr. Michael Zellman-Rohrer, of Oxford University for helping me locate these texts and also helping me now as a colleague with translating them precisely. Carlin Barton helped me considerably with nuances of the Latin, a language with respect to which I am quite the *rudis*. Of course only I am responsible for the results such as they are, since I have modified and otherwise mangled their translations.

130. Recensuit Georgios Fatouros, *Theodori Studitae Epistulae*, Corpus Fontium Historiae Byzantinae (Berolini: W. de Gruyter, 1992), epist. 314, lines 11–15.

131. Eutyhmius, "Encomium in Conceptionem Annae, §3, Ed," in *Homélies Mariales Byzantines: Textes Grecs*, ed. and trans. Martin Jugie, Patrologia Orientalis (Paris: Firmin-Didot, 1922–1926), 500.

132. Ambrosiaster, *Ambrosiastri Qui Dicitur Commentarius in Epistulas Paulinas. Recensuit Henricus Iosephus Vogels*, Corpus Scriptorum Ecclesiasticorum Latinorum 81 (Vindobonae: Hoelder-Pichler-Tempsky, 1966–1969), vol. 3, 15.

133. Franco Gori, ed., *Marii Victorini Opera. Pars Posterior, Opera Exegetica*, Corpus Scriptorum Ecclesiasticorum Latinorum 83. Marii Victorini Opera Pars II (Vindobonae, 1986), preface to Ephesians.

134. Nirenberg, *Anti-Judaism*, 175.

135. Nirenberg, 387–422.

136. Nirenberg, 5. See too, "It was the logic of art criticism that produced 'Judaism,' not the real beliefs or genealogy of its object" (456).

137. Nirenberg, 3.

138. See too Nirenberg, 417–418, on Nietzsche.

CHAPTER 5 — FROM *YIDDISHKAYT* TO *JUDENTUM*; FROM *JUDENTUM* TO *YAHADUT*; OR PHILOLOGY AND THE TRANSFORMATION OF A FOLK

1. Max Weinreich, *History of the Yiddish Language*, trans. Shlomo Noble, the assistance of Joshua A. Fishman, and the editorial assistance of Paul Glasser, Yale Language Series (New Haven: Yale University Press, 2008), 196.

2. This position is held by Weinreich himself as well as by the important Yiddishist, Mordkhe Shekhter. Mordekhai Shekhter and Shikl Fishman, *Laytish Mame-Loshn: Observatsyes un Rekomendatsyes* (New York: Yidish-lige, 1986), 148–149. Finally, it is the position endorsed by the current dean of Yiddish lexicographers, Yizhoq Niborski, in his dictionary of Hebrew words in Yiddish tsunoyfgeshtelt durkh Yitshak Niborski, mit der mithilf fun Shim'on Noyberg, and tsugegreyt tsum druk Eli'ezer Niborski, *Verterbukh Fun Loshn-Koydesh-Shtamike Verter in Yidish* (Pariz: Medem-bibliyotek, 1997), ad loc. I wish to thank my brother Jonathan Boyarin, who helped me find the Shekhter (spelling varies even with a single work) text and to Professor Zohar Weimann-Kelman, who insured that I had understood it correctly. On the supposed problem of nasalization without the *ayin* consonant in the root, Amos Noy has offered *danges* "worries" from Hebrew *da:gus*, in a personal communication dated March 2, 2017. Noy also referred me to the online (and very learned) comment by my teacher, Professor Mikhl Herzog of Columbia University:

> It's apparently because the "ayin," itself, is not the decisive factor. It's the "hataf-patah" (a very short a vowel) that counts. That's why nasalization occurs with "alef" and "hey" as well: "ka:nsher," "ba:nsher," "ya:ndes." (https://www.ibiblio.org/pub/academic/languages/yiddish/mendele/vol3.308)

We may take the problem as solved!

3. From Shekhter, it seems that the earliest attestation of the word in Yiddish is in the writings of Y. L. Perets (1852–1915) (Shekhter and Fishman, *Laytish Mame-Loshn*, 148). See also Amos Noy, "Those Who Pass Over: Do Not Forget Yahandes? An Examination of a Word from Avot Yeshurun's Poetry," *Theory and Criticism* 41 (2013): 206, in Hebrew.

4. Responsa of Rabbi Shmuel, son of Rabbi Moshe Kalei c. 1500–1585. We find this usage in other contemporaneous rabbinic writings (only among Sefaradim?). My friend, Professor Elchanan Reiner, has suggested that *yahadut* in this context means circumcision, remembering that in the Bible such an oath was not uncommon in Israel. One comparandum of interest can be found in England, as in Shakespeare's writing:

> *Gads. We four set upon some dozen–*
> *Fal. Sixteen at least, my lord.*
> *Gads. And bound them.*
> *Peto. No, no, they were not bound.*
> *Fal. You rogue, they were bound, every man of them; or I am a Jew else, an Ebrew*
> *Jew. (1 Henry IV, 2.4.174–179)*

Falstaff here is swearing that what he says is true, or he *is* a Jew; an oath on my *Yahadut* could mean an oath else I am *not* a Jew. Even more exact and compelling is the following from *Merchant of Venice*: "Now by my hood, a gentle, and no Jew" (2.6.53). Gratiano is swearing by his foreskin (hood), the structural equivalent of the Jew swearing by his circumcision! but also, perhaps, by his own Gentile-hood, thus matching the double entendre of swearing by one's *yahadut*.

5. Jonathan Boyarin, *Thinking in Jewish* (Chicago: University of Chicago Press, 1996), 196. Shekhter himself had referred to the giant demonstration in Tel Aviv following the massacres at Sabra and Shatila as "an outpouring of traditional Jewish *yandes.*"

6. Weinreich, *History of the Yiddish Language*, 199.

7. Severin M. Fowles, *An Archaeology of Doings: Secularism and the Study of Pueblo Religion* (Santa Fe: School for Advanced Research Press, 2013), 76.

8. Matthias Mieses, *Die Entstehungsursache de Jüdischen Dialekte* (Wien: R. Löwit, 1915).

9. Weinreich, *History of the Yiddish Language*, 163.

10. Weinreich, 164.

11. Weinreich, 202.

12. Timothy Fitzgerald, *Discourse on Civility and Barbarity: A Critical History of Religion and Related Categories* (New York: Oxford University Press, 2007).

13. Weinreich, *History of the Yiddish Language*, 175.

14. Some Jewish languages were closer to the majority tongue and others further but they were always *Jewish* and, for instance, not Christian in their vocabulary and thus, as argued in the first chapter, in their conceptual / semantic apparatus.

15. Weinreich, *History of the Yiddish Language*, 176.

16. In earlier oral iterations of this argument, I had actually supposed that Luther *invented* the word *Judenthum* to gloss Paul's *Ioudaismos*. A very, very helpful intervention of Daniela Schmidt (Potsdam) spared me the embarrassment of such an error. While I am sorry to have to renounce my rhetorical flourish, I am, of course, very happy for the accuracy, which seems not to affect my argument at all. See the excursus to this chapter for Schmidt's comment.

17. See "-thuon Abstraktsuffix. Mhd. ahd. -tuom, errtsprechend as. ae. -döm. Ursprünglich selbständiges Wort, das in Komposita immer stärker abgeschwächt

wird." Friedrich Kluge, *Etymologisches Wörterbuch der Deutschen Sprache* (Berlin: De Gruyter, 1989), 744.

18. See OED ad loc. I thank Professor Ralph Hexter for seeing the import of this source for supporting my conjecture.

19. See the following excursus, a detailed pre-Luther history of this word in German by Daniela Schmidt, candidate for PhD at Potsdam University, to whom I am very grateful for it.

20. It is equally fascinating to observe (with the OED) that in the sixteenth to twentieth centuries "Judaism" appears also as a count noun, meaning a practice of Jews or even a so-called ritualistic practice that has some imaginary correspondence to what Christians call "Judaism." So someone could be accused of committing several "Judaisms." Thus from Milton (Milton Reason Church-govt. 54): "As if the touch of a lay Christian . . . could profane dead judaisms." This is, I reckon, a hearkening back to the earlier Greek usage.

21. Johannes Müller, *Judaismus oder Judenthumb, das ist: Außführlicher Bericht von des jüdischen Volckes Unglauben, Blindheit und Verstockung, darinne sie wider die prophetischen Weissagungen* (Hamburg: Hertel, 1644). I am grateful to Professor Michael Brenner, who, on answering a question of mine about the history of *Judenthum*, sent me to this title and offered other helpful information as well.

22. Johannes Andreas Eisenmenger, *Entdecktes judenthum, oder, Gründlicher und whrhaffter bericht, welchergestalt die verstockte Juden die hochheilige Drey-einigkeit. verunehren, die heil. mutter Christi verschmähen. die christliche religion sp?ttisch durchziehen, und die gantze christienheit* (Königsberg in Preussen: Gedruckt im jahr, 1711).

23. Traditionally, in historical scholarship, termed "the Jewish Enlightenment," but now Olga Litvak, *Haskalah: The Romantic Movement in Judaism*, Key Words in Jewish Studies 3 (New Brunswick: Rutgers University Press, 2012), *must* be consulted on this question, which lies beyond the scope of the present book. On the other hand, and just to correct the record, I think she has misunderstood my earlier remarks on this figure somewhat. See too in this series Cynthia M. Baker, *Jew*, Key Words in Jewish Studies (New Brunswick: Rutgers University Press, 2017), 57–60. Of course, Mendelssohn scholarship is prodigious and far outside of the scope of this book.

24. Moses Mendelssohn, *Jerusalem; oder, über religiöse Macht und Judentum* (Berlin: F. Maurer, 1783); Moses Mendelssohn, *Jerusalem, or, On Religious Power and Judaism*, trans. Allan Arkush, introduction and commentary by Alexander Altmann (Hanover: Published for Brandeis University Press by University Press of New England, 1983).

25. Aaron Halle Wolfssohn, *Jeschurun: Oder unparteyische Beleuchtung der dem Judenthume neuerdings gemachten Vorwürfe. In Briefen, etc.* (Breslau, 1804).

26. Much of the information in these two sentences was supplied to me by Professor Marion Aptroot of the Yiddish department of the Henrich Heine Universität Düsseldorf, for which I am grateful.

27. Leora Batnitzky, *How Judaism Became a Religion: An Introduction to Modern Jewish Thought* (Princeton: Princeton University Press, 2011)

28. Talal Asad, *Genealogies of Religion: Discipline and Reasons of Power in Christianity and Islam* (Baltimore: Johns Hopkins University Press, 1993).

29. Cited in Batnitzky, *How Judaism Became a Religion*, 82.

30. Elizabeth Eva Johnston, "Semitic Philology and the Wissenschaft Des Judentums. Revisiting Leopold Zunz's Etwas ber die Rabbinische Litteratur (1818)," *Philological Encounters* 2 (2017): 314–315. Not so incidentally, we should probably stop speaking of "rabbinic Judaism" for much the same reason.

31. Leon Wieseltier, "Etwas über die Judische Historik: Leopold Zunz and the Inception of Modern Jewish Historiography," *History and Theory* 20 (1981): 141. "In our time the most influential exponent of the view that the Jew is entirely a reactive being has been Sartre, whose discussion of the subject displayed all the ignorance of history befitting a man of his philosophical persuasion" (Wieseltier, 146).

32. Leopold Zunz, *Gesammelte Schriften von Dr. Zunz* (Berlin: I Gerschel, 1875–1876), 99.

33. I am grateful to Dr. Nora Schmidt for helping me construe some of the more difficult German passages quoted in this chapter.

34. Amos Bitzan, "Leopold Zunz and the Meanings of Wissenschaft," *Journal of the History of Ideas* 78 (2017): 253.

35. More than that, Stern carried on an intense conversation with me about these matters over the course of two days—I in Berlin and he in New Haven—that much stimulated these final conclusions. ‏!עלי ייאמר ומתלמידי יותר מכולם‎

36. Eliyahu Stern, "Catholic Judaism: The Political Theology of the Nineteenth-Century Russian Jewish Enlightenment," *Harvard Theological Review* 109, no. 4 (2016): 487.

37. ‏החלק העיוני‎.

38. Once again, I wish to thank Professor Stern for pointing me in the direction of the database that includes this publication, *JPress*, the database of the historical Jewish press cosponsored by Tel Aviv University and the National Library.

39. The allusion is to the pronouncing of the Holy Name by the High Priest on Yom Kippur, a kind of mock heroic.

40. This has to be interpreted, I think, as arguing that the concept referred to by contemporary writers of Hebrew as *yahadut* was precisely what the Prophets were referring to, and if there had been such a word, they would surely have used it, so clearly it did not exist.

41. The claim to Europeanness was the calling card of the *haskalah* (Noy, "Those Who Pass Over," 215; see note 3 in this chapter).

42. I am grateful to my friends, Profs. Chana Kronfeld and Elkhanan Reiner and Dr. Yair Furstenberg, for correcting my text and interpretation of this passage, saving me from shame and embarrassment.

43. I am not at all certain regarding my interpretation of the last clause here.

44 Flensberg was an obscure figure compared to his associates Brill and Salomon. He is mentioned as the author of this very piece in אוצר בדויי השם, that is the *Treasury of Pseudonyms*, of Shaul Chayyes (Vienna, 1933) and mentioned in a Memorial Volume for his daughter, the Rebbetzin Esther Rubenstein, edited by S. L. Citron and published in Vilna (1926–1927). I am grateful to my young and learned friend, Tal Chever-Chybowski for this information. He wrote a commentary on the Song of Songs, published in Vilna (n.d.), a volume of sermons, published in Vilna in 1894–1895, a volume of Responsa, published also in Vilna in 1896, as well as a commentary on Exodus, published in Vilna in 1909. In short, he was a very learned Litvak savant.

45. I am grateful to my once-student, Dr. Shlomo Fischer, for helping me sharpen and clarify this point.

EPILOGUE — THEORY AS *ASKESIS*

1. Talal Asad, "The Concept of Cultural Translation in British Social Anthropology," in *Writing Culture: The Poetics and Politics of Ethnography*, ed. James Clifford and George E. Marcus (Berkeley: University of California Press, 1986), 161.

2. For this, if for no other reason, referring to the history of modern Hinduism as its Semiticization is both inaccurate and disturbing. Daniel Boyarin, "Jewish Cricket," *PMLA* 113, no. 1 (January 1998): 40–45. Not that the term "Jews" is itself not at all unproblematic, on which point see now the brilliant Cynthia M. Baker, *Jew*, Key Words in Jewish Studies (New Brunswick: Rutgers University Press, 2017).

3. Jonathan Boyarin, "Introduction," in *Powers of Diaspora: Two Essays on the Relevance of Jewish Culture*, by Daniel Boyarin and Jonathan Boyarin (Minneapolis: University of Minnesota Press, 2002), 23.

4. Jacques Derrida, *Glas*, trans. John P. Leavey Jr. and Richard Rand (Lincoln: University of Nebraska Press, 1990), 189b.

5. Sheldon Pollock, "Philology in Three Dimensions," *Postmedieval: A Journal of Medieval Cultural Studies* 5 (2014): 411.

6. Anna Boncompagni, "Elucidating Forms of Life: The Evolution of a Philosophical Tool," in "Wittgenstein and Forms of Life," special issue, *Nordic Wittgenstein Review* (2015): 168.

7. See too Naomi Scheman, "Forms of Life: Mapping the Rough Ground," in *The Cambridge Companion to Wittgenstein*, ed. Hans Sluga and David G. Stern (Cambridge: Cambridge University Press, 1996), 383–410, whose argument I deem deeply compatible with my own.

8. Ludwig Wittgenstein, *Philosophical Occasions, 1912–1951*, ed. James C. Klagge and Alfred Nordmann (Indianapolis: Hackett, 1993), 379.

Bibliography

Abulafia, Abraham. *Imrei Shefer*. Edited by Amnon Gross (Jerusalem, 1999). In Hebrew.

———. *Otsar Eden Ganuz*. Jerusalem, 2000. In Hebrew.

Acadia, Lilith. "Discourses of 'Religion.'" Unpublished manuscript. Berkeley, 2016.

Adorno, Theodor W. "The Essay as Form." In *Notes to Literature. Vol. 1*, European Perspectives. Edited by Rolf Tiedemann. Translated by Shierry Weber Nicholsen, 1–23. New York: Columbia University Press, 1991.

Ambrosiaster. *Ambrosiastri Qui Dicitur Commentarius in Epistulas Paulinas. Recensuit Henricus Iosephus Vogels*. Corpus Scriptorum Ecclesiasticorum Latinorum 81. Vindobonae: Hoelder-Pichler-Tempsky, 1966–1969.

Amir, Yehoshua. "The Term Ιουδαϊσμός: On the Self Understanding of Hellenistic Judaism." In *Proceedings of the Fifth World Congress of Jewish Studies, the Hebrew University, Mount Scopus-Givat Ram, Jerusalem, Jerusalem [Sic], 3–11 August, 1969*, edited by Pinchas Peli, 263–268. Jerusalem: World Union of Jewish Studies, 1972–1973.

Asad, Talal. "The Concept of Cultural Translation in British Social Anthropology." In *Writing Culture: The Poetics and Politics of Ethnography*, edited by James Clifford and George E. Marcus, 141–164. Berkeley: University of California Press, 1986.

———. *Genealogies of Religion: Discipline and Reasons of Power in Christianity and Islam*. Baltimore: Johns Hopkins University Press, 1993.

Baker, Cynthia M. *Jew*. Key Words in Jewish Studies. New Brunswick: Rutgers University Press, 2017.

Baker, G. P. *Wittgenstein: Understanding and Meaning: Volume 1 of an Analytical Commentary on the Philosophical Investigations, Part II: Exegesis 1–184*. Hoboken: Wiley, 2008.

Barrett, C. K. "Jews and Judaizers in the Epistles of Ignatius." In *Jews, Greeks and Christians: Religious Cultures in Late Antiquity. Essays in Honor of William David Davies*, edited by Robin Scroggs, 220–244. SJLA 21. Leiden: E. J. Brill, 1976.

Barton, Carlin A. "The 'Moment of Truth' in Ancient Rome: Honor and Embodiment in a Contest Culture." *Stanford Humanities Review* (1998): 16–30.

———. *Roman Honor: The Fire in the Bones*. Berkeley: University of California Press, 2001.

Barton, Carlin A., and Daniel Boyarin. *Imagine No Religion: How Modern Categories Hide Ancient Realities*. Bronx: Fordham University Press, 2016.

Batnitzky, Leora. *How Judaism Became a Religion: An Introduction to Modern Jewish Thought*. Princeton: Princeton University Press, 2011.

Beard, Mary, John A. North, and S. R. F. Price. *Religions of Rome*. Cambridge: Cambridge University Press, 1998.

Benjamin, Walter. "The Task of the Translator." In *Walter Benjamin: Selected Writings. Vol. 1, 1913–1926*, edited by Marcus Bullock and Michael W. Jennings.[1913–1926.] [Selections. English], 253–275. Cambridge, MA: Belknap Press of Harvard University Press, 1996.

Ben-Yehuda, Eliezer. *Milon Ha-Lashon Ha-ʿIvrit Ha-Yeshanah Veha-Ḥadashah*. Yerushalayim, 1910–1959.

Bhabha, Homi K. *The Location of Culture.* London: Routledge, 1994.

Bloch, Marc. *The Historian's Craft: Reflections on the Nature and Uses of History and the Techniques and Methods of Those Who Write It.* Translated by Peter Putnam. New York: Vintage Books, 1953.

Bloor, David. *Wittgenstein, A Social Theory of Knowledge.* Contemporary Social Theory. London: Macmillan, 1983.

Boncompagni, Anna. "Elucidating Forms of Life: The Evolution of a Philosophical Tool." In "Wittgenstein and Forms of Life," special issue. *Nordic Wittgenstein Review* (2015): 155–175.

Bowen, Elenore Smith, pseudonym. *Return to Laughter.* New York: Harper, 1954.

Bowersock, G. W. *Hellenism in Late Antiquity.* Jerome Lectures, Eighteen. Ann Arbor: University of Michigan Press, 1990.

Boyarin, Daniel. "Beyond Judaisms: Meṭaṭron and the Divine Polymorphy of Ancient Judaism." *Journal for the Study of Judaism in the Persian, Hellenistic, and Roman Periods* 41 (July 2010): 323–365.

———. *Border Lines: The Partition of Judaeo-Christianity.* Divinations: Rereading Late Ancient Religions. Philadelphia: University of Pennsylvania Press, 2004.

———. "The Christian Invention of Judaism: The Theodosian Empire and the Rabbinic Refusal of Religion." *Representations* 85 (2004): 21–57.

———. "Daniel 7, Intertextuality, and the History of Israel's Cult." *Harvard Theological Review* 105, no. 2 (2012): 135–162.

———. *Dying for God: Martyrdom and the Making of Christianity and Judaism.* The Lancaster/Yarnton Lectures in Judaism and Other Religions for 1998. Stanford: Stanford University Press, 1999.

———. "The Gospel of the Memra: Jewish Binitarianism and the Crucifixion of the Logos." *Harvard Theological Review* 94, no. 3 (2001): 243–284.

———. "Jewish Cricket." *PMLA* 113, no. 1 (January 1998): 40–45.

———. "Justin Martyr Invents Judaism." *Church History* 70, no. 3 (September 2001): 427–461.

———. "Semantic Differences: Linguistics and 'the Parting of the Ways.'" In *The Ways That Never Parted: Jews and Christians in Late Antiquity and the Early Middle Ages,* edited by Adam H. Becker and Annette Yoshiko Reed, 65–85. Texte und Studien Zum Antiken Judentum 95. Tübingen: Mohr Siebeck, 2003.

Boyarin, Jonathan. "Introduction." In *Powers of Diaspora: Two Essays on the Relevance of Jewish Culture,* by Daniel Boyarin and Jonathan Boyarin, 1–33. Minneapolis: University of Minnesota Press, 2002.

———. *Thinking in Jewish.* Chicago: University of Chicago Press, 1996.

Brown, Peter. *Authority and the Sacred: Aspects of the Christianization of the Roman World.* Cambridge: Cambridge University Press, 1995.

Burrus, Virginia. "'In the Theater of This Life': The Performance of Orthodoxy in Late Antiquity." In *The Limits of Ancient Christianity: Essays on Late Antique Thought and Culture in Honor of R. A. Markus,* edited by William E. Klingshirn and Mark Vessey, 80–96. Recentiores: Late Latin Texts and Contexts. Ann Arbor: University of Michigan Press, 1999.

Burrus, Virginia, Richard Kalmin, Haim Lapin, and Joel Marcus. "Boyarin's Work: A Critical Assessment." *Henoch* 28 (2006): 7–30.

Castelli, Elizabeth A. *Martyrdom and Memory: Early Christian Culture-Making.* New York: Columbia University Press, 2004.

Cavell, Stanley. *The Claim of Reason: Wittgenstein, Skepticism, Morality, and Tragedy.* Oxford: Clarendon Press, 1979.

Chidester, David. *Savage Systems: Colonialism and Comparative Religion in Southern Africa.* Charlottesville: University Press of Virginia, 1996.

Cohen, Shaye J. D. *The Beginnings of Jewishness: Boundaries, Varieties, Uncertainties.* Hellenistic Culture and Society 31. Berkeley: University of California Press, 1998.

———. "Judaism without Circumcision and 'Judaism' without 'Circumcision' in Ignatius." *Harvard Theological Review* 95, no. 4 (2002): 395–415.

———. "Pagan and Christian Evidence on the Ancient Synagogue." In *The Synagogue in Late Antiquity,* edited by Lee I. Levine, 159–181. Philadelphia: American Schools of Oriental Research, 1987.

Collins, John J. "Cult and Culture: The Limits of Hellenization in Judea." In *Hellenism in the Land of Israel,* edited by John J. Collins and Gregory Sterling, 38–61. Christianity and Judaism in Antiquity. Notre Dame, IN: University of Notre Dame, 2000.

Copeland, E. Luther. "Nomos as a Medium of Revelation—Paralleling Logos—in Ante-Nicene Christianity." *Studia Theologica* 27 (1973): 51–61.

Cover, Robert M. "Supreme Court, 1982 Term—Foreword: Nomos and Narrative," 1983.

Davies, Philip R. *On the Origins of Judaism.* BibleWorld. London: Equinox, 2011.

Derrida, Jacques. *Glas.* Translated by John P. Leavey Jr. and Richard Rand. Lincoln: University of Nebraska Press, 1990.

Deutsch, Nathaniel. *Guardians of the Gate: Angelic Vice Regency in Late Antiquity.* Brill's Series in Jewish Studies 22. Leiden: E. J. Brill, 1999.

Dmitrieva, L. A. [sostavlenie i obshchaia redaktsiia], and D. S. Likhacheva. *Pamiatniki Literatury Drevnei Rusi: Konets XV-Pervaia Polovina XVI Veka.* Pamiatniki Literatury Drevnei Rusi. Moskva: "Khudozh. lit-ra," 1984.

Dover, K. J. *Aristophanic Comedy.* Berkeley: University of California Press, 1972.

Drake, Hal A. "Lambs into Lions: Explaining Early Christian Intolerance." *Past and Present,* no. 153 (1996): 3–36.

Dubuisson, Daniel. *The Western Construction of Religion: Myths, Knowledge, and Ideology.* Translated by William Sayers. Baltimore: Johns Hopkins University Press, 2003.

Eisenmenger, Johannes Andreas. *Entdecktes Judenthum oder, Gründlicher und wahrhaffter Bericht, welchergestalt die verstockte Juden die hochheilige Drey-einigkeit . . . verunehren, die heil. Mutter Christi verschmähen . . . die christliche Religion spöttisch durchziehen, und die gantze Christenheit . . . verachten und verfluchen; dabey noch viel andere . . . nur zum Theil bekant gewesene Dinge und grosse Irrthüme der jüdischen Religion und Theologie, wie auch viel lächerliche und kurtzweilige Fabeln . . . an den Tag kommen. Alles aus ihren eigenen . . . Büchern . . . kräfftiglich erwiesen, und in zweyen Theilen verfasset . . . Allen Christen zur treuhertzigen Nachricht verfertiget, und mit volkommenen Registern.* Königsberg in Preussen: n.p., 1711.

Elze, Martin. "Irrtum und Häresie." *Kairos* 71 (1974): 393–394.

Epiphanius of Salamis. *The Panarion of Epiphanius of Salamis, Book I, Sections 1–46.* Translated by Frank Williams. Leiden: E. J. Brill, 1987.

Eusebius. *Preparation for the Gospel.* Translated by Edwin Hamilton Gifford. Grand Rapids: Baker Book House, 1981.

———. *The Proof of the Gospel.* Edited and translated by W. J. Ferrar. Translations of Christian Literature. London: SPCK, 1920.

Eutyhmius. "Encomium in Conceptionem Annae, §3, Ed." In *Homélies Mariales Byzantines: Textes Grecs*, edited and translated by Martin Jugie. Patrologia Orientalis. Paris: Firmin-Didot, 1922–1926.

Fatouros, recensuit Georgios. *Theodori Studitae Epistulae*. Corpus Fontium Historiae Byzantinae. Berolini: W. de Gruyter, 1992.

Fitzgerald, Timothy. *Discourse on Civility and Barbarity: A Critical History of Religion and Related Categories*. New York: Oxford University Press, 2007.

———. *The Ideology of Religious Studies*. New York: Oxford University Press, 2000.

Flatto, David C. "Theocracy and the Rule of Law: A Novel Josephan Doctrine and Its Modern Misconceptions." *Dine Yisrael* 28 (2011): 5–30.

Foschia, Laurence. "Le Nom du culte, et ses derives a l'epoque Imperiale," In *L'HELLENISME D'EPOQUE ROMAINE: NOUVEAUX DOCUMENTS, NOUVELLES APPROCHES (Ler s. a. C.—111e s. p. C.) Actes du Colloque international la memoire de Louis Robert Paris, 7–8 Juillet 2000*. Paris: De Boccard, 2004.

Fowles, Severin M. *An Archaeology of Doings: Secularism and the Study of Pueblo Religion*. Santa Fe: School for Advanced Research Press, 2013.

Frankfurter, David. "Comparison and the Study of Religions in Late Antiquity." In *Comparer en histoire des religions antiques: controverses et propositions*, edited by Claude Calame and Bruce Lincoln, 83–98. Religions 1. Liège: Presses universitaires de Liège, 2012.

———. *Religion in Roman Egypt: Assimilation and Resistance*. Princeton: Princeton University Press, 1998.

Fredriksen, Paula. *Augustine and the Jews: A Christian Defense of Jews and Judaism*. New Haven: Yale University Press, 2010.

———. "Mandatory Retirement: Ideas in the Study of Christian Origins Whose Time Has Come to Go." *Studies in Religion* 35, no. 2 (2006): 231–246.

Gieseler, Johann Karl Ludwig. "Über die Nazaräer und Ebioniten." *Archive für alte und neue Kirchengeschichte* 4, no. 2 (1819): 279–330.

Ginzberg, Louis. *The Legends of the Jews*. Translated from the German manuscript by Henrietta Szold. Philadelphia: Jewish Publication Society of America, 1909–1938.

Glei, Reinhold, and Stefan Reichmuth. "Religion between Last Judgement, Law and Faith: Koranic Dīn and Its Rendering in Latin Translations of the Koran." *Religion* 42, no. 2 (April 2012): 247–271.

Goldstein, Jonathan A., trans. and ed. *II Maccabees: A New Translation with Introduction and Commentary*. The Anchor Bible 41a. New York: Doubleday, 1983.

Goodenough, Erwin R. *By Light, Light: The Mystic Gospel of Hellenistic Judaism*. New Haven: Yale University Press, 1935.

Gruen, Erich. "Hellenism and Persecution: Antiochus IV and the Jews." In *Hellenistic History and Culture*, edited by Peter Green, 238–264. Berkeley: University of California Press, 1993.

Hacker, P. M. S. "Forms of Life." In "Wittgenstein and Forms of Life," special issue. *Nordic Wittgenstein Review* (2015): 1–20.

Hacker, P. M. S., and G. P. Baker. *Wittgenstein: Understanding and Meaning. Part I, Essays*. Analytical Commentary on the Philosophical Investigations 1. Oxford: Blackwell, 2005.

Hacking, Ian. "'Style' for Historians and Philosophers." *Studies in History and Philosophy of Science Part A* 23, no. 1 (1992): 1–20.

ha-Levi, Judah. *Judah Hallevi's Kitab al Khazari*. Translated by Hartwig Hirschfeld. The Semitic Series. London: G. Routledge, 1905.

HaLevi, Yehudah. *The Kuzari: In Defense of the Despised Faith.* Newly translated and annotated by N. Daniel Korobkin. Jerusalem: Feldheim, 2009.

———. *Sefer Hakuzari: Maqor Wetargum.* Edited and translated by Yosef ben David Qafiḥ. Kiryat Ono: Mekhon Mishnat ha-Rambam, 1996.

Hall, Jonathan M. *Hellenicity: Between Ethnicity and Culture.* Chicago: University of Chicago Press, 2002.

Harries, Jill, and I. N. Wood. *The Theodosian Code.* Edited by Jill Harries. Ithaca, NY: Cornell University Press, 1993.

Hengel, Martin. "Die Synangoninschrift von Stobi." *ZNW* 57, no. 3 (1966): 145–183.

Hill, Charles E. "Ignatius, 'the Gospel', and the Gospels." In *Trajectories through the New Testament and the Apostolic Fathers,* edited by Andrew F. Gregory and Christopher M. Tuckett, 267–285. Oxford: Oxford University Press, 2005.

Himmelfarb, Martha. "Judaism and Hellenism in 2 Maccabees." *Poetics Today* 19 (1998): 19–40.

Honigman, Sylvie. *Tales of High Priests and Taxes: The Books of the Maccabees and the Judean Rebellion against Antiochos IV.* The S. Mark Taper Foundation Imprint in Jewish Studies. Oakland: University of California Press, 2014.

Honoré, Tony. *Law in the Crisis of Empire, 379–455 AD: The Theodosian Dynasty and Its Quaestors; with a Palingenesia of Laws of the Dynasty.* Oxford: Clarendon Press, 1998.

Hopkins, Keith. "Christian Number and Its Implications." *Journal of Early Christian Studies* 6, no. 2 (1998): 185–226.

Horowitz, Elliott S. "The Rite to Be Reckless; on the Perpetration and Interpretation of Purim Violence." *Poetics Today* 15, no. 1 (1994): 9–54.

Humfress, Caroline. "Religion." In *The Evolution of the Late Antique World,* by Peter Garnsey and Caroline Humfress, 135–170. Oxford: Orchard Academic Press, 2001.

Hunter, J. F. M. "'Forms of Life' in Wittgenstein's 'Philosophical Investigations.'" *American Philosophical Quarterly* 5, no. 4 (1968): 233–243.

Idel, Moshe. "Abraham Abulafia and the Pope: An Account of an Abortive Mission." *AJS Review* 7 (1982): H1–H17. In Hebrew.

Jacobs, Andrew S. "The Imperial Construction of the Jew in the Early Christian Holy Land." PhD diss., Duke University, 2001.

Jerome. *Correspondence.* Edited by Isidorus Hilberg. Corpus Scriptorum Ecclesiasticorum Latinorum. Vienna: Verlag der Osterreichischen Akademie der Wissenschaften, 1996.

Johnson, Aaron P. "Greek Ethnicity in Eusebius' 'Praeparatio Evangelica.'" *American Journal of Philology* 128, no. 1 (Spring 2007): 95–118.

Jones, C. P. "Ἔθνος and γένος In Herodotus." *Classical Quarterly,* n.s., 46 (1996): 315–320.

Josephus, Flavius. *Against Apion. Translation and Commentary.* Edited by Steve Mason. Translation and commentary by John Barclay. Josephus, Flavius. Works. English. 2000, vol. 10. Leiden: E. J. Brill, 2007.

———. *Judean War 2.* Translation and commentary by Steve Mason and Honora Chapman. Josephus, Flavius. Works. English. 2000, vol. 1B. Leiden: E. J. Brill, 2008.

Julian, and Wilmer Cave France Wright. "Against the Galileans." In *The Works of the Emperor Julian,* translated by Wilmer Cave France Wright. Loeb Classical Library, 313–433. London: Heinemann, 1913.

Justin. *Dialogus Cum Tryphone.* Edited by Miroslav Marcovich. Patristische Texte und Studien Bd. 47. Berlin: Walter de Gruyter, 1997.

Kluge, Friedrich. *Etymologisches Wörterbuch der Deutschen Sprache*. Berlin: De Gruyter, 1989.

Koch, Glenn Alan. "A Critical Investigation of Epiphanius' Knowledge of the Ebionites: A Translation and Critical Discussion of *Panarion 30*." PhD diss., University of Pennsylvania, Philadelphia, 1976.

Koester, Helmut. "Ancient Christian Gospels: Their History and Development." Harrisburg: Trinity Press International, 1990.

———. *Synoptische Überlieferung bei den Apostolischen Vätern*. Berlin: Akademie-Verlag, 1957.

Krinis, Ehud. "The Arabic Background of the *Kuzari*." *Journal of Jewish Thought and Philosophy* 21 (2013): 1–56.

Krupat, Arnold. *Ethnocriticism: Ethnography, History, Literature*. Berkeley: University of California Press, 1992.

La Barre, Weston. *The Ghost Dance: Origins of Religion*. London: Allen and Unwin, 1972.

Lasker, Daniel J. "Translations of Rabbi Yehuda Halevis Kuzari." http://seforim.blogspot.com/2017/06/translations-of-rabbi-judah-halevis.html.

Levine, Lee I. "The Jewish Patriarch (Nasi) in Third Century Palestine." In *Aufstieg und Niedergang der Römischen Welt II, Principat 19,2*, 649–688. Berlin: Walter de Gruyter, 1979.

Liebeschuetz, J. H. W. G. *Antioch: City and Imperial Administration in the Later Roman Empire*. Oxford: Clarendon Press, 1972.

Lienhardt, Godfrey. "Modes of Thought." In *The Institutions of Primitive Society, a Series of Broadcast Talks*, edited and compiled by E. E. Evans-Pritchard, et al., 95–107. Glencoe, IL: Free Press, 1954.

Lieu, Judith. "'I Am a Christian': Martyrdom and the Beginning of 'Christian' Identity." In *Neither Jew Nor Greek? Constructing Christian Identity*. Edinburgh: T & T Clark, 2003.

———. *Image & Reality: The Jews in the World of the Christians in the Second Century*. Edinburgh: T & T Clark, 1996.

Limberis, Vasiliki. "'Religion' as the Cipher for Identity: The Cases of Emperor Julian, Libanius, and Gregory Nazianzus." *Harvard Theological Review* 93, no. 4 (2000): 373–400.

Linder, Amnon. *The Jews in Roman Imperial Legislation*. Edited by Amnon Linder. Translated by Amnon Linder. Detroit: Wayne State University Press, 1987.

Litvak, Olga. *Haskalah: The Romantic Movement in Judaism*. Key Words in Jewish Studies 3. New Brunswick: Rutgers University Press, 2012.

Lyman, J. Rebecca. *Christology and Cosmology: Models of Divine Activity in Origen, Eusebius, and Athanasius*. Oxford Theological Monographs. Oxford: Oxford University Press, 1993.

MacRae, Duncan. "Diligentissumus Investigator Antiquitatis? 'Antiquarianism' and Historical Evidence between Republican Rome and the Early Modern Republic of Letters." In *Omnium Annalium Monumenta: Historical Writing and Historical Evidence in Republican Rome*, edited by Christopher Smith and Kaj Sandberg. Leiden: E. J. Brill, 2017.

Marcus, George E., and Michael M. J. Fischer. *Anthropology as Cultural Critique: An Experimental Moment in the Human Sciences*. Chicago: University of Chicago Press, 1986.

Mason, Steve. *The Jewish-Roman War of 66 to 74: A Historical Inquiry*. Cambridge: Cambridge University Press, 2016.

———. "Jews, Judaeans, Judaizing, Judaism: Problems of Categorization in Ancient History," *Journal for the Study of Judaism* 38, no. 4–5 (2007): 457–512.

Matthews, John. *Laying Down the Law: A Study of the Theodosian Code*. New Haven: Yale University Press, 2000.

McCutcheon, Russell T., ed. *The Insider / Outsider Problem in the Study of Religion: A Reader*. Controversies in the Study of Religion. London: Cassell, 1999.

Mendelssohn, Moses. *Jerusalem; oder, über religiöse Macht und Judentum*. Berlin: F. Maurer, 1783.

———. *Jerusalem, or, On Religious Power and Judaism*. Translated by Allan Arkush, introduction and commentary by Alexander Altmann. Hanover: Published for Brandeis University Press by University Press of New England, 1983.

Mieses, Matthias. *Die Entstehungsursache de Jüdischen Dialekte*. Wien: R. Löwit, 1915.

Molland, Einar. "The Heretics Combatted by Ignatius of Antioch." *Journal of Ecclesiastical History* 5 (1954): 1–6.

Momigliano, Arnaldo. "The Rules of the Game in the Study of Ancient History." Translated by Kenneth W. Yu. *History & Theory* 55, no. 1 (2016): 39–45.

Moore, George Foot. "Intermediaries in Jewish Theology: Memra, Shekinah, Metatron." *Harvard Theological Review* 15, no. 1 (January 1922): 41–85.

———. *The Rise of Normative Judaism*. Cambridge: Reprinted from *Harvard Theological Review* XVII, no. 4 (October 1924) and XVIII, no. 1 (January 1925). Includes bibliographical references. I. To the reorganization at Jamnia–II. To the close of the Mishnah., 1925.

Müller, Johannes. *Judaismus oder Judenthumb, das ist: Außführlicher Bericht von des jüdischen Volckes Unglauben, Blindheit und Verstockung, darinne sie wider die prophetischen Weissagungen*. Hamburg: Hertel, 1644.

Needham, R. "Polythetic Classification: Convergence and Consequences." *Man*, n.s., 10 (1975): 349–369.

Neusner, Jacob. *The Way of Torah; an Introduction to Judaism*. The Religious Life of Man Series. Encino, CA: Dickenson, 1974.

Neuwirth, Angelika. *Wie Entsteht eine Schrift in der Forschung und in der Geschichte? Die Hebräische Bible und der Koran*. Lucas-Preis. Tübingen: Mohr Siebeck, 2017.

Newman, Hillel. "Jerome's Judaizers." *Journal of Early Christian Studies* 9, no. 4 (December 2001): 421–452.

Niborski, Yitshak, tsunoyfgeshtelt durkh, mit der mithilf fun Shim'on Noyberg, and tsugegreyt tsum druk Eli'ezer Niborski. *Verterbukh Fun Loshn-Koydesh-Shtamike Verter in Yidish*. Pariz: Medem-bibliyotek, 1997.

Nirenberg, David. *Anti-Judaism: The Western Tradition*. New York: W. W. Norton, 2013.

Nongbri, Brent. *Before Religion: A History of a Modern Concept*. New Haven: Yale University Press, 2013.

———. "Paul without Religion: The Creation of a Category and the Search for an Apostle beyond the New Perspective." PhD diss., Yale University, 2008.

Noy, Amos. "Those Who Pass Over: Do Not Forget Yahandes? An Examination of a Word from Avot Yeshurun's Poetry." *Theory and Criticism* 41 (2013): 199–221. In Hebrew.

Paulsen, Henning, and Walter Bauer. *Die Briefe des Ignatius von Antiochia und der Brief des Polykarp von Smyrna*. Handbuch zum Neuen Testament. Tübingen: Mohr Siebeck, 1985.

Pearson, Birger. "The Emergence of the Christian Religion." In *The Emergence of the Christian Religion: Essays on Early Christianity*, 7–22. Harrisburg: Trinity Press International, 1997.

Pharr, Clyde. *The Theodosian Code and Novels, and the Sirmondian Constitutions a Translation with Commentary, Glossary, and Bibliography.* In collaboration with Theresa Sherrer Davidson and Mary Brown Pharr, with an introduction by C. Dickerman Williams. Princeton: Princeton University Press, 1952.

Pollock, Sheldon. "Philology in Three Dimensions." *Postmedieval: A Journal of Medieval Cultural Studies* 5 (2014): 398–413.

Pourkier, Aline. *L'Hérésiologie chez Épiphane de Salamine.* Christianisme Antique 4. Paris: Editions Beauchesne, 1992.

Pritz, Ray A. *Nazarene Jewish Christianity: From the End of the New Testament Period until Its Disappearance in the Fourth-Century.* Jerusalem: Magnes Press, 1992.

Reed, Annette Yoshiko. "'Ancient Jewish Sciences' and the Historiography of Judaism." In *Ancient Jewish Sciences and the History of Knowledge in Second Temple Literature,* edited by Jonathan Ben-Dov and Seth Sanders, 197–256. New York: New York University Press, 2013.

———. "Categorization, Collection, and the Construction of Continuity: 1 Enoch and 3 Enoch in and Beyond 'Apocalypticism' and 'Mysticism,'" 2016. Unpublished paper.

Reischl, Wilhelm Karl, and Joseph Rupp. *Cyrilli Hierosolymarum Archiepiscopi Opera Quae Supersunt Omnia.* Edited by Wilhelm Karl Reischl. Hildesheim: Olms, 1967.

Rius-Camps, Josep. *The Four Authentic Letters of Ignatius, the Martyr: A Critical Study Based on the Anomalies Contained in the Textus Receptus.* Xpictianicmoc. Rome: Pontificium Institutum Orientalium Studiorum, 1979.

Sachot, Maurice. "Comment le Christianisme est-il devenu *religio.*" *Revue des sciences religiuses* 59 (1985): 95–118.

———. "«*Religio/Superstitio*»*.* Historique d'une subversion et d'un retournement." *Revue d'histoire des religions* 208, no. 4 (1991): 355–394.

Saler, Benson. *Conceptualizing Religion: Immanent Anthropologists, Transcendent Natives, and Unbounded Categories.* Studies in the History of Religions 56. Leiden: E. J. Brill, 1993.

———. "Religio and the Definition of Religion." *Cultural Anthropology* 2, no. 3 (1987): 395–399.

Salzman, Michele R. "'Superstitio' in the Codex Theodosianus and the Persecution of Pagans." *Vigiliae Christianae* 41 (1987): 172–188.

Satlow, Michael. "Defining Judaism: Accounting for 'Religions' in the Study of Religion." *Journal of the American Academy of Religion* 74, no. 4 (2006): 837–860.

Schäfer, Peter, ed. *The Talmud Yerushalmi and Graeco-Roman Culture III.* Texte und Studien Zum Antiken Judentum 93. Tübingen: Mohr Siebeck, 2002.

Scheman, Naomi. "Forms of Life: Mapping the Rough Ground." In *The Cambridge Companion to Wittgenstein,* edited by Hans Sluga and David G. Stern, 383–410. Cambridge: Cambridge University Press, 1996.

Schoedel, William R. "Ignatius and the Archives." *Harvard Theological Review* 71 (1978).

———. *Ignatius of Antioch: A Commentary on the Letters of Ignatius of Antioch.* Edited by Helmut Koester, translated and edited by William R. Schoedel. Hermeneia—a Critical and Historical Commentary on the Bible. Philadelphia: Fortress Press, 1985.

Schwartz, Daniel R. *Jewish Background of Christianity.* Wissenschaftliche Untersuchungen Zum Neuen Testament. Tübingen: J. C. B. Mohr, 1992.

———. "'Judean' or 'Jew'? How Should We Translate *IOUDAIOS* in Josephus?" In *Jewish Identity in the Greco-Roman World = Jüdische Identität in der Griechisch-Römischen*

Welt, edited by Jörg Frey, Daniel R. Schwartz, and Stephanie Gripentrog, 3–27. Ancient Judaism and Early Christianity 71. Leiden: E. J. Brill, 2007.

———. *Judeans and Jews: Four Faces of Dichotomy in Ancient Jewish History*. Kenneth Michael Tanenbaum Series in Jewish Studies, 2014.

———. "More on Schalit's Changing Josephus: The Lost First Stage." *Jewish History* 9, no. 2 (Fall 1995): 9–20.

———. *2 Maccabees*. Commentaries on Early Jewish Literature (CEJL). Berlin: Walter de Gruyter, 2008.

Schwartz, Seth. "How Many Judaisms Were There? A Critique of Neusner and Smith on Definition and Mason and Boyarin on Categorization." *Journal of Ancient Judaism* 2, no. 2 (2011): 208–238.

———. *Imperialism and Jewish Society from 200 B.C.E. to 640 C.E.* Princeton: Princeton University Press, 2001.

Seidman, Naomi. *Faithful Renderings: Jewish-Christian Difference and the Politics of Translation*. Afterlives of the Bible. Chicago: University of Chicago Press, 2006.

Shawver, Lois. "Commentary on Wittgenstein's Philosophical Investigations." http://users .rcn.com/rathbone/lwtocc.htm.

Shekhter, Mordekhai, and Shikl Fishman. *Laytish Mame-Loshn: Observatsyes un Rekomendatsyes*. New York: Yidish-lige, 1986.

Skinner, Quentin. "The Idea of a Cultural Lexicon." *Essays in Criticism* 29 (1979): 205–224.

———. "Meaning and Understanding in the History of Ideas." *History and Theory* 8 (1969): 3–53.

Smith, Jonathan Z. *Imagining Religion: From Babylon to Jonestown*. Chicago: University of Chicago Press, 1982.

———. *Relating Religion: Essays in the Study of Religion*. Chicago: University of Chicago Press, 2004.

———. "Trading Places." In *Relating Religion: Essays in the Study of Religion*, 215–229. Chicago: University of Chicago Press, 2004.

Stemberger, Günter. *Jews and Christians in the Holy Land: Palestine in the Fourth Century*. Edinburgh: T & T Clark, 1999.

Stern, Eliyahu. "Catholic Judaism: The Political Theology of the Nineteenth-Century Russian Jewish Enlightenment." *Harvard Theological Review* 109, no. 4 (2016): 483–511.

Thiessen, Matthew. *Contesting Conversion: Genealogy, Circumcision, and Identity in Ancient Judaism and Christianity*. Oxford: Oxford University Press, 2011.

Urbach, E. E. "*Yahadut* in the Language of the Sages." *Leshnonenu* 25 (1961): 145. In Hebrew.

Vinzent, Markus. *Tertullian's Preface to Marcion's Gospel*. Studie Patristica Supplementa. Leuven: Peters, 2016.

Viveiros de Castro, Eduardo. "Perspectival Anthropology and the Method of Controlled Equivocation." *Tipití: Journal of the Society for the Anthropology of Lowland South America* 2, no. 1 (2004): 3–22.

Weinreich, Max. *History of the Yiddish Language*. Translated by Shlomo Noble, with the assistance of Joshua A. Fishman and the editorial assistance of Paul Glasser. Yale Language Series. New Haven: Yale University Press, 2008.

Werman, Cana. "On Religious Persecution: A Study in Ancient and Modern Historiography." *Zion* 81, no. 3–4 (2016): 463–496. In Hebrew, with English summary.

Wierzbicka, Anna. *Understanding Cultures through Their Key Words: English, Russian, Polish, German, and Japanese*. Oxford Studies in Anthropological Linguistics. New York: Oxford University Press, 1997.

Wieseltier, Leon. "Etwas über Die Judische Historik: Leopold Zunz and the Inception of Modern Jewish historiography." *History and Theory* 20 (1981): 135–149.

Williams, A. Lukyn, ed. and trans. *Justin Martyr: The Dialogue with Trypho*. Translations of Christian Literature. London: SPCK, 1930.

Williams, Raymond. *Keywords: A Vocabulary of Culture and Society*. Oxford: Oxford University Press, 2015.

Williams, Rowan. "Does It Make Sense to Speak of Pre-Nicene Orthodoxy?" In *The Making of Orthodoxy: Essays in Honour of Henry Chadwick*, edited by Rowan Williams, 1–23. Cambridge: Cambridge University Press, 1989.

Wittgenstein, Ludwig. *Philosophical Occasions, 1912–1951*. Edited by James C. Klagge and Alfred Nordmann. Indianapolis: Hackett, 1993.

———. *Philosophische Untersuchungen = Philosophical Investigations*. Translated by G. E. M. Anscombe, P. M. S. Hacker, and Joachim Schulte. Chichester, West Sussex, UK: Wiley-Blackwell, 2009.

———. *Preliminary Studies for the "Philosophical Investigations," Generally Known as the Blue and Brown Books*. Oxford: Blackwell, 1969.

Wolfson, Elliot R. "Textual Flesh, Incarnation, and the Imaginal Body: Abraham Abulafia's Polemic with Christianity." In *Studies in Medieval Jewish Intellectual and Social History: Festschrift in Honor of Robert Chazan*, edited by David Engel, Lawrence Schiffman, and Elliot Wolfson, 189–227. Supplements to the Journal of Jewish Thought and Philosophy 15. Brill: E. J. Leiden, 2012.

Wolfssohn, Aaron Halle. *Jeschurun: Oder unparteyische Beleuchtung der dem Judenthume neuerdings gemachten Vorwürfe. In Briefen, etc.* Breslau, 1804.

Young, Frances. "Did Epiphanius Know What He Meant by 'Heresy'?" *Studia Patristica* 17, no. 1 (1982): 199–205.

Young, Robert. *Colonial Desire: Hybridity in Theory, Culture, and Race*. London: Routledge, 1995.

Zunz, Leopold, *Gesammelte Schriften von Dr. Zunz*. Berlin: I Gerschel, 1875–1876.

Index

Index of Works Cited

About the Author

DANIEL BOYARIN is the Taubman Professor of Talmudic Culture at the University of California, Berkeley. His work for the last fifty years has been devoted to figuring out why there are Jews, inquiring into that question by studying (mostly) rabbinic texts as well as Christian texts, history, archaeology, literary criticism, feminism, ethnography, queer theory, and postcolonial studies in search of the meaning(s) of Jewishness. The present book, following hard upon the book cowritten with Carlin Barton, *Imagine No Religion*, inquires into the different constructions of Jewishness from "inside" (Jew-identified Jews) and "outside" (Christian and Christianizing Jews) and thus is a further step along the way that always only leads to the next question.